MW01073509

Second Spring

The Complete
Topeka Capital-Journal Columns,
1997-2012

NAOMI B. PATTERSON

(Naomi Patterson and son David, 1962)

Second Spring
Table of Contents

(Naomi Patterson and daughter Carol Patterson Baldwin, 2011)

to have put just such a collection together and offer it both to those who want to remember a dear friend and colleague from days past, as well as to those as of yet unfamiliar with Naomi Patterson's writings. (You are in for a treat.)

You need not hear from us that this is the voice of a special writer; this will become patently obvious as the pages turn. We hope that whoever you are, you enjoy this collection and the glimpses that these essays provide into the unique, humorous, poignant, and insightful mind of an extraordinary woman and deeply talented writer (or as we called her, "Mom").

– David Patterson and Carol Patterson Baldwin

NAOMI B. PATTERSON, PH.D.
1934-2012

Age is more a state of mind than a number
August 14, 1997

My grandmother could have posed for the dictionary picture illustrating the word "Grandma." Rotund, white hair in a bun atop her head, her face as soft and welcoming as her spirit, she invented all the classic grandmotherly traits – cooking, baking, story telling, lap holding, and unconditional love. But Grandma showed a bolder, more independent side as well. She dared teach in a one-room schoolhouse when a teacher's duties included bringing in coal, stoking the fire, shoveling snow, and single-handedly disciplining students bigger than she. She made bold speeches to the Women's Christian Temperance Union, denouncing the evils of liquor in a time when most women remained seen but unheard. In later years, without complaint, she stubbornly fought back from half a dozen strokes, courageously kneading a little red ball in her affected hand, the only physical therapy prescribed. Sometimes reliant upon a walker, she dubbed it her "horse" and valiantly walked or trotted it around the house while seeing to her duties.

My favorite photograph of my grandmother was taken when she was about eighty years old. The picture shows her wearing one of her trademark house dresses, sitting on a large stump several feet into shallow water at the ocean's edge, her bare feet submerged in tiny waves. In one hand, she waves a long walking stick high above her head. Her smile is zestful and free.

Grandma was ahead of her time. In 1997 it's almost a cliché to say that being over sixty isn't what it used to be. Indeed, dare we say over one hundred? One colorful current-day t-shirt proclaims, "Over the hill? What hill? I didn't see a hill!" All those years ago, Grandma didn't see the hill either. She had lived all her life as a land-locked Ohioan, knowing no water body greater than country creeks. Whatever qualities allowed her to remove her shoes, to wade to the stump, and to wield her stick like a conquering hero, are the qualities that made her oblivious to the hill and invited her to explore a broader world with excitement. I'm learning that everyone, regardless of age, has a stump – to sit on, to leap from, to sing or shout from, to carve.

Have you ever tried to buy a birthday card designed specifically for someone who is turning sixty or more? Good luck! There are a multitude of greets for those going "over the hill" at forty, and for those celebrating the half-century mark at fifty. There is virtually nothing for those who are sixty, and positively nothing for seventy and eighty. What do the greeting card companies think happens to us? Have they not read the statistics on longevity? Fifty is not the end anymore. Reaching that point, we are, as Dante described in his *Inferno*, "Nel mezzo del cammin di nostra vita" – in the midway of this our mortal life. Bernard Baruch wisely defined old age as always fifteen years older than he was. Zsa Zsa Gabor was reportedly asked during an interview which of the Gabors was the oldest. She replied, "Well, she'd never admit it – but it's Mama." I like Mama's style!

And do the greeting card moguls assume that with advancing age the sense of humor evaporates, and that we henceforth prefer card designs of flower baskets and somber verses? Entrepreneurs would be wise to introduce a greeting card series celebrating the energy, the spunk, the bawdy spirit, the optimism and wisdom that propel us beyond that mythical hill after fifty.

Of course, for seniors as well as any other age group, our gifts and burdens vary. Some of us are luckier than others in terms of genes, health, and opportunities. It's fashionable to say that age is all in the mind, but that isn't so. Sometimes it's in the legs, the hands, the eyes, the heart. French pundits claim that, "A man is as old as his arteries." It would be foolish to deny age or infirmities, but we might do well to remember that sometimes age is fatal only if it spreads to the spirit. In spite of limitations, we can at least determine to use what we've got left to the fullest. Edward Weston observed, "How ironic that we pay others to dance when we should be dancing – to sing when we should be singing." Life and my grandmother urge us to choose dancing and singing – whether that means stubbornly kneading a little rubber ball in feckless hands or slamming a ball into the wall on a racquetball court.

Over sixty: is it winter or a Second Spring?

* * * * *

[2]

True measure of ourselves is our kindness to others
Sept. 11, 1997

If you're ready for some light reading with a heavy message, and if you've already read Cat in the Hat, consider looking deeply into a lesser-known Dr. Seuss book, *The Sneetches*. In just the first four lines of this sad, rhyming tale the good doctor describes the social/cultural problem in which these tall, feathery, yellow creatures find themselves embroiled. He sets the stage for conflict and drama when he tells us that:

"The Star-Belly Sneetches had bellies with stars.
The Plain-Belly Sneetches had none upon thars."

It's made clear from the outset that those distinguishing marks were quite small and shouldn't have made any difference, but the creatures with stars snubbed and vilified the others and boasted that, because they were adorned with stars, they were the best Sneetches on the Beaches.

Sensing turmoil, and knowing a good thing when he saw it, an entrepreneur named Sylvester McMonkey McBean showed up to help. He encouraged feelings of inferiority on the part of the Sneetches without stars and then, not surprisingly, offered a remedy for which he charged handsomely. After completing his self-serving shenanigans, eventually bilking both Sneetches with stars and Sneetches without, he concluded as he drove away with everyone's money:

"They never will learn. No. You can't teach a Sneetch!"

Fortunately, human beings are smarter than Sneetches. (Well, aren't we?) Though most people remain gracious in spite of station or condition, by middle age we have all met a couple or three Sneetches enamored with the stars on their bellies who feign superiority or actually believe in their own supremacy. We've learned that such Sneetches can come in several varieties and that their belly stars are not immediately visible. They might be concealed beneath an expensive suit, a white collared shirt, a graduation gown, a size six skirt, a star athlete's jersey, or beneath some dangling religious medallion.

And, strangely, after all these years, although we feel wise and sophisticated, we can find ourselves still cowering in the presence of one or the other of these pretenders, dazzled by their shining belly ornament. Intellectually, we know that things like money, size, color, education, and physical prowess "don't matter," in terms of our worth as human beings. At some level we know these things are all excess baggage that we won't be able to take on our final train out of here. Yet sometimes we succumb to feelings of inferiority.

It starts early. Even grade school children fret about name brands on tennis shoes, and jeans have to have the "right" name emblazoned across the seat. Teenagers binge and purge to emulate an impossible idealized image. Adults struggle to keep up with those mythical Joneses who are probably, in turn, trying to keep up with some other starred Sneetch.

Age teaches, however, that life is too short to allow others to make us feel second best; and energy is too valuable to waste on mimicking those who flaunt their stars. We're old enough and wise enough to know which sort of Sneetch we allow to make us cower and, on the other hand, to identify who among us makes it easy to feel good about ourselves.

And while we're checking stars, it can't hurt to see if there are some old ones on our own bellies that might best be peeled off. Perhaps it's time to consider removing any unnecessary barriers that separate us from fellow human beings.

Is achievement not important? Does nothing at all matter? Of course it is. Of course it does. But if there's going to be a criteria to determine the best Sneetches on the Beaches, maybe the true measure of one's worth is a willingness to appreciate the value of every human being… and to be kind. These are the only stars worth their points, the only sparkles that endure.

Surely we're basically kind. We ordinarily find it easy to be accepting and pleasant to family members and our circle of friends. But offering that respect and kindness for all of those with whom we come in contact takes a little more thought. Author Naomi Nye singles out for attention: "the people we meet only once, the lives that spin out in vast rings from the moment they clicked together, stones, jumbled in a hand, then tossed."

Do you recall some moment in which you caught the gaze of a total stranger – and in that two seconds of contact were acutely reminded that we are all the same – that it didn't matter if we belonged to the county club, or were fat, or had a college degree; that it didn't matter what we had in our pockets, on our backs, or emblazoned on our bellies?

In the same essay collection, *Never in a Hurry*, Nye continues, "People come to us whom we have not beckoned… I can believe we are ultimately judged, if such reckoning there be, by how we treat them."

Clearly, there are plenty of Sylvester McMonkey McBeans among us as well – those who make their livings inventing inadequacies and then preying upon us, selling stars for our bare bellies. But once we care about ourselves and can extend that same acceptance and kindness to others, those shops of horror close down.

You'll have to read Seuss' book yourself for the exciting, exasperating details of the Sneetches' adventure, but he assures us at the close of his story:

"That day, all the Sneetches forgot about stars
And whether they had one or not, upon thars."

His stories always have happy endings.

* * * * *

[3]

Old dogs must learn new tricks
October 9, 1997

When interplanetary exploration recently made headlines, I received a message from a savvy friend saying she had been in touch with Mars tracking stations and was sending the address in case I wanted to visit there, too. It occurs to me that most of us reading this *Age* page are old enough to remember when it wasn't a good idea to admit we were contacting other planets. The few who did spent lots of subsequent hours talking with therapists.

Welcome to the brave new world! Welcome to the internet!

Many years ago, I vowed that when knowledge of computers and mastery of the metric system became obligatory on this planet, I'd pack and move to Mars. This old dog wasn't about to learn such fancy new tricks. The determination was serious, but a funny thing happened on the way to my suitcase.

It was my son who cajoled me into buying a computer that would not only type, but could perform all sorts of other amazing functions including dusting and cooking. (I swear he promised that). Twenty years earlier, I had been traumatized when I disposed of my ancient manual typewriter, turning it in for an electric one. But when I finally succumbed to his sales pitch and bought a computer, I found it surprisingly easy to master. Within two weeks of the purchase, I unplugged the electric typewriter for good and relegated it to the attic museum along with the dial telephone and souvenir penny postcards.

The first thing I discovered a computer could do that the typewriter couldn't was to play games with me. An addictive game called Crystal Quest lured me into chasing sparkly crystals in the computer sky, earning points for some prize that was never specified. In the process, bizarre screen monsters tested my frustration and tolerance and periodically blew me up. Tiring of routine annihilation, I dared enter the realm of artwork – and found myself drawing absolutely horrible, colorful pictures on the screen with "spray paint, brushes, and pencils."

Ten months ago, my son determined to rescue me once again from the jaws of antiquity and sprinkled his new campaign with words like "E-mail" and "internet." Eureka! Once assured that I would blow nothing up if I made an error, I quickly trod where angels didn't, and began my voyage into the wider world of the net. Previously not a seasoned traveler, from my desk chair I now tracked elephants in Africa, listened to the national anthem of Greece, read The New York Times, and, if I chose, could make flight and hotel reservations to visit exotic sites in person.

But most of all, the people…

Relatives and long-time, long-distance friends who used to be in touch only on holidays were now "talking" with me regularly on the computer. I soon made myself at home in a chat room for seniors only and met people from all over the United States and beyond – "senior-netters" between the ages of fifty-five and eighty who also had exchanged their typewriters for cyberspace. What a zany, caring bunch! It was obvious that the internet was rescuing many seniors from what otherwise would be an isolated life. Some were housebound due to illness or the illness of their spouse. Others sought relief from boredom, or relished just plain fun and good conversation. Friendships (yes, real ones), blossomed through this medium and, with appropriate precautions, I dared travel to meet in person some of those whom I had met "online." My mother, nearing ninety, remains convinced that the folks I meet via computer all belong to the Mafia and warns me regularly about "those internet people." I try to break the news gently that I *am* one of "those internet people."

Across the United States, senior learning centers have been established to introduce us over-fifties to computers and to exorcise the demons that we sometimes fear reside inside. But I've learned that we can't push the wrong key and inadvertently launch missiles or break into the Pentagon's secret files. I discovered after my brief initial trepidation that there are no demons. There is magic!

Internet sites are filled with health care information, financial news, movie reviews, legal tips, jokes, maps, and a multitude of newspapers and magazines. There are even tutorials on line to teach us to use the internet itself! Seniornet is one web site specifically for those over fifty-five and holds a wealth of information in addition to sponsoring the chat room.

If you're not already on line, the next time a grandchild wants to demonstrate something for you on the computer, or your son/daughter gives a gentle sales pitch, don't hesitate to look and listen. Our children and grandchildren are often far ahead of us in the realm of computer expertise. Even contemporary four-year-olds know that every mouse isn't Mickey. If your children haven't suggested it themselves, tell them when they conspire to buy you a recliner or offer you a birthday vacation that you'd rather have a computer. Tell them you'll forgo the cruise to Barbados and cruise the universe instead. Dare to inquire of an electronics store clerk, "Show me what this thing will do," and prepare to be amazed.

My grandfather said television wasn't possible and regularly voiced disbelief even as he watched his favorite programs. I don't believe computers are possible either, but fortunately, we don't have to understand how they work to use them. Someday we might be ordering our groceries from the computer. Who knows what will come next? With so much to see and learn, why should we be left behind as technological fossils?

Buying a computer, taking this step into the twenty-first century, definitely won't solve all our problems. I'm still leaving this planet if someone makes me learn the metric system. But at least now, when I'm ready for the exodus, I know how to contact Mars for reservations.

* * * * *

[4]

Thanksgiving: a holiday or an attitude?
November 13, 1997

The smartest turkeys in the barnyard are already running for cover hoping to avoid the ax. Thanksgiving simply isn't their favorite holiday.

Results of my informal survey suggest that Thanksgiving also fares poorly in the holiday popularity contest among some of us higher on the food chain than turkeys. We soon will hear mutterings about too much time in the kitchen, too much company, too much football, too many leftovers, too many squabbles at the children's table, and too much geography between the dinner table and loved ones who couldn't attend the feast.

Some of us might even be tempted to join the chorus of mutterers.

Thanksgiving loses any aura of sentimentality when we conjure up those worst possible scenarios. We could dwell on hours of preparation for a meal no one fully appreciates, or the animated bickering among relatives who sprinkle salt in old wounds as they season the peas. Husbands and wives might confer sharply about where to spend the holiday, while hopeful extended families pull them in both directions.

From its humble, laudable origin, Thanksgiving seems more recently to have been assigned the role of keeping Halloween from bumping into Christmas and Hanukkah, a respite before the biggest shopping day of the year. One immediately senses the holiday's relative insignificance when noting that single day is designated for this celebration, as opposed to the seven generous days allotted for National Pickle Week. Surely this isn't what Thanksgiving was meant to be.

What ever happened to the Waltons? Remember John Boy and Grandpa and the rest of the clan? Now there's a Thanksgiving! What ever happened on our way to the table?

For the best possible Thanksgiving scenario, consider this: last Spring, I had the pleasure of talking with a nine-year-old boy whose mother had just bought him a new pair of shoes. He showed them to me, beaming, and spent a full ten minutes elaborating on why he liked the shoes, how he came to get them, and what he would do to take care of them. Such a refreshing monologue! I sat transfixed, just listening. Sadly, it has become commonplace for us, in our relative affluence, to adopt an attitude of entitlement; to feel so deserving that we expect the world's gifts rather than appreciate them, that we automatically claim title to all things bright and beautiful, taking health, love, and comforts for granted.

Each of us recalls moments of genuine gratitude, when we experienced that sense of being blessed beyond measure. Everyone can remember having been sick for a week with the flu or worse, and the exultation on that first day of recovery. And most of us have expressed thanksgiving for a good night's rest after a week of insomnia. Similarly, in times of crisis, we are deeply moved when we recognize the circle of love and friendship in which we reside. Several years ago, during moments of insightful appreciation, I made a list of the people most influential in my life and decided to express my thanks in letters to them. Unfortunately, four of them didn't wait for my belated recognition. They had already died. At such turning points in our lives we vow nevermore to take gifts for granted; and we don't... at least until the world moves in again and we forget. George Canning asks, "When our perils are past, shall our gratitude sleep?"

In spite of disappointing holiday scenes elsewhere, many families do genuinely enjoy Thanksgiving the way it's pictured in story books... the way Norman Rockwell painted the scene. Admittedly, it's a good idea to set aside at least one day a year for counting our blessings out loud. But I have a feeling that those who wholeheartedly relish the Thanksgiving holiday are those who maintain a grateful nature all year long. For even though Thanksgiving is designated a national feast day, we know that families can't miraculously wax grateful and enjoy each other on cue. Whether dining alone, with extended family, friends, or total strangers, those celebrate best who are grounded in genuine thankfulness, practiced from November to November. Maybe in its purest sense, Thanksgiving is an attitude more than a holiday.

Someone told me about a four-year-old in her neighborhood who was visiting a young friend. Shortly after arriving, he demanded of his friend's mother, "Give me a cookie." Intending to remind him gently of his manners, she asked, "Oh, but what is the magic word?" And he sternly replied, "Now!" Four-year-olds can be forgiven with a smile. The rest of us have learned that the magic word isn't "Now." It's "Please." And it's "Thanks."

We still have a week or so to begin serious holiday preparation. But before searching for the elusive turkey, we might brush up on our Olde English and spend a thoughtful moment with Robert Burns:

"Some hae meat, and canna eat,
And some wod eat that want it;
But we hae meat and we can eat,
And sae the Lord be thankit."
Happy thanks giving… all year long!

* * * * *

[5]

A victim of vocabulary
December 11, 1997

Please refer me to the twelve-step program for unrepentant word addicts. I discovered the magical power of words and picked up the habit as a youngster. Having three brothers, I learned early on that I couldn't assert my rights by beating them up or outrunning them. But if they pilfered something that belonged to me, they would sometimes give it back when I warned in a horrified voice, "Stop, or you'll break the flemander!" Don't bother to look it up. There's no such word. But they didn't know that.

By the time I turned twelve, fascination with words had escalated and I was hooked. A friend and I created and memorized a scholarly paragraph that we spouted to peers at the slightest provocation. Building our paragraph by adding one word each day, the recitation began: "You are a provocative, egotistical, prevaricator from a bedlamite's dwelling. You are ostreiform and look like a cockatrice. You are a terpsichorean person with many idiosyncrasies and you would be infatuated if you capitulated." It's embarrassing to contemplate how many times we must have imposed this pedantic display on peers, since I remember it after fifty years. No doubt my friend and I appeared more obnoxious and peculiar than erudite. But we didn't know it at the time.

Although I no longer make a habit of using words to intimidate, and although the unsolicited recitations have stopped, my addiction lives on. Willard Espy warns that, "words choose their lovers arbitrarily," and I have been willingly seduced. Do you want to make me get up from the dinner table before dessert is served? Want to watch me crawl out of bed when the alarm won't be going off for hours? If so, just casually wonder aloud, "Gee, I wonder what valetudinarian means." Words that recently sent me scurrying to the dictionary include sesquipedalian, poltroon, zaftig, and the beautiful pastiche. Rest assured. I'm not developing a new recitation paragraph.

Please don't misunderstand. I forget most of the definitions shortly after the dictionary slams shut. It's simply enticing to swirl these words around in the head for a while – to let them slip off the tongue like "slither" or stick in the throat like "ugly." Even if they aren't absorbed into my vocabulary, they refresh the synapses and delight the eye and ear. Fellow word-junkie Paul Dickson reminds us that, "there is no such thing as 'mere words,'" and Espy recommends that we "treat words as a Victorian gentleman treated a lady… Defer to them. Tell them how beautiful they are. Give them your seat in the subway."

Anne Soukhanov estimates that U.S. English grows by five thousand new words per year. I haven't personally counted, but will take her word for it. Most of us get lazy and chatter through our days using the same one thousand words over and over. Crossword puzzle fans and avid readers regularly put me to shame with their actual working vocabulary. One friend is trying to save me from disgrace by e-mailing me a new word daily, and I sincerely hope there isn't going to be a test!

Although not routinely called upon to use it, most of us keep at least one show-off word in reserve, and in emergencies we can always rely on "antidisestablishmentarianism." But Rudolf Ondrejka lists a fifty-two-letter mouthful that starts with "spirofuran" and ends with "thiazepine" with thirty-two more letters in the middle. Even if the word were pronounceable, it would be difficult to work into dinner conversation. Espy advises that to communicate with authority, one should always include a long, exotic word. For instance, he suggests referring to "karimata," a two-headed Japanese arrow that whistles, even if it has nothing to do with the point being made. Well, perhaps not, Willard.

Instead of emphasizing length, other word lovers seek the most beautiful sounding words. Ululation, melodious, rendezvous, philanderer, urethra, scenario, and diarrhea make the list. Obviously, the qualifying characteristic in this case is pure acoustics.

Words aren't merely the tool of poets and the faint of heart. Even the more feisty among us need an extraordinary vocabulary in time of battle. The "Shakespearean Insult Kit" (compliments of an internet friend) makes it possible to insult others with confidence and erudition. Just think! We can confront our enemies with, "You mewling, tickle-brained fustilarian," or "You dankish, ruttish, mammet," instead of stammering, "You… you… you!"

Word pushers have written volumes to feed my addiction. Among them are *The Connoisseur's Collection of Old and New, Weird and Wonderful, Useful and Outlandish Words* by Paul Dickson and *The Highly Selective Thesaurus for the Extraordinarily Literate* by Eugene Ehrlick. Ehrlick's book includes monstrosities like "catachresis," "dissepiment," and "balop" – which, together, sound strangely like a law firm. I'm considering these books and word-a-day calendars as holiday gifts for closet addict friends. They are legal, non-fattening, and require no batteries, but I'll enclose the Surgeon General's warning that they are potentially addictive.

My own addiction will follow me to the grave. If some tormentor isn't content with simply getting me up from the table from dessert or enticing me out of bed with an unfamiliar word, let him design my tombstone. Engrave on it the customary scroll and rose buds. Record my name and dates of my birth and death. Then at the bottom, carve "muniment, retrousse, tergiversation." You will hear an agitated rumbling from below, then one faint, hopeful, final request: "Please – give me another minute. Let me check the dictionary one more time."

* * * * *

[6]

It's your time: use it wisely
January 8, 1998

It's January again. Just when we've learned to write "1997" on checks and letters, 1998 showed up. And with a new century arriving in only two years, the younger generation will soon ask us for stories about the "olden days" – meaning the 1900s.

I'll introduce my own stories by explaining that time passes more quickly than it used to – that apparently something drastic happened in the solar system to speed everything up. Then, while they are riveted to every word, I'll divulge two truths about Time that I gleaned from years of accumulated wisdom and assorted wild guesses.

First I'll tell them (with profound apologies to our founding fathers) that all men are not created equal. We could easily list advantages some of us have over others at birth and thereafter. But we are unequivocally equal in at least one respect: regardless of race, creed, sex, economic status, or dimpled charm, each of us has twenty-four hours a day. Period. Yet we frequently hear otherwise intelligent people lament, "I don't have time." In a frantic, resentful tone of voice, they imply as they rush past that others may have twenty-four hours a day, but that somehow they personally were gypped and have to manage with just twelve or sixteen. Convinced they have no control over their time, they feel victimized and resent not being allotted sufficient time to do the things they truly want to do.

Although we want to sympathize politely with their plight, "I don't have time" is a deceptive thing to say. We (and they) have nothing but time. No one has found a way to retrieve the past or borrow hours from the future, and none of us gets gypped. The issue is not how much time we have but how we decide to use it; how we elect to invest that particular minute, hour, day... that "now." As complex as it may seem on the surface, we simply choose to use our time differently, each of us making dozens of choices every day – to sleep or bake cookies, to watch television or phone a friend, to play golf or do volunteer work. The thing most difficult to accept is that when we make these choices, our priorities are revealed, whether we like to acknowledge those priorities or not. Most of us would say that family is top priority, but in the midst of our busyness, family members are often the first to feel neglected.

Sure, buying food and paying rent are healthful habits! We can't often quit our paying jobs to pursue other ventures full-time; but working outside the home means we have to be extraordinarily careful how we choose to use the rest of our twenty-four hours. Loved ones can't be kept on dry ice to preserve them for a relationship at some more convenient time. They will go on living and growing with or without us. As a modern-day philosopher cautions, "No one on his death bed ever lamented, 'If only I had spent more time at the office!'" It certainly isn't a new quandary. Virgil's contemporaries (70-19 BC) faced the same dilemma, so he reminded them: "meanwhile it is flying, irretrievable time is flying."

"Yes," my young listeners will say, "we understand! What is truth number two?"

Well, remember death and taxes? Apparently there are those who manage to avoid the "certainty" of taxes, but we are still unquestionably equal in the sense that we can count on death. In spite of fantasies of invulnerability and in spite of sips from the fountain of youth, the second truth is that we all will die someday. As one contemporary comedian irreverently exclaims, "In a hundred years, all new people!"

No, I don't take death lightly. Though it's never surprising that someone dies, the when and how are sometimes tragic, always sad, and often heart-breaking. None of us is immune to the grief of losing someone we love or untouched by the death of another fellow being. But in my speech about Time, I'll explain that the central tenet of my life is that I'm going to die someday – that I don't have unlimited time – and that I live best remembering this truth.

That isn't a morbid or depressing thought! And I don't regularly bring up the subject at dinner parties. But this realization about Time, that we are all allotted an indefinite, finite number of years, is the best vantage point I've found for looking at the world. It means living with an awareness of my temporary status here; considering myself a transient at best. My hope is to leave as little unfinished business as possible when I die – whether that be ten days, six months, or twenty years from now. It requires keeping things current and helps me decide how to invest individual minutes and hours. If there's a conflict, I want to work it out. If I love someone, I make certain they know it. If there's a puddle to splash in, I probably will choose to splash. And if someone else feels pinched by Time, maybe I can let him cut ahead of me in line.

In spite of their fascination with my philosophizing, the younger generation shouldn't be expected to sit still for so long a dissertation. After all, they are busy making choices for their own time. If I have to settle for a brief summary statement, I'll advise, "You have twenty-four hours a day and you aren't going to live forever. Write it down so you won't forget."

* * * * *

[7]

What's in a name?
February 12, 1998

The fall of ancient Rome was triggered when a young boy hailed his waitress by shouting, "Hey, Mabel!" That disrespectful salutation launched the Empire's tragic cultural decline. I think we're still on that downward skid.

What ever happened to "Mr." and "Mrs.?" As children, we called our school custodian "Mr. Fisher," and the piano teacher, "Miss Firestone." The neighbors were "Mr. and Mrs. Moore." I'm sure if they lived today they'd be demoted to Harry, Maggie, Joe, and Tish. Young people simply don't address adults formally anymore unless muscles qualify us as "Mr. T." or our great pies as "Mrs. Smith."

Form of address will never rate the designation of most significant cause on the planet, and I promise to save time for worrying about nuclear proliferation, world hunger, and the ozone layer. But right now it's February and it's cold. I've resolved to warm my spirits by airing this pet peeve. Does anyone else even care? Will I find others to endorse my petition and help unload picket signs from the truck?

Showing zero decorum, a doctor's young office nurse, who has never met me, shouts my first name from across the crowded waiting room, mispronouncing it for good measure. Is this meant as a friendly gesture? Is it a way of leveling us in the name of equal opportunity? Physicians sometimes encourage patients to address them informally, too. But believe me, as a patient I'd rather have my physical examination done by someone I know as "Dr. Zweebach," than as "Skip." Physicians are so young anymore! Their title is the only thing that keeps me from fearing I'm contributing to the delinquency of a minor as I sit on the exam table in skivvies or less.

Children call aunts, uncles, neighbors, and other adult acquaintances by their given names. Young men and women address their college professors as "Jim," or "Judy," and their probation officer as

"Shelly." As adults, we ignore titles of position as well. The U.S. President answers to just plain "Bill." We used to call our minister "Chuck" and our mayor "Butch." I conscientiously, albeit fruitlessly, object to this pretense of familiarity and instant camaraderie.

While it's easy to gripe about the situation, it's harder to know what to do. And where do we draw the line in making decisions about formality vs. informality? Certainly, I painstakingly avoid using first names if the addressee is wearing papal robes or an obvious crown. On the other hand, I don't advocate children's addressing adults as "sir" and "ma'am" – a nicety that smacks of the nineteenth century and oppression of children. But as a general rule, if I'm speaking with someone old enough to be my parent, I address him/her as "Mr.," "Mrs.," or Ms." until specifically invited to do otherwise. And it doesn't matter whether that person invests my money or cleans my furnace. I tried to teach our children to refer to elders respectfully, and I gently let children of my acquaintance know what I prefer being called myself. I'm also working on a politely assertive request for the young nurse in the doctor's office – something I'll perhaps shout across the waiting room to her – and I plan to continue referring to her boss as "Dr. Zweebach."

Although I like to think of myself as "cool" and "with it," introducing this subject marks me as old fashioned at best and snobbish at worst. Old fashioned, maybe. But I lack both the temperament and training to carry off snobbery. When I call an elderly neighbor "Mr. Barnes," that title is a mental curtsey; a verbal bow indicating respect. I don't even have to respect the man personally – sometimes his behavior may not warrant it – nonetheless, I choose to acknowledge his age or station in life. "What's in a name?" you and Shakespeare ask. Well, my relationship with that neighbor will definitely differ depending upon whether I call him "Mr. Barnes," "Sweetie," or something in between.

I might be fighting a losing battle, but the issue is not frivolous or academic. When Henry Stanley located Livingstone in Ujiji in 1871, history would have taken a decidedly informal turn had he inquired upon his discovery, "Dave, I presume?" In the face of their enormity, we don't even know the first names of Dr. No and Dr. Strangelove. Nor would we demean Mrs. Miniver or Mr. Tibbs by referring to them as – well, we can't even guess, can we?

My plea is not for stuffy elitism, and the use of titles doesn't imply that one person is better than another – not at all. I generally agree with Daniel Defoe that, "Titles are shadows, crowns are empty things." But I also applaud Laurence Sterne's eighteenth-century reflection, and urge that it be printed in leaflets and dropped from helicopters: "Hail, ye small, sweet courtesies of life! for smooth do ye make the road of it."

Granted, we struggle with more earthshaking issues than this one, and how we address each other is just the beginning of mutual respect. But it had better start somewhere – soon. At this very moment some twentieth-century adolescent in a Denver restaurant is shouting, "Hey, Mabel!"

And another column of civilization trembles.

* * * * *

[8]

Health tips dangerous – all that stress
March 12, 1998

A motivational sign hangs over my desk. It reads, "If you don't take care of your body, where will you live?" I put the sign there to help realign my previous attitude, aptly summarized by Robert Orben, who advised, "Quit worrying about your health. It'll go away." Since becoming a convert I've paid homage to all sorts of healthful habits and strive to do what the experts recommend.

In this new health-conscious mode, keeping track of which foods to eat presents a perpetual challenge. Sugar is bad for us, but so are artificial sweeteners. We substitute margarine for butter only to learn later that one is as bad as the other. "Eat oat bran!" they clamored. Perhaps my cholesterol level dropped, but my arteries clogged with oat bran. And then a friend cited research that people with low cholesterol have more accidents and are more often suicidal. Coffee causes breast cancer? What's the latest? Even my picnics took a bland turn when the powers that be advised not to grill meat because of the carcinogens in charcoal. Meats in general pose a problem. I've studiously tried to avoid spoiled sushi, diseased chicken, and mad cow. But switching to more fruits, I had to worry about poisonous raspberries. All that remains safe are roots and nuts. Summer time isn't bad; but foraging gets tedious in the winter.

A healthy diet creates economic problems as well. First of all, I had to turn down a part-time job because it takes much of the week to read labels in the grocery store. And, secondly, foods cost more when they remove the salt, sugar, fat, and cholesterol. Go figure. You'd think they would be cheaper.

While following the recommended diets du jour, I also embarked on an exercise program. After first undertaking weight training, I decided to participate in sports. It's been amazing. Although I've played tennis for just a few months, I have already learned the forehand ground stroke, lob, volley, and treatments for tennis elbow and bursitis. Smoking research also accelerated my exercise regime. Having long ago decided not to smoke, new findings about harmful second-hand effects kept me active outrunning smoke that other people generated. Then, just when I felt good about this new fitness life style, I read a list of "prominent people who died while exercising." Do I really want to die tangled up in a net?

Although I harkened years ago to evangelists who spoke against the Demon Rum and all his relatives, researchers often make claims that one drink a day does wonders for health and longevity. I was nearly ready to drink to that when a February study concluded that one drink a day increases the risk of breast cancer by one third.

Medicines themselves create confusion. Take estrogen and risk cancer, or don't take it and risk heart attack. I try to read the list of possible side effects that comes with any prescription, but the print is so fine that I fear not living long enough to find the magnifying glass. The information isn't always reassuring. One prescription drug I took listed, "possible death." Talk about your adverse side effects!

And remember, I am trying to follow all these recommendations and keep current with the latest bulletins while I juggle the schedule to see my dentist twice a year, have an annual physical exam, keep track of my body fat, and squeeze in a mammogram.

Well, I've encountered the last unbelievable straw. I kid you not that recent medical research claims that flossing teeth regularly can lower the risk of heart disease. Never mind how it happens. This finding simply marks the latest in a lengthy series of confusing advisories. I propose a new Surgeon General warning: "Reading medical bulletins is dangerous to one's mental health." And I'm seriously thinking of giving up reading because they're playing with our minds here. How am I supposed to take care of myself? I feel like a failure. I don't even know the shampoo pH level that's best for my hair.

Long before I ever read what researchers had to say about staying healthy, two family experts had shared their wisdom with me. My grandfather didn't believe in either calories or germs because he couldn't see them. He lived a relatively healthy life for nearly ninety years. My mother had always advised against being too germ conscious, reminding me occasionally that, "You have to eat a peck of dirt before you die." She's 88.

Perhaps they were right. Perhaps it's that simple. It's obvious I can't follow all the recommendations flowing out of research laboratories, and if I keep up this fitness regime, I may have to be subdued at age ninety-five by being struck with one of my own dumbbells. Otherwise, I'll just have to sort out all the medical alerts and decide what I want to die from. Right now, I think it will have something to do with an overstuffed recliner and tubs of real ice cream.

* * * * *

[9]

Just remember: Mother Teresa was a little old lady
April 9, 1998

A recent press release sang the praises of some U.S. political muckety-muck, and specifically noted that in spite of his demanding schedule, this paragon of virtue often took time to answer letters from "little old ladies." High praise indeed! Question: if his behavior warrants such applause, why does it awaken my hackles from their ordinarily sleepy haze?

Surely, "little" holds no demeaning implication unless referring to moral stature. "Old" describes a simple fact of life and beats the alternative. And most twentieth-century women wouldn't object to the "lady" moniker. But these three words strung together smack of ageism and make me want to yodel in response, "Little old lady who?"

I wondered, upon reading the article, whether some of his letters could have come from little old ladies whose IQs reached high into three digits and who had more education than he did. I wondered if they might have kept a critical eye on the political scene since before he was born. It occurred to me that Golda Meir and Mother Teresa technically qualified as little old ladies. So do many in my own circle of friends, but I don't advise letting them know if you call them that.

I dared ask one young man to list synonyms for older people and he responded with a litany of "seniors, golden agers, old folks, snow birds, old fogies, geezers, codgers, coots... " He continued the recitation as I headed in another direction.

Those over sixty in our culture (little old men as well as little old ladies) are usually not directly maligned or openly mistreated, but are frequently overlooked – diminished and dismissed as being harmless.

Recently, I visited a lingerie shop, looking for a long, slinky, silk nightgown. In spite of the young saleslady's help, I couldn't find exactly what I wanted. Eventually she asked, "Is this for you?" And when I answered in the affirmative, she rejoiced, "Oh well, then! Here! We have some flannel gowns left over from Christmas!"

We were not amused.

Physicians sometimes rush to blame patients' ailments on age. When my eighty-year-old neighbor experienced pain in her left leg, the doctor advised that her discomfort was a function of age. She informed him, "My right leg feels fine, and it's just as old as the left one." I've bottled a gallon of her spunk to uncork in emergencies.

What has happened here? Having had distinct personalities and individual interests until we turned sixty, some would now hand us a vanilla script to follow, a bland identity to adopt. But one of the advantages of age is that we can write our own scripts – with more humor and freedom and confidence than ever before. I had always wanted to mature into a salty old woman, and even bought the appropriate red velvet hat. Then a caring young friend cautioned that there was one place I shouldn't wear it – "outside of the house." Younger generations occasionally gape at our antics in amazement and amusement, not knowing we blaze trails they shortly will follow.

Television characterizations of "golden agers" have recently become more realistic. No longer always portrayed as incompetent and incontinent, over sixties can be found in marathons, in congress, or in love. And those four little old ladies sitting in the booth at your neighborhood restaurant have nearly three hundred years of accumulated information, stories, and experience. Perhaps they haven't just awakened from a nap. Check their bags for dance shoes, lap top computers, or golf balls.

In moments of creative sarcasm, I wonder if after blowing out the sixty candles on our birthday cakes we should be required to have "l.o.l." (little old lady) or "l.o.m." (little old man) tattooed on our foreheads so others can be formally advised to pay no attention to us. Besides, when we look into mirrors, the tattoos would remind us of our place when, otherwise, we might forget and feel young. Rubber stamps with those identifying initials could be issued as well. When we write to elected officials or other genuinely important people, stamping the envelopes before mailing them would save them from having to read our mail except in the event of photo opportunities.

In more mellow moods, I propose that it be arranged for people of all ages to look as old as their spirit. If oldsters sparkle on the inside, let them sparkle on the outside. Likewise, if someone is stodgy and unimaginative at age thirty, Mother Nature should color him old. She might have implemented this system long ago, being one of the original senior citizens.

Although I'd never claim that age automatically brings wisdom, in feistier moments I admittedly enjoy the caveat that "youth and skill are no match for old age and treachery."

But as long as we inhabit the same planet, we might as well strike a workable bargain. If the next generation learns to appreciate little old ladies (those of us who are "chronologically experienced"), I'll make allowances for young whippersnappers. I'll insist, however, that they sit down for a chat with Walt Whitman, and he'll inquire of them:

> "Youth, large, lusty, loving –
> youth full of grace, force, fascination,
> Do you know that Old Age may come after you
> with equal grace, force, fascination?"

* * * * *

[10]

Motherhood is a lifetime occupation
May 14, 1998

Another Mother's Day came and went. Once again, the authorities spurned me when choosing Mother of the Year, but I take comfort in guessing I'd get at least passing marks from my own grown children. Perhaps children are the only qualified voters in that selection process anyway. Nonetheless, Mother's Day, bless its commercial little heart, always renders me a bit nostalgic.

Do you remember the early parenting years when we sometimes collapsed on the couch after hectic days with our children and fantasized about an "empty nest?" We pictured grown children clearing eighteen years of debris from their bedrooms, handing back the car keys, maybe giving us gold retirement watches, and then flying off to feather their own nests. But we eventually learned, as all parents do, that when offspring leave the nest they leave little piles of treasured twigs in the attic to mark their territory and hold their spot. Little do they know how much room they continue to take up in our hearts as well as in our storage spaces.

When we talk now with parents of young children, we shouldn't disillusion them. They'll learn soon enough. But we older folks know that in many ways, parenting is harder after our children turn eighteen. We care just as much about them then, but can do relatively little. We hope we've done enough in spite of our imperfections to carry them through; hope they'll be making smart choices; hope the world will be kind. We try to walk the tightrope of showing care and concern without intruding with criticism or unsolicited advice, knowing that we can't ground them anymore, make them get sufficient sleep, or bribe them to eat broccoli. We recall those times we had more faith in them than they did in themselves – and times their daring left us secretly shaking in our boots as we bit our tongues and wished them well.

Elizabeth Stone reminds us that, "Making the decision to have a child is momentous. It is to decide forever to have your heart go walking around outside your body."

My own emphasis is on the "forever."

We lived in Colorado when our son turned three. During one early winter night that year, the first snow fell, and by morning was several glistening inches deep. I knew he wouldn't recall the previous winter and that this would be his first real experience of snow. So when he awoke that morning, I told him there was a big surprise. I positioned him in front of the draped patio doors, then stood aside and dramatically pulled the drapes open to reveal the back yard, completely transformed by white hills and valleys. He stood transfixed for a moment, then gasped, "For me?"

I felt magical. In his grateful mind, he credited me not only with showing him that magnificent scene, but with creating it as well.

I occasionally think about that episode, because when children are grown, parents inevitably lose their magical powers. We used to kiss away "owies" and make the unbearable bearable with a caring conversation or well-timed hug. Erma Bombeck's children once thought she was able to turn red lights green just by blowing on them, and all of us were able to banish nighttime monsters from bedroom closets. We took some comfort in knowing we could keep our children safe by letting into their lives only those bits of the world that would be generous and kind. But it didn't take long for the rest of the world to creep in, too, and our sorcerer days were over.

When the children are grown, something in us would still like to guarantee them smooth sailing. When they run into difficult situations, we'd like to be able to pull back the drapes and create a peaceful, sparkling season. But even though we sometimes long for that old omnipotence, we all know too much for that to work anymore. We have to turn in our magic wands, confident these new adults will be able to handle whatever season arrives.

In watching the winter Olympics on television earlier this year, I kept one eye on parents of the athletes – parents who were not merely cheering, but who were experiencing every triple axel and ski jump, every crash through the fence. Surely they were wishing they could turn red lights green for this cherished part of them that was out there risking, daring, gliding, and flying... wishing to be magical just once more.

We don't graduate from parenting. There is no ceremony, no tassel. Even though I've long since left home, my own mother still worries about me and only half-jokingly concludes her letters with a reminder to wear my boots.

Funny, isn't it? We once yearned for quiet afternoons, tidy rooms, and the relaxed schedule of the empty nest. But in spite of all the ups and downs, there's a magnet, fixed for life, that holds our children close. They often weren't aware of the kisses we planted on their foreheads after they were asleep – or of those wordless or wordy little prayers we said for them. Would they be surprised to know that we still do? Ursula LeGuin writes:

"Walk carefully, well loved one,
Walk mindfully, well loved one.
Return with us, return to us,
be always coming home."

* * * * *

[11]

Trips to the auto and body shop
June 11, 1998

I hate to sound ungrateful because it served me well for many years. But it's begun causing so many problems that I'm faced with having to make drastic decisions.

Lately, if I leave it parked over the weekend, it grumbles about starting up on Monday morning. More and more frequently, I have to take it in for repairs. It runs out of gas quickly and every year emits more squeaks and creaks. I've been told it might well develop leaks or start overheating. Besides, it looks less classy than before, having accumulated several unattractive dents and faded spots. I routinely keep it clean and usually apply extra polish on special occasions, but onlookers don't "ooh" and "aah" anymore. And even though I'm conscientious about meeting its maintenance needs, things are falling apart all at once. Talk about planned obsolescence!

Cars? Oh, yes! Cars, too. But I'm talking about my body here.

I can see why it would be confusing. Whether discussing auto bodies or our own, we're dealing with an eternal, universal question: Do we ride around in the old jalopy as it is or do we spend money, time, and energy doing something about its dilapidated condition?

It's no secret that our culture worships youth and that thousands of businesses make a good living winning converts to that religion. For some reason, we don't want our skin or our hair to age as fast as we do, and as much as we loved Grandma and Grandpa, we don't want to look like them. When we encounter that fawning old acquaintance for the first time in twenty years, we want to believe him when he lies, "You haven't changed a bit!"

I attended a college class reunion several years ago; and although all of us were pointed toward 60, just half a dozen of us had any gray hair. Only their hairdressers knew for sure, but I felt certain that Mother Nature got lots of help. They looked great! No question about it. I've decided I'm simply too lazy and too cheap to intercept advancing white roots every few weeks and have them re-dipped... or whatever beauticians do to them.

While dyeing hair probably ranks as the most common intervention, the world offers dozens of tactics for fooling ourselves and the world about our age. We can schedule facelifts, nose jobs, tummy tucks, and liposuction. Or, we might buy special girdles to hold parts of us in or padded bottoms and tops to make parts of us stick out. We can have a new chin installed when the old one begins to sag.

Some opt for electrolysis to remove unwanted hair while others have hair imported when there isn't enough to cover bald spots. We wear contact lenses to conceal the fact that newspaper print is getting smaller, and fake nails to hide years of hard work that chip and peel. We zap spider veins from our legs – those colorful road maps of where we've been – or put lifts in our shoes when yet another vertebra collapses and makes us shorter.

Cosmetics employees at the mall peddle wrinkle removers and offer "complete makeovers," promising to exchange old faces for young ones. Although "Just for Men" products clamor for attention, plastic surgeries and hair preparations are now unisex. What a sad state of affairs if all women over fifty still looked thirty and men over fifty looked… well, their age. Somewhere, it is written, "Vanity of vanities. All is vanity." The reference must be biblical, because I'm certain it isn't from an Avon brochure.

Now don't get me wrong. There's no "right" decision here, and I like to look at well-chiseled chins, tucked tummies, and color-perfect hair as much as the next person. I'm just trying to get some perspective as I enter these later years of middle age. I want to do everything that will enhance my wellbeing and even a few things to bolster my youthful image. But where to draw the line? (Not on my forehead, please.) First of all, I don't like to be such trouble to myself that inordinate amounts of time are spent in the pursuit of camouflage. And I'm hesitant to contemplate procedures that will make me completely over. It would be spooky having a face younger than the rest of me. And what if I had my tummy tucked and nails sculptured, and still was a stubborn and irritable person?

We're not the only culture hooked on beautiful veneers. When I need renewed perspective, I look at old copies of *National Geographic Magazine*. I picture myself in the jungle among members of some featured primitive tribe, painting red and black designs on my face, stretching my earlobes with wooden disks, and polishing a bone for my nose – trying to stay young and attractive for primitive men busy painting their own stripes and polishing their own bones. Then it's easier to chuckle and ask, "What's this all about, anyway?"

I don't know the answer for anyone else. For now, I've decided just to keep it running as smoothly as possible, without expecting too much from the poor old thing. I'll protect it from the elements, keep it clean and well oiled, and won't race the engine. Occasionally, I'll buy it new seat covers.

And that goes for the car, too.

* * * * *

[12]

We reap what we sow
July 9, 1998

No one intends to have accidents. That's why we call them accidents. No one deliberately behaves carelessly, purposely makes errors in judgment, or plans stupid mistakes. That's why we fondly call ourselves "only human."

I could have forgiven any of those foibles quickly, even graciously. But she ran a stop sign at the intersection and crashed into my car with me in it, sending us both spinning across the street like an arcade game-ball. And after pausing briefly to contemplate the best course of action, she sped off in the opposite direction. Fortunately, gratefully, I didn't sustain serious injuries, but she didn't know that when she ran.

When a police officer responded to the call, I told him I didn't understand how someone could leave the scene of an accident. He quickly curtailed any discussion with a crisp, flat pronouncement: "It happens all the time." I think in filling out the report he wrote "naive" beside my name.

So I'm left to ruminate on my own, hoping to reap something more from the trauma than repair bills. Mostly I wonder what went through the perpetrator's mind as she decided to run, and how long she had unwittingly been in training to make that decision.

The scenario reminded me of an occasion several years ago when a couple of my friends went to an upscale restaurant, taking their two young children along for the first time. The evening was a fiasco, with the children soon disrupting the restaurant's advertised ambiance. Their manners were prehistoric, their volume excessive, and their bickering incessant. Embarrassed and annoyed, both parents tried to teach etiquette on the spot. Of course, it didn't work.

Unfortunately, as those children so aptly illustrated, we don't develop manners (or ethics and moral responsibility) when traumatic events occur. During these crises, whether in a restaurant or an intersection, we simply discover what we have already become.

Well, "the accident" was a great place to observe what people had become. I learned first of all that many had become Good Guys. Five truly human witnesses chose to interrupt their lives to help, and I swear they wore white hats. I wish a posse of them would follow me everywhere. They reaffirmed my faith in people and proved once again that Good Guys outnumber Bad Guys by at least five to one.

It's easy to see what my assailant had become – but harder to understand how she got that way. Occasionally, news stories carry accounts of tragedies in which bystanders remain aloof, hesitating to "get involved" in other people's problems. But hit-and-run drivers go a step beyond that, refusing to be involved even in their own dramas, refusing to accept responsibility for their own behavior.

Are there "bad seeds?" Just evil, uncaring people? If that explanation suffices, we should issue black hats to the Bad Guys so we can identify them early and swerve accordingly. Well, it worked in cowboy movies, but I doubt the answer is that simple.

Or, could it be, as S. J. Lec says, "No snowflake ever feels responsible for an avalanche." Sadly, there are those whose lives do resemble avalanches. They gradually come to feel powerless, believing they have no control over how far and fast they fall. How desperate do people become in that landslide, and to what extreme would they go to survive?

I'm no "bleeding-heart liberal" blaming genes, drugs, abuse, poverty, or avalanches for misdeeds. Civilization is possible only if each person is ultimately held responsible for his/her own behavior. Though some of us have been far more fortunate than others, we could all find excuses for shortcomings if we searched desperately enough.

Of course I had a chance to observe what I had become, too. I took pride in the fact that I didn't go home and vent my frustration on the neighbor's cat. And although I soon learned the name and address of the perpetrator, I didn't send an emissary to seek revenge. On the other hand, I noticed that my cup of righteous indignation did, indeed, runneth over.

It has to make us wonder. No one wears Tennyson's "white flower of a blameless life." It's interesting to guess where each of us in a crisis would draw the line. We like to picture ourselves with moral standards that aren't tailored on a daily basis in the name of expedience. But are we certain we would stop at the scene of our accidents if we had no money and no insurance? Benjamin Franklin observed long ago that it's "hard for an empty sack to stand upright." Perhaps the next time I peer into a mirror I'll double-check the color of my own hat – just to make sure it isn't gradually fading to some indeterminate shade of gray.

Thanks to eyewitness Good Guys, the police will locate my hit-and-runner and chat with her about responsibility. While I'm making phone calls to the insurance company, filling out accident reports, getting estimates for repairs, and temporarily bumming rides, I'll be wondering what happened to her.

I should be so lucky in return.

* * * * *

[13]

If a woman answers, hang up
August 13, 1998

In the early 1960s, as I organized our first real apartment and fine-tuned my June Cleaver act, a vacuum cleaner salesman came to the door. Since Ward was at work and The Beaver was taking a nap, I greeted the salesman alone. He explained that he had a new product to demonstrate, but that he could divulge no further detail until the *Man of the House* was there to listen to the spiel along with me. Well, I sensed that a feisty edge was beginning to develop when June's apron untied itself and dropped to the floor. I explained that I was competent enough to make a household appliance decision myself and convinced him to go ahead and throw dirt on the floor and sweep it up again even if I was his only audience. I can acknowledge nearly forty years later that I probably made the purchase just to show him I could do it. Since the vacuum cleaner still works, I apparently made a good decision, albeit for the wrong reason.

Later, salespersons became more politically aware and began asking, instead, to speak with the *Head of the Household*, not specifying male or female. This terminology probably created a lot of bickering between couples after the salesman was out of earshot. Many couples probably hadn't known they had to designate one of them as "head." Besides, I understand that when people filled out financing forms and came to the question, "Who is the head of your household?" some wrote "God" or "Jesus." Although both are worthy sentiments, the information wasn't especially helpful for billing purposes.

Several years later, again in an effort to get the wording just right, solicitors began asking to deal with the *Responsible Party*. This implied, first of all, that there could be only one – and they didn't ever specify responsible for what. Responsible for preparing dinner? For solving national defense problems? For mowing the lawn? Their new jargon didn't deal adequately, either, with the fact that some unfortunate households boasted no responsible person at all.

Well, I thought I had heard the last of it. But this summer when we needed major repair work on the house and I phoned to request bids, one of the companies told me they wanted to talk with the family's *Decision Maker*. Initially, I told them I would do nicely. But when they called later to confirm the appointment, they said they needed to talk with *both Decision Makers*.

Again, they didn't specify which decisions they were interested in. But regardless of the lingo they've used through the years, and even though they won't ask it directly, what they want to know is, "Okay. Who has the

25

authority to spend money in your house?" Perhaps we should applaud their efforts to be diplomatic and politically correct. But the bottom-line implication is that the *Man of the House* is still that person. Can you imagine a husband contracting to have his roof replaced and being told that the company representative will first have to talk with the *Woman of the House?* Give me a break!

Banks and investment corporations are high on the list of those who need to get a clue. When their agents phone to solicit our business, they consistently ask to speak to the "Mr." of the household. These aren't people who already know us. These are people who simply take for granted that husbands are more knowledgeable and have more authority in money matters.

Believe me, I'm not a strident feminist and certainly not a man-hater. I'm not even working right now toward female domination of the planet. But businesses seem to be late in getting the message. Surveys have documented what a large percentage of the nation's money is handled by women, and most of us aren't in the dark anymore about contracts, interest, payment plans, and scams. Most of us, in the '90s, are qualified both intellecttually and financially to purchase more than Tupperware and Underware.

Besides, even in less egalitarian marriages, who qualifies as decision maker anyway? Is it the out-front husband who strides up to the salesman and says, "I'll take that car?" Or is it his quiet, unassuming wife who rolls close to him in bed and whispers, "I think that's the car we should buy, honey?"

Businesses deserve to be paid for their services. But I suggest they quit trying to find out who is "boss" in the household and just get on with their sales pitch. They don't have to identify the responsible person, head of the household, or the decision maker. Let them present their case and then retreat to let couples talk it over, fight it out, flip a coin, pray over it, kiss over it, or read tea leaves to reach their decision – however they usually resolve such issues. All we need from the company is an explanation of their product and service. If I choose, I should be allowed to enlist an intelligent cockatiel to gather information for me, regardless of how responsible the bird is or how many of the decisions it usually makes around the house.

So I don't know how the same old question will be phrased five years from now. But having confessed to the vacuum cleaner incident, I want to make sure salesmen know that June Cleaver doesn't live here anymore.

* * * * *

[14]

Reading, writing, and rampage
September 10, 1998

As a thirteen-year-old, I had visited the principal's office before, but mostly to deliver polished apples or to kiss the hem of her garment. This particular time, however, she summoned me there, along with a couple of my cohorts. Reviewing our transgressions, she made us sit in her cramped office while she read aloud from the Bible (in the public schools, no less.) The passage she selected listed seven things that are an abomination to God, and she insisted we choose the one that fit us best. I hate multiple choice, but knew right away I didn't have "hands that shed innocent blood." After eliminating five other loathsome possibilities (like lying tongue and wicked imagination), I admitted by default to having "feet that be swift in running to mischief." To merit this particular chastisement, we had immobilized all the white keys on our choir director's piano by tacking them down with scotch tape.

Few students are entirely angelic during the course of their school years. But when did foolish, annoying pranks progress to violence? I refuse to believe that the piano key episode precipitated this downward spiral. But it's scary out there, and it's that time of year again.

Yellow school busses pull up to the corner and students rush to meet them in sneakers that haven't been broken in yet. Flashing lights warn cars to slow down in school zones, and neighborhood streets settle into silence. Witnessing this transition from my front step, I find myself wishing students well as they hoist their backpacks for another year.

Sadly, I have to wish first of all for them to be safe… safe in the places we once considered certain sanctuaries, the place where infractions included gum-chewing in class and hogging the playground swings. But smiley faces and welcome signs on the schools' front doors have been replaced by signs declaring "zero drug tolerance" and "gun free zone." What ever happened to spit wads? And how do we get them back?

Before students arrive on the scene each year, teachers gather for faculty meetings. They still discuss where to find art supplies and how to proceed during fire drills. But the agenda has expanded to include emergency procedures in case someone brings a weapon to school. Some may have to alternate playground duty with security camera monitoring.

Parents send their children to school dreading not only the possibility of head lice and scraped knees, but unspeakable, random tragedy. Children wear brave smiles, sheltered, perhaps, by their philosophy that it won't happen here… just like it could never happen in Mississippi, Kentucky, Pennsylvania, Oregon, or Virginia.

Understandably, lots of conversation is focused on this problem, the dialogue accompanied by head-shaking and bewildered expressions. Obviously there is no simple explanation, and it would be foolish to undertake vast solutions with half-vast ideas. But I'm wondering if we don't know more than we think we do.

We've all seen how toddlers act if they need a parent's attention and get no response. They first call out, then tug at skirts or pant legs, then cry. If we're still too busy to pay attention, they might climb the drapes or do something unfriendly to the cat. When children need us, they need us. Older children might have to throw rocks at streetlights or set their hair on fire to make a point, but they will be heard.

We already know that behavior speaks when words fail. Children themselves usually don't know what's behind their violence, and frankly, I don't really know either. But troubled children are sending messages we haven't translated yet, and we're in danger until we do. One danger is that we become so used to schoolyard mayhem that we are numbed into indifference rather than being shocked and outraged. In June, after yet another shooting in which a student and two teachers were hit by gunfire, a TV news anchor reported, "The two teachers were just in the wrong place." I suggest they were in the right place, doing the right thing. Something else was amiss.

Newsweek Magazine quotes a middle-school principal's effort to explain schoolyard violence. "Like cakes that should be allowed to bake slowly in a warm oven, our children too often get the heat turned up and the time cut back. On the outside they look finished, perhaps even crusty, but inside, they have not had time to coalesce. Under stress they are likely to collapse."

Short of knowing the ultimate solution, I hope students everywhere will have quiet, disciplined classrooms in which to work; that both the administration and parents allow teachers to maintain order, offering respect for each student and insisting upon that same respect for themselves and fellow classmates. I hope that beginning with kindergarten, life at school will give children a chance to learn they can count on having reasonable consequences for both good and bad behavior, so they won't have to learn this later in a tragic crash course.

For the rest of us, I hope we'll remember how desperately children need our attention, time, and direction and that we listen carefully enough to translate what a few troubled children are telling us in the language of violence. Theirs are not "feet that be swift in running to mischief." Theirs are "hands that shed innocent blood."

* * * * *

[15]

Inquiring minds want to know – thank goodness
October 8, 1998

It looks like a prop from some 1930s horror movie.

On an otherwise blank wall in a local medical facility, and within easy reach of patients, there's an ominous looking metal panel about three feet tall and two feet wide. Hardly inconspicuous! On its face is a huge red knob attached to an equally huge pointer that can be turned to indicate either "ON" or "OFF." The day I visited, its pointer was nearly, but not quite, aimed at "ON." I asked the technician what that imposing switch controlled and, although she'd worked there several years, she said she didn't know.

Well, my brain started making those piercing beeps that big trucks make when they back up, and I suggested we experiment. What if we turned it completely on? Maybe the sun would come out! Or if we dared turn it off, gravity might shut down! She declined my offers to flick the switch and didn't make any guesses of her own. Actually, she seemed relieved when I left and escorted me past the switch to an exit.

Curiosity. It's gotten a bad name. As children, we poked fingers in light sockets, tasted earthworms, and tested whether Lincoln Logs would flush down the toilet. Parents cautioned us against exploring too far and told us, of course, about all those dead cats who sacrificed themselves by nosing in where they didn't belong.

Even as adults, we hear dire warnings. Adam and Eve lost their lease in Eden just because they wanted to know what apples taste like. Poor Lot's wife, unable to resist peeking over her shoulder, ended up as a salt lick. We often frown on intellectual curiosity as well. What child hasn't heard, "Don't ask so many questions?" What adult hasn't been chided at least once for challenging accepted truths whether on the topic of politics, religion, or science? St. Augustine describes a dialogue between two unnamed discussants long before our own time. When a curious man asked what God had been doing all those years before he made heaven and earth, the other admonished, "He was fashioning hell for the inquisitive."

John Clarke warned in 1639 that if we insist upon prying into every cloud, we might be struck with a thunderbolt. But although the wrong sort of exploration could be disastrous, most of us live to tell about any downside of our curiosity. I recall once sticking my finger into a bucket of manure to see if it was frozen – and it definitely wasn't.

In general, however, I'm wondering if Clark's admonition isn't more a promise than a threat. I'd remind him that curious people aren't limited to sticking their fingers into manure buckets. Those who pry into loftier clouds are the inventors, explorers, and philosophers in our midst. They sailed ships to the edge of the world when it was still flat, found out what makes things tick and what makes them stop ticking. They wondered hard enough about what was on the moon that they arranged to go look. They unearthed the Dead Sea Scrolls and King Tut's tomb. And who, for heaven's sake, was that hungry adventurer who ate the first raw oyster? Lucky for us all, they had been struck by thunderbolts – every curious one of them.

We probably don't have to worry about that ultra-select, inquisitive group. They're born with an extra curiosity gene and feed it regularly with imagination and wonder. As for the rest of us, we might want to be careful. Dorothy Parker once said she'd like to get rid of her curiosity and her freckles. Well, bleach out freckles if you like. Just hang on to curiosity. Even the brightest and most inquisitive among us probably won't discover another planet. But when we quit wondering about ourselves and the world, we become vegetables; and all we'll need then is a periodic watering.

Curiosity can be stifled, quickly and early in life. It's as easy as telling a child not to put his hands in mud or to waste the morning following an ant. As easy as, "Don't ask so many questions." Or sometimes, when we get older, we're too busy and tired to take the long way home to explore country roads. Or we're too settled in our theology to think about what members of that seemingly strange church believe. We shake our heads at those new-fangled computer things, never daring to sit in front of one, to touch it, to let it do its magic.

Human minds stay fresh long past their usual expiration dates when we ask questions and aren't afraid to look under rocks or peek around new corners… or stick our fingers where they technically don't belong. Somehow we need continually to renew and nourish this spirit in ourselves and encourage it in others. Most of us don't turn into pillars of salt for trying.

I'm still concerned about that big switch on the wall since I've heard no explanation. Someone should rotate the pointer completely to its "ON" position. Who knows? It might ignite everyone's curiosity.

* * * * *

[16]

Little girls know, somewhere in the blue sky is peace
November 12, 1998

Veterans Day always reminds me of my first war.

Grandpa was cupping his ear with his hand, leaning close to the radio, listening to the news through persistent static. Hearing just bits and pieces of the bulletin myself, I whispered excitedly, "Grandpa! They said the Germans are coming!" He admonished me with a "Shhh."

I'm told that about twenty-five years earlier World War I advertised itself as being the war to end all wars. But apparently everyone forgot. By the time I was eight years old, all those promises had fallen apart and World War II began teaching us things we didn't even want to know.

In spite of Grandpa's "Shhh," I knew a little bit about war. I knew that grownups were afraid the Germans would attack our little Ohio town, because they volunteered for Civil Defense, wore white hard-hats, and painted shelter insignia on basement rooms in the courthouse. At home, we shut off all the lights for blackouts when practice air-raid sirens blew at night. In school, we held air raid drills, crawling under desks and covering our heads to keep imaginary bombs from hurting us. I contemplated the horror of war, but didn't' tell adults. I consoled myself by reasoning that even if everything were destroyed in battle, the sky would still be blue, and that some determined flower (always blue, too) would manage to survive and push itself up through a sidewalk crack.

In the meantime, I learned about ration coupons for sugar and how to compute red and blue tokens we got back as change for purchases. I knew about "A and B cards" for gasoline and about buying war bonds to defeat the enemy. Sometimes I took ten cents to school to buy a savings stamp, needing an impossible one hundred eighty-five of them to get a bond. We sacrificed our school playground, turning it into a junkyard for scrap metal, tinfoil balls, and rubber tires, all of which would magically turn into airplanes or tanks and go into battle for our side.

No one flinched at name-calling or worried about being politically correct when it came to the war. I could sing all three verses of "Heil, Pfft, Heil Pfft, Right in der Führer's Face" and frequently did so. We spoke in a unified, horrified voice about "Japs" and watched Saturday propaganda newsreels at the movie theater. There was no question about who the good guys were.

For the duration (a term I heard a lot), we could buy only white margarine with dye pellets to color it yellow, trying to fool ourselves into thinking butter. Young women painted their stockings on with brown leg makeup, sometimes marking a darker stripe up the back for seams. We planted a Victory Garden behind our house, and I pulled weeds to help the war effort.

We children chanted slogans of the day: "Lucky Strike green has gone to war," "Uncle Sam wants you," and "Loose lips sink ships." I tried not to divulge any military secrets and always wondered if I knew any. But I did have one dreadful secret of my own.

In my image of the war, our good-guy tents stood in a row on one side of a battle line about ten feet from the enemy's row of tents on the other side of the line. Soldiers from both sides emerged refreshed each morning to fight in hand-to-hand combat. Scenes from Saturday newsreels should have taught me otherwise, but I preferred that my fantasies follow this Civil War battle model. So I wondered what would happen if, instead of sleeping, one camp or the other sneaked out of bed at night, crossed the line, and attacked their enemy in the dark. I felt sure I had invented this plan, and it presented such horrifying possibilities I vowed never to tell anyone, and I didn't (not even our side); not for the duration.

Thanks to many whom I didn't know to thank at the time, the Germans didn't attack Ohio. I recall few of the war's specifics and remained childishly sheltered from tragedies and separations that others endured. I knew, however, that this war thing was something very big, because on V-E day and V-J day, my Aunt Mary danced in the middle of Washington Street, whooping and hollering in a decidedly uncharacteristic way.

World War II wasn't the war to end all wars, either. Since then we've endured conflicts not only in Korea and Vietnam, but also in Nigeria, Cambodia, India, Afghanistan, Indonesia, Iraq; nearly everywhere but here. It's likely that if there's another Big One, we won't be as much concerned about who's right as with what's left. And although it's popular to say that peace is not just the absence of war, it seems to be a reasonable place to start.

I wonder what today's children think about the evening news, and whether little girls still comfort themselves by imagining blue skies and courageous flowers blossoming in war's debris.

* * * * *

[17]

Making a list and checking it twice
December 10, 1998

My brothers and I, occasionally ingenious, developed a surefire method of predicting one November what Santa Claus would bring for Christmas. Our mother unintentionally made it easy. All we had to do to spoil the surprise was search our mail-order catalogs for the two tiny check marks she made beside each item being ordered.

Since another gift-giving season is upon us already (and whether you plan to ply me with gifts for Hanukkah, Christmas, my birthday, or simply because you can't resist), let me make it easier for you and less challenging for me.

I offer this assistance while recalling several years ago how a distant, desperate acquaintance sent me an obligatory gift that, try as I might, I haven't been able to forget. It was a ceramic cow's head with a little round hole drilled in its nose. After a reasonable bout of guessing, I decided it might be meant to dispense string, but I really didn't want to adorn my kitchen with a cow dribbling something from it's nose. She didn't buy it to be funny, because she definitely wasn't the funny kind. I pictured her grabbing that strange token from some curiosity shop shelf then, with considerable relief, crossing me off her list for another year. I know it's the thought that counts. I just had trouble deciphering the thought. I don't remember what eventually happened to the thing or exactly how I worded her thank you note, but I remained polite since one should never look a gift cow in the nose (or something like that.)

So if you examine your mail order catalogs this year, you'll find I've double-checked several items as gift suggestions for myself. While these are particularly for your holiday consideration, feel free to consult them at any time during the year.

(1) Give me something to reflect my quirks and peculiarities; something that shows how well you know me, even if you shake your head in wonderment. I'm remembering how a Colorado friend special-ordered a thirteen-scoop ice cream cone (yes, 13) from Baskin Robbins for me, knowing it would touch my heart, although eventually both hips as well.

(2) Give me something you made yourself; something that shows you care enough to get glue on your fingers, flour on your apron, or dirt on your hands. We're talking breads, stews, plants, sketches, or a whittled whistle – even if the results are as amateur as the clay bowls and paper chains we treasured as gifts from our kindergartners long ago. Effort and thoughtfulness wrap themselves like ribbons around hand-made gifts.

(3) Give me something that will make me laugh. Give me God's ugliest cheap jewelry on purpose or a wind-up toy chicken that cackles. Give me the gift of your own laughter all year long. Tell me bad jokes and tolerate some of mine.

(4) Give me something sentimental, even if it makes me cry. Write me a poem, dedicate a song to me, send me a tape of your favorite music or photographs of people I love. Write something tender that's true. Touch my heart with recollections of some sweet memory that I thought you had forgotten.

(5) As the neighbor children do, bring me fairy tokens. Give me treasures like their gifts of a delicate golden cicada wing and pinecone doll with pebble head. Give me a shiny stone and tell me where you found it. Give me something to feed my backyard birds, something to feed my spirit.

(6) Bring me a pack of gum or a carryout cappuccino for no special occasion. Send me postcards from France or California or Wichita to let me know you were thinking of me even when I was out of sight.

(7) Give me that clothespin bag or book of poems you heard me wish for last February so I know you were listening. Give me something you noticed I needed because you were looking and seeing. Sometimes I don't notice how raggedy my long-suffering house slippers have become.

(8) Mostly, give me your time because then you give part of yourself. And that's the real definition of love. Don't mail me expensive gifts or ceramic cows' heads and then ignore me the rest of the year. A true friend, they say, is one you can call at four in the morning – the one who always seems to have time and enjoys sharing it with others – the one who gives the ultimate gift of being there.

Christmas, Hanukkah, and birthdays find us digging into our wallets, sometimes deeper than we should. I don't intend to discourage anyone who wants to give me a big screen television set or sports car this year. Certainly don't cancel the order if you've already gone to the trouble. But when you deliver them, stay long and sit deep. Give me a welcoming hug; not the light-pat-on-the-shoulder kind, but the bear-hug kind. Laugh with me, cry with me, share with me… gifts I'll savor long after you're gone.

[18]

Count her among the forgetful
January 14, 1999

Oh no! Another January! They've changed the year again! Just a few weeks ago I got used to writing "1998" and now the world insists upon "1999" and talks excitedly about "2000." I tell you true, whichever side of my brain stores numbers is already full, and they're oozing through the cracks and cascading over the edges.

Making a list of numbers we're expected to remember is a scary project, and the list grows longer every day.

For instance, even if we don't particularly care, it's critical that we remember today's date and year because if we get hauled in for a surprise psychiatric examination the intake worker will ask. And if we don't know, someone in a white coat will write "disoriented" in the chart beside our name. For the same reason, we'd best remember our age and probably the ages of our children. Those in charge of the keys won't consider it a good sign if we need paper and pencil to figure it out.

Even if the authorities declare us competent, family members become surly if we don't remember a few additional birthdays and anniversaries. Namely, theirs.

And phone numbers. Remember when we dialed poetic numbers like Elm 5238? In those grand old days we cranked the telephone handle and let an operator do the work. Now, as a minimum, we dial seven unpoetic digits for local calls, and at least eleven for long distance, while phone companies periodically change our area codes to keep us alert and amused. If I use my telephone calling card, touted as a major convenience, I have to punch thirty-five numbers before reaching my party. To renew our mental competency rating, the world holds us responsible for remembering at least our own phone number and probably a couple others. I am working desperately just to remember 911.

Addresses used to be easier, too. When five-digit zip codes were added, I became mildly anxious. Since then we progressed to "zip code plus four," and any way you count it, that makes nine numbers. Tack on an apartment designation and it's even worse. Recently, I added insult to injury by moving, and still have to practice my new address and phone number like a kindergartner before her first day of school.

Let's don't forget Social Security! Everyone in town asked me for that number sometime within the last year. It appears that on any given day I can remember either my Social Security number or phone number, so I constantly pray that no one wants both and that they aren't particularly fussy about which one they get.

I have numbers for the combination on my gym locker, a PIN number for the bank, a numerical code for the house alarm and one for the car door lock. Things recently came to a head when I tried to get into my gym locker using my house alarm code. And, no joke, when I tried to set the house alarm, the first number that sped through my mind was that often elusive Social Security number. I simply surrender and plead ignorance when motel desk clerks request my car's license plate number when I register. As if I ever knew!

It's wise to recall some historical dates as well. An insistent high school history teacher etched the year 1066 so deeply on my mind that I'll remember it until the day I die. Unfortunately, I long ago forgot what significant event occurred that year, but I'm saving that date as a possible answer for the day I'm on a quiz show.

And can you believe it? When I recently arranged for dental work, the oral surgeon's receptionist asked me the number of the offending tooth. I've known forever that the hairs of my head are numbered, but my teeth too?

I don't want to give up on numbers and be considered senile. So I routinely recite important number facts to keep my memory limber. A stitch in time saves nine. Seventy-six trombones. Sixteen tons and what do ya' get? And that thirty days hath September thing. I've looked into the possibility of having the most vital numbers tattooed on some inconspicuous but accessible body part and am researching the cost in terms of both money and pain.

T.S. Eliot, wiser and more obtuse than I, might have been experiencing a similar forgetfulness when he wrote, "Midnight shakes the memory as a madman shakes a dead geranium." In spite of my own memory lapses, I am somehow comforted by the fact that I haven't the foggiest idea what Eliot is talking about.

Anyway, I'm determined to cling to those numbers I already know, but there simply isn't room for more. Not even one. As I recently stood in line at a busy bakery, the harried clerk shouted, "Take a number!"

No thanks! I forfeited the bagels and ran.

* * * * *

[19]

Is there a doctor in the house?
Feb. 11, 1999

I'm sixty-five and I'm scared.

My physician just left private practice and I am left to find a new one. Friends offer advice regarding whom to see or not see – their advice as mixed as their experiences. Office receptionists provide a list of those who are accepting new patients. Insurance companies don't care whom I see but will pay for services only if the physician is on their own list.

I'm smart enough to know that all physicians aren't alike any more than their patients are alike. And I reject the assumption that it doesn't matter which physician I choose as long as a diploma hangs on the wall. Diplomas don't say whether doctors graduated at the top or bottom of the class and what grades they got in Bedside Manner and Caring 101. They don't specify whether they have specialized interests that fit my medical needs and surely don't divulge their attitude toward patients over sixty.

With all this in mind, and willing to spend at least as much time choosing a physician as I would a hair stylist, I called the office of one recommended physician. I asked the receptionist for a ten- or fifteen-minute appointment, explaining that I wanted to meet the doctor and ask some questions. She told me that this just wasn't done. She said I'd have to schedule an "initial appointment" during which time "all I'd have to do" would be to give my medical history. I, in turn, explained that I didn't want to give a medical history to someone before I knew whether they were going to be my doctor. The receptionist quickly decided I should talk with the nurse. But since an answering machine spoke for the nurse, I left my taped inquiry and requested that she call back.

The call wasn't returned. I surmise that they weren't interested in someone taking such interest in her own health care, and I quickly lost all interest in them.

It's no secret that changes in the health care system have severely compromised what we once knew as the patient-physician relationship. Physicians themselves are victimized by pressures of time, patient-load, insurance restrictions, and the ever-changing system. But when everyone is a victim and no one benefits, who is to do something about it? Most of us can't go to Washington to take a stand and, I have noticed, no one asks even at a local level what we consumers want or need. I'd do battle personally, but first I have to find a physician.

So back to what scares me.

I'm afraid at sixty-five that doctors will lump us all together in their mental file as "old people, "those folks with gray hair who have Medicare cards and won't live much longer anyway. I'm afraid they will forget we have a past – not just a medical past, although that's scary enough, but a personal past as well; and a future.

Especially with new patients, I'm too savvy or cynical to think the new doctor will wade through sixty-five years of a medical chart before that initial visit, and afraid of the day we won't be well enough to remind him of our strokes, meds, surgeries, or heart palpitations. And, since most procedures short of brain surgery are now done on an outpatient basis, I'm worried whether physicians will know what help waits or doesn't wait at home when dismissing us from their care. I'm concerned that we might not even see our regular physicians when we are hospitalized because hospitals are beginning to hire their own physicians for that purpose. If so, we'll be faced with a new doctor just when we need the security of our regular physicians the most.

I guess I'm concerned that younger physicians don't even know what older patients mean when we talk about what medical care used to be. They can't empathize with our perception of the insurance maze and complications that have arisen. They don't know what it means to the elderly to get a phone message instructing, "Press one if you think you have pneumonia, press two if you are gasping your last breath, press three if you are tired of pressing buttons."

Actually, I consider myself unusually fortunate. Even after more than six decades, I am healthy and energetic and ordinarily keep my faculties intact. I take care of my body, am not a hypochondriac, and literally have no current medical problems except for occasional stiffness in my right index finger. I can't imagine the anxiety of chronically ill or debilitated patients when they have to search for a new physician.

To solve my own problem, I'm thinking of placing a classified ad.

Wanted: A general practice physician or internist. Must be able to peer beyond my bifocals to see the sparkle. Must realize that I haven't always been 65, and that they will be 65 themselves someday, too. Must know the cost of medications and not prescribe $12 pills that I can't afford, and not offer pills at all if something else will do. Must not only tolerate my taking an active role in my own medical care, but encourage and insist upon it. References are available from my previous physician upon request.

Only the caring need apply.

* * * * *

38

[20]

Showing up is half the fun
March 11, 1999

The same day I bought my first tennis racquet, I announced that one year hence I'd compete in the Senior Olympics. It was just a joke – a declaration as unsubstantial as the $20 tennis racquet. Playing for the first time at age sixty-three, I amused myself and horrified others with my bravado, but no one thought much about it again until I actually signed up for the competition twelve months later.

Astounded friends tried to save me from myself. "Oh, don't do that. Some of those senior women have played tennis for thirty or forty years. You're going to lose. You will be embarrassed in public." I told them I didn't mind losing, even in public, and reminded them that opponents might enjoy annihilating a rank amateur. My friends sighed (as they often do) while, outfitted like a pro, I signed in on match day.

You've probably already heard about Senior Olympics. Senior athletes, fifty and older, compete in five-year age groups. In addition to team sports of volleyball, basketball, and softball, participants can choose to compete in track and field, archery, bowling, tennis, cycling, horseshoes, badminton, swimming, racquetball, golf, or table tennis. In Kansas alone, 750 men and women enrolled for the festivities this past year and brought their own group of family spectators to cheer them on. So I realized competition could be tough.

I'll have to admit there had been impressive improvements in my tennis game after just a year. I learned to keep the ball within my own court most of the time and, when the net didn't get in the way, I actually returned balls to surprised opponents. I still underwhelmed others with my two-mile-per-hour serve and regularly lost track of the score. But determined to look professional, I bought sweatbands, a more expensive racquet, an arm brace to prevent tennis elbow, and swingy little tennis skirts meant to distract attention from my game. I felt ready.

Well, as it happened this year of my tennis debut, for whatever reason, only one woman in the state of Kansas in my age group chose to compete in singles tennis – me. I'd like to think that when potential opponents learned I had signed up, they withdrew in fear. In more lucid moments, however, I acknowledge that hundreds of Kansas women between ages sixty and sixty-five play tennis infinitely better than I. But I received the gold medal in my age group... simply for showing up.

Now I'm not the sort who would lord this over my nay-saying friends or flash my medal around in their presence. Admittedly, I cruised the city with my trophy protruding from the sunroof of my car. And I guess

I rubbed it in by informing them that this "win" qualified me for national competition in Orlando this fall. They've tried to hold their tongues but can't help warning me again that women at nationals definitely will be way out of my league. It seems to me I've heard that song before.

Well, with zero expectation and a wide grin, I'm seriously contemplating the trip.

Woody Allen claims that eighty percent of success is just showing up, so you have to wonder why we don't show up more often; why we don't risk something new, put timidity on the back burner, and venture into unfamiliar territory. One vital gentleman, when asked if he could play the violin, answered, "I don't know. I've never tried." He's definitely the sort who would show up just to try.

Who told us we can't? Where did we learn that it's bad to fail or to appear awkward in our attempts? Who convinced us we're too old? And why, for heaven's sake, do we perpetuate the myth that everything worth doing has to be done well? What ever happened to adventure and experimentation just for the fun of it?

Last November, John Glenn showed up for a space ride at age seventy-seven. But fortunately we don't often have to leave the planet for new vistas. Not confined anymore to knitting, whittling, and reading, adventurers over fifty show up to clog, ice skate, tap dance, bike, swim, and play basketball. One zany over-fifty local group holds weekly workshops for improvisational comedy. The hardiest among us find ourselves running for office, starting a new business, or joining the Peace Corps.

Before scholars established that the world is round, cartographers incorporated conspicuous warnings on the maps they drew. They first outlined the land mass as they knew it, endless ocean on all sides. Then, at each edge of their flat rectangular world, they printed in bold letters, "Here be dragons." Prudent folk knew to venture no further.

Most of us have lived long enough to realize that the dragons we fear usually don't materialize. If they do, they ordinarily tend to their own business like the Loch Ness monster.

If they get feistier, we can slay the vicious ones and tame the rest. True, a rare and particularly grizzly dragon could eat us alive or take one fine chunk out of us, but a good folly is often worth what we pay for it.

Without risk, we sit on the shores of the commonplace. Never getting our feet wet. Never showing up.

* * * * *

[21]

Who's afraid of the Y2K?
April 8, 1999

"Who's afraid of the big bad wolf, the big bad wolf, the big bad wolf?" I remember having sung that song years ago, but hadn't thought of it since childhood until Y2K came along. Now we're threatened with yet another wolf at the door, huffing and puffing and ready to blow our house down.

We laymen can't begin to comprehend what dreadful possibilities await the dawn of this millennium, and I'd hate to minimize the problem out of ignorance. The big event already earned itself the acronym TEOTWAWKI; The End Of The World As We Know It. It simply wouldn't be wise to scoff or feign indifference while surrounded by global panic.

I just don't feel ready to take this on when I'm still reeling from the bicentennial. But ready or not, here it comes, and nearly everyone voices some concern. A thoughtful ten-year-old recently confided her own puzzlement to me. "Everyone says to prepare for Y2K," she observed. "But what are we supposed to do?"

Well, I don't really know. My problem in deciding what action to take is that I have trouble fitting the Y2K meltdown into the lengthy list of other crises to worry about. Besides attending to the ongoing stream of health warnings, financial advisories, and product recalls, I try to keep abreast of less advertised threats. Publishers of the *Bulletin of Atomic Scientists*, scholars who keep track of our progress in the nuclear arms issue, recently set the Doomsday Clock five more minutes closer to midnight – proclaiming that it's now 11:51 p.m. That nine-minute interval doesn't leave sufficient time for decent preparation, let alone goodbyes and confessions.

El Niño messed with the clock, too, and temporarily increased the length of our days by one tenth of a millisecond each. I have no idea what I did with the extra time, but it certainly threw my routine off schedule.

Sometimes one learns even more than they want to know, and this creates anxiety too. One long-standing, personal worry arises from the fact that the Catholic Church established its Legion of Decency in 1934, the same year I was born. I tell myself that the timing was strictly coincidental, but it wears on a person's mind anyway and eats up thinking time.

And speaking of anxiety-provoking warnings, I read recently that the only parts of our bodies that keep growing as we age are our ears and our nose. If that's true, it's one ugly trick and not a prediction to pass off lightly.

Then, Heaven help us, there's global warming and those tiny little fish facing extinction. What are we supposed to be doing about that?

When I do have time to think about preparations for Y2K, advice from the experts varies. From some quarters I'm told to gather up flashlights, peanut butter, generators, toilet paper, bottled water, my vital records, and a shotgun. Then I'm to wait in the basement. Others encourage me to withdraw my money from the bank and bury it in the back yard. Archeology enthusiasts suggest that I bury a time capsule for Y3K, and Y4K revelers will dig it up during their own celebrations. They might also discover my can of money if I forget where I put it.

Most prognosticators seem to agree that it's risky to be undergoing surgery, flying in an airplane, or riding in an elevator when Y2K strikes. No one's mentioned it yet, but what if the Y2K bug gets into things other than computer systems – things like dresser drawers, flour canisters, or the vegetable garden?

I genuinely fear that overzealous devotees might buy new tennis shoes and lie down to meet their Maker halfway when 2000 arrives. As recently as March 1998, a Texas group announced that God would appear on Channel 18 before visiting earth later that month. I had cable TV temporarily installed to watch that program, but because He didn't show, I'll probably just wait to see His Y2K appearances on the six o'clock news. I hope everyone gets the word that Y2K is not an event worth dying for.

I understand that foolhardy, defiant folks are actually planning parties to celebrate the advent of 2000. These are probably the same people who watch for tornadoes from their rooftops. It's not that I'm scared, but you can't be too careful. Friends will have to talk fast to convince me to wear a funny hat and help usher this one in, but if they miss me at the party, they can always reach me on my basement phone.

So I don't know exactly what to tell my young friend to do to get ready for this long-heralded event. I'll have to rely on others to deal with any potentially tragic consequences and trust they'll find the solution in time. In the meanwhile, there are so many other things to worry about that I'm just hoping the cataclysm won't affect my hair dryer or the VCR.

January 1, 2000, TEOTWAWKI, falls on a Saturday. That gives us the weekend to peer out of our basements and assess damage – or sleep off the celebrations – or lament the downfall of civilization.

Then again, maybe we'll just go to work as usual on Monday.

* * * * *

[22]

That's the way the dust ball bounces
May 13, 1999

It's May. Time for Spring Cleaning. I know this because I over-heard a conscientious homemaker say so. Apparently during this season, I'm supposed to experience an uncontrollable urge to move furniture, wash quilts, and wallpaper the refrigerator. Fortunately or otherwise, I lack that gene. Erma Bombeck warned us all that, "Housecleaning, if you do it right, will kill you." If I drank, I'd drink to that.

Several months ago, as a friend and I chatted at the supermarket, our conversation took a strange turn to the subject of dust, and we enjoyed listing everything we'd rather do than clean house. On my way home, I wondered why most women fall heir to exclusive ownership of the dirt in their houses and how each decides the amount of energy she wants to exert chasing dust bunnies. Frankly, those critters multiply so rapidly that I've long since made pets of mine.

Some homemakers manage to keep perspective. One clever mother told her young children she didn't care if they wrote their names in the furniture dust as long as they didn't write the date. And most of us have heard about the little boy who, after learning "from dust you came and to dust you shall return," told his mother that someone under his bed was either coming or going.

If we live next door to Mrs. Clean, or inherited her as our mother-in-law, the pressure escalates. Phyllis Diller used to complain that the excessively tidy woman next door even bleached her snow. I guess at one time or another we've all felt obliged to measure up against the neighbor-hood equivalent of Mrs. Clean. Well, perhaps those few can legitimately boast that their kitchen floors are so sterile one can eat off them. But, fortunately, most of the rest of us have tables. I remember an allergist once seriously recommending I keep my home dust free. I gave him my address and told him I'd furnish all the dust cloths, but he never showed up. And even as we speak, one long cobweb dangles defiantly from my bedroom ceiling, but I notice it only from bed at night. I've forgotten all about it by morning and gradually have grown rather fond of it.

Perhaps I come by this casual attitude naturally. In the house where I grew up, our bathroom floor was patterned with alternating white and black linoleum blocks, each about twelve inches square. As a college student, I once got a letter from my mother saying that she had worked especially hard that day. Down on her knees with brush and cleanser, she had scrubbed all the white tiles. Not the black ones, just the white ones. Surely a woman after my own heart.

But in spite of bad jokes on the subject, housekeeping issues easily become battlegrounds and aren't amusing in many domestic quarters.

Well, I've developed several theories about housework and am glad to share them while my neighbor is busy polishing the leaves on her houseplants.

* First of all, it's important to remember that if *Better Homes and Gardens* photographers plan to visit and take pictures of our home for their magazine, they will phone first and make an appointment. Consequently, we don't have to scrub under the stove or keep people from stepping on our clean throw rugs until we get the call. I've been puzzled by those who insist upon an immaculate household at all times "in case someone drops in," but who admit that it seldom happens. If someone does ring the doorbell unannounced, it's a neighborhood child selling candy, or it's a friend escaping her own sink of dirty dishes. We can't live comfortably in a furniture store display window and could spoil a perfectly good life trying to create that illusion.

* Secondly, years of personal research prove that it requires exactly the same number of swipes to whisk away a whole week's worth of dust as it does to whisk away one day's worth. We needn't be there with the cloth to catch each particle as it lands.

* We've all heard that housework is a dirty job, but that someone has to do it. Well, maybe not just some one. Maybe everyone who lives there owns an equal portion of the dirt and can share in wiping it up. If one person has already been elected to permanent cleanup duty, it's certain that others won't welcome further nominations. But what the heck, families aren't democracies. Form a job squad for everyone's sake.

* The most fascinating characteristic of dust, grit, and grime is that they wait. We are not in danger of forfeiting the opportunity if we don't clean the sink or wash the windows this very minute. None of us wants to delay so long that Public Health decorates our kitchen with a condemned sign, but we might comfortably settle for some relaxed medium between bleached snow and squalor.

* Finally, one of the grim realities of housework is that it's never finished. If a sparkling house becomes an end in itself, the vacuum cleaner will suck up time that might well be spent on something more lasting.

I like the bit of wisdom that compares life to a circus act in which we juggle many balls at once. Since it gets complicated and we often get overloaded, we have to remember which of our pursuits are rubber balls and which are the glass balls that we must never drop. Families and friends, caring and laughter, are glass.

Dust balls bounce.

* * * * *

[23]

All the cats in Zanzibar
June 10,1999

Travel and tourism haven't always been my areas of expertise. While friends stayed home just long enough to repack for their next trip, I rarely shattered the city limits barrier. And although I took some teasing about this idiosyncrasy, my staying at home worked out pretty well for friends. Someone had to pick up their newspapers and receive incoming postcards. I also kept everyone's door keys and next of kin lists in case of emergency. I had become Block Mother for the nomadic.

It's not that I wouldn't have liked visiting all those exotic places. It's just that in my own mind, the hassle of getting there outweighed the pleasure of being there. Thoreau agreed with me about travel and post-humously offered comfort when my spirits flagged. "It's not worthwhile," he maintained, "to go round the world to count the cats in Zanzibar."

On the other hand, Robert Louis Stevenson apparently loved traveling for itself. "I travel not to go anywhere," he said, "but to go... the great affair is to move." I always wondered which part of that "great affair" would thrill him today. Perhaps he would be amused by two-hour delays on airport runways awaiting a mechanic or entertained by the screaming toddler across the aisle who is slightly too large to stuff into an overhead compartment. He could occupy himself by guessing whether his luggage will visit the same city he does, and whether the airline lunch will be peanuts or pretzels. He'd perhaps enjoy five hours in a seat not quite as wide as his own, and surely smile to imagine his cushion as a flotation device.

It's hard to characterize travel as pleasurable when we are honest about airports, train depots, and bus stations, because the truth is that absolutely no one who is there wants to be there. Everyone is suspended in those bleak terminals like blank pages between chapters, wanting to escape to resume the trip home or awaiting more transportation to carry them to some Far Better Place. Ah, yes. The great affair is to move.

Well, at any rate, all this logic notwithstanding, I determined to lay aside my inertia and succumb to the pressure to travel. In fact, I've already arranged for the visa and shots necessary to escape the city limits and have scheduled a full summer itinerary. As you can imagine, this required significant research since I had to uncover destinations so enticing that I'd forget the downside of getting there. If your own vacation schedule isn't yet full, and if you've already seen the Taj Mahal and the Barbed Wire Museum, feel free to come along.

Two June events particularly caught my eye. On the third Saturday of June, I will be travelling to Spivey's Corner, North Carolina, for the National Hollerin' Contest. This event is dedicated to reviving "the lost art of hollering as a means of communication." Rather than simply being part of the audience, I'm contemplating whether I might qualify as a contestant. Neighbors emphatically insist, however, that I not practice any more after 10 p.m.

The next leg of my June trip takes me to Baltimore, MD. The drawing card is a Chicken Clucking Contest in which human "amateur cluckers" compete for trophies and "poultry-related" prizes. There is something poultry-related that I've always dreamed of having, so this might be my chance. (Don't even ask.)

In July, I'm off to Pelican Rapids, Minnesota, site of the Ugly Truck Contest. Though onlookers ordinarily scowl, my old truck finally has a chance to win points for things like rust, dents, lousy paint job, excessive exhaust smoke, and over-all worst appearance. And I'll bet you never thought that truck in my driveway could be a winner.

Then, when the heat of summer subsides, I'll pack the suitcase again for September adventures.

In Dawson City, in the Yukon, I'll compete in the Great Klondike Outhouse Race. I can construct my own outhouse on wheels or could rent one at the contest site. Creative juices already stirred by the challenge, I'm designing a half-moon decor for the door of my double occupancy architectural masterpiece.

Next, in Reedpoint, Montana, I'll participate in what promoters advertise as "a safe alternative to Spain's running of the bulls" by joining the "Running of the Sheep." I've always been a little timid about cavorting with bulls, but have plenty of time to practice sheep racing before fall. After such strenuous activity during the actual contest, according to the schedule of events, competitors relax in the evening, listening to sheepherders read their poetry.

Finally, to cap off my summer activities, I added Yuba City, California, to the September itinerary. As citizens of the prune capital of the world, these folks proudly sponsor the California Prune Festival. Here I'll sample such taste treats as prune chili and prune ice cream; then I will hurry home – yes, hurry home.

As I said, I don't ordinarily enjoy traveling, but these extravaganzas were too enticing to resist. Now all I have to do is find some neighbor who will be home long enough to pick up my newspapers and collect my mail. After all, it's their turn.

* * * * *

[24]

The inside story
July 8, 1999

"It's just a routine screening," he said. "I recommend it for my patients every five years after age fifty."

Being sixty-two at the time, I already felt lucky, since my previous physician hadn't introduced me to that procedure. I accepted the brochure my new physician offered, promised to schedule an appointment with the specialist, and heard him suggest something like, "Stay near a bathroom." Thus, I agreed to this "routine screening" quicker than you can say flexible sigmoidoscopy.

As procedure day approached, I read the brochure and gaped at anatomical illustrations that were, as usual, worth a thousand words. The text prescribed a liquid diet for a couple days and, at two designated hours, a potion with the suspicious name of Fleet.

As my whining stomach attested, liquids didn't fill the void where bananas, granola bars or bagels belonged. It turned out, however, that anything was a taste treat compared to those two half-cup servings of Fleet. Superfluous instructions on the bottle ordered me to drink eight ounces of clear liquid as a chaser. Twenty-four ounces later, the noxious taste had just begun to fade, and I forgot about food for a while.

My bathroom is a comfortable place to visit, but you wouldn't want to live there. I did, so I know. It had by now dawned on me that the special potion was called "Fleet" because you'd better be. Certain there would be an upside to this adventure, I weighed myself periodically and enjoyed the temporary loss of about five pounds. Not yet familiar with what was to come, I didn't realize that the day in my bathroom would turn out to be the upside.

On the day of the procedure, after a too-short respite in the office waiting area, the nurse called me into an examining room and told me that my gown should open in the back. I had already guessed that. A television monitor with my name and number printed at the top of the screen sat near the exam table where I, for the moment, sat protectively on the anatomical point of interest.

I nearly left when I saw the physician. He was so young I feared being arrested for contributing to the delinquency of a minor. He greeted me cheerfully and then, holding his hands about twelve inches apart, explained that he'd be examining me with "a short rod." I asked to see the instrument.

"Do you want to see it before or after?" he inquired.

"Before," I insisted.

Looking rather sheepish, I thought, he produced the allegedly flexible rod from behind the table and I saw that it was at least thirty inches long.

"I lied," he confessed.

Nonetheless, he went on to show me a colorful diagram, pointing out exactly how far into my system he would explore. I was hoping the thirty-inch rod would be more than sufficient.

The Oscar for Best Costumes went to the doctor and nurse who donned helmets that looked like welders' masks except that instead of being metal they were made of see-through plastic.

"Good grief," I exclaimed. "You're wearing splash guards!" The doctor's credibility being what it was, I'll never know if, as he claimed, the headgear really was required by OSHA, or was simply part of the ambiance.

The procedure began.

Suffice it to say, I'll probably never again lie on my left side to watch TV. This particular set was apparently tuned to the Discovery Channel. While I watched the spectacle on the screen, the physician called, "Lights, camera, action," and conducted a narrated ten-minute tour down a meandering pink tunnel with a couple sharp, memorable curves. It was so real, I felt like I was actually there.

"Sorry," he said, lying again.

When not focused on some particularly scenic view of my interior, we conversed further.

"How in the world did you choose this specialty?" I asked. "Surely you didn't plan this as a child."

Tongue firmly in cheek, I hope, he explained that his mother had been "retentive" and frequently criticized him for the way he squeezed toothpaste tubes; hence a profession requiring hundreds of KY Jelly tubes. Freud would have loved it.

After the tour, the doctor retrieved the rod, and concluded, "Negative." My sentiments exactly! Offering another confession, he added, "And by the way, I explored farther than I told you I would, because you were a good patient."

Rather like climbing the mountain just because it's there, I thought.

As the doctor left the room, his nurse tethered me to the exam table to prevent my ascent. She discharged me with some hints about getting rid of the ballast as my day progressed, a protracted event that neither she nor the doctor chose to attend.

I dressed and left for home, still floating several inches off the ground.

Yes, I know. Refusing this examination could be dangerous to one's health, and I don't want to dissuade anyone from doing what's best for them. In the meantime, I have a couple more years myself to reflect on the fact that when I turn sixty-seven, my primary care physician will recommend the guided tour again and will hand me that explanatory brochure. I'm deciding where to put it.

* * * * *

[25]

In search of the write stuff
August 12, 1999

The imminent millennium poses tough competition for the limelight, but I'm holding a quiet celebration anyway to mark the second anniversary of this column, "Second Spring."

I began my column-writing adventure not knowing exactly in what direction we would take each other, and it's been a fascinating ride.

So I decided for this anniversary celebration to indulge in a time of reflection about two years of Second Spring and fifty years of writing that preceded this column. Never fear. I'll summarize.

First of all, even though my essays get more exposure, I'm really a poet moonlighting in prose and have three volumes of poems poised for publication. I'd share samples here occasionally, but newspaper policy discourages using the column for poetry. (If I sneak some in as prose, will they notice? No one knows.) Frankly, my Muse just doesn't understand why I'm allowed to quote Shakespeare but not myself. Poetry apparently sells better posthumously, but that's an awfully long time to wait.

I remember the first serious poem I ever wrote. It erupted along with mortifying adolescent blemishes when I was thirteen.

My America / where each new morning with its light recalls the glory of the night.

After recopying its several verses several times, I handed the finished product to my homeroom teacher before class. She read it silently, snickered, and without a word handed it back.

Years later in graduate school, I lamented to my adviser that during a recent move I had lost all the poetry, prose and journal entries I had written since childhood. He said, "Good. That means you're growing up." I didn't think so. Still don't.

Luckily, my Muse and I are often more energized than squelched by naysayers. When I mentally rehearse my Pulitzer Prize speech, I always mention those two detractors by name and fantasize their slouching in the front row at the award presentation.

Notwithstanding those early attempts to dissuade me and my poetry bent, the recent possibility of becoming a columnist left me more eager than anxious. It felt peculiar at first, writing without knowing who the readers were or if there actually were any. But reader feedback encouraged me from the outset, and there was always that core of friends who'd appreciate even dangling participles if I chose to let one dangle.

Letters from readers I hadn't known personally were pleasant surprises. I've answered each one and now count those readers as friends. It's fun hearing from out of state folks who see the column online, or learning that someone sends my column to friends and relatives or posts them on the refrigerator. Some have sent funny, articulate anecdotes of their own, worthy of wider readership.

Occasionally, someone unexpectedly baptizes me with a healthy sprinkling of humility. One woman approached me at the gym to ask, "Aren't you the person whose picture I see in the newspaper every once in a while?" I said, "Yes, I am. It's nice to have feedback from readers." "Oh no," she explained. "I don't read the articles. I just see your picture."

Fortunately, many people actually read the column and regularly let me know which one is my "best one yet." The one reprinted most often in other publications was an early one about senior citizens learning to use computers. My e-mail response from readers as old as ninety clearly reconfirms our generation's growing expertise on that newfangled machine.

Readers appeared to identify most strongly with two columns. They first had lots to say about my sad commentary on memory problems, but their own memories remained well enough intact to share amusing tales of their occasional lapses.

More recently, they were simultaneously repelled and amused by the flexible sigmoidoscopy escapade. My brother hoped aloud, however, that the column didn't launch a continuing series about my intestinal tract.

The column eliciting the most sober response described my efforts to find a new physician. I received numerous supportive and helpful calls, several of them from physicians and other medical clinic personnel who obviously understood the predicament of older patients. The public responded with stories of similar frustration, and some recommended physicians whom they trust with their own medical care.

That column also generated my first anonymous "fan mail" (apparently from a physician) suggesting that if I got psychotherapy I would no longer feel the need to be an active participant in my own health care. (Run, patients, run!) Well, they say if you don't step on anyone's toes, you must be standing still. So in spite of all the applause that column generated, I apparently crushed some sensitive, horse-and-buggy toes. But even that experience turned into a productive one when I wrote a column about the anonymous letter itself and sold it to another publication.

Occasionally I've wondered what it is that drives someone to write and keeps writers motivated even in the face of uncertain reward. I'm reminded of the story of Aeschylus, a Greek poet and playwright born about 500 B.C. Tradition has it that an eagle had seized a tortoise and was looking for something on which to smash the reptile's shell. The eagle mistook the poet's bald head for a stone and dropped the tortoise on him. In Aeschylus' case, the tortoise bomb killed him. For the rest of us, it knocks us just senseless enough to keep plugging away at this wonderful business.

Thanks and all good wishes to my readers as we continue sharing our Second Spring.

* * * * *

[26]

Summer went along swimmingly
September 9, 1999

As a lifelong, landlocked, landlubber, intimidated by large bodies of water and even ambitious puddles, I surprised myself last year by falling in love with an entire ocean. I waded into it, floated on it, challenged its waves, and cried when I left.

The fact that I didn't drown buoyed my confidence considerably. So I decided this summer to conquer the water and signed up for swimming lessons.

My childhood hometown had no swimming facilities, and the creeks we waded in were only ankle deep. Consequently, I had neither motive nor opportunity to learn to swim. When deeper bodies of water occasionally presented themselves, we hung our clothes on a hickory limb, as the nursery rhyme advises, and didn't go near.

I vaguely recall splashing around in the shallow end of a city pool somewhere, but details elude me except for one peculiar habit. I distinctly remember that every time I accidentally slipped under water and surfaced again, I'd spontaneously exclaimed, "Wichikoo!" Don't ask why or what it means; I certainly don't know. I do feel fortunate that no one tried to teach me to swim by tossing me into a lake, because I probably would have Wichikooed myself right to the bottom.

So after weighing the pros and cons of private versus group lessons, and deciding I'd rather not go under without being noticed, I chose private lessons and searched for an instructor.

A competent and pleasant young woman one-third my age undertook the challenge. She said she had been swimming since she was five months old, and, judging from her expertise, I suspect that since then she has emerged from the water only for meals.

My old bathing suit had developed a hole in the knee, so I purchased a couple new outfits for the lessons. I settled for styles that wouldn't actually frighten young children but would make them think twice before splashing me. That turned out to be a good move, because children dipped and dived everywhere and made my first pool experience somewhat intimidating.

In the kiddie-pool, some three-year-old show-off put his face in the water and blew bubbles. When he finally came up for air, I sneered at him and hissed; "I can do that."

Even five-year-olds frolicked in the deep end of the pool and none of them called for help. There was one blood-curdling moment when someone screamed, but regardless of what the instructor says, it wasn't I.

In spite of my protests, the lessons began in water nine feet deep. Being vertically challenged already, even my imagination couldn't touch its toes on the bottom. But that depth definitely guaranteed I wouldn't contemplate giving up in the middle of an attempted lap across the pool. I recalled one little boy who used to engage his instructor in discussions of buoyancy to avoid having to swim. I filed his evasion plan in my head in case of emergency.

I quickly learned to keep my eyes open under water, if for no reason other than to make sure the instructor hadn't left. I thought I already knew how to breathe in and out with regularity, but it was hard to cling to that fantasy as I siphoned chlorine through my nostrils and out my ears.

After my having spent a lifetime trying to affect a relatively human gait, the instructor asked me to make leg movements like a frog. And when teaching the backstroke, she insisted that I stick my chest out, something good girls absolutely never did on dry land. I tried my best to coordinate body parts that had suddenly developed minds of their own. It was like teaching a caterpillar to waltz.

Way back in 40-something B.C., Virgil wrote about seeing "odd figures" swimming in the water. Apparently some things never change.

Altogether, however, I survived admirably and progressed quickly. As alternatives to sinking, I learned to tread water, do the backstroke, and breathe through my own brand of freestyle, all without a Wichikoo. I'd have advanced further had they agreed to salt the water. I practiced regularly at city pools and remembered my age when children splashed past me with an "Excuse me, ma'am." But I'll always cherish the reunion with my ocean at summer's end when I showed off my new tricks. She was impressed.

I'm still not ready for the Olympics or cavorting with dolphins. Nor am I ready for the challenge of an emergency swim from sinking boat to beach. But I figure if all else fails, I'll just drop to the bottom and run like the devil toward shore.

Friends cheer me on as they always do. My niece, amused at my new athletic lifestyle, said that learning to swim would come in handy if the tennis courts are ever under water.

But I have other motivations.

First of all, it's time that I got to play in the deep end with the big kids. And secondly, if the Earth ever floods again, and some Noah builds an ark, I doubt I'll be one of the righteous few invited on board.

Then it will definitely be sink or swim.

* * * * *

[27]

Please don't play it again, Sam
October 14, 1999

In the beginning, while tracking down a mastodon, some hulking prehistoric man accidentally struck his wooden club on a rock and like the way it sounded. He hummed a few guttural ughs in time with the beat and thus created music.

That primitive musician had no way of knowing what he started, and to him I remain eternally grateful. Well, at least I used to be grateful. William Congreve and I once agreed that, "Music hath charms to soothe a savage breast, to soften rocks, or bend a knotted oak." Lately, however, it's lost some of its charm and, under siege, I've been ready to wave the white flag and surrender. But before giving up completely, I'm promoting a campaign against noise pollution in which music has risen to status of major offender.

Although I know what sorts of music I personally like, be assured that I wouldn't presume to dictate taste. "One man's trash is another man's treasure" doesn't apply only to garage sales. Arguments about the relative merits of classical, jazz, rap, rock, alternative, and country music would end as they began. There would be no converts made and no prisoners taken.

But let's not forget that music, which has charms to soothe the savage breast, also stirs men to battle. We recognize at least intellectually that background music for movies helps set the mood. Though it's called "incidental" music, there is nothing incidental about it, and composers manipulate feelings both blatantly and subtly as audiences watch the story unfold. Music for horror shows and adventure tales frazzles nerves and keeps us on the edge of irritability. What happens if someone is raised from infancy on an auditory diet of music that keeps them on that edge? And what happens to serenity when that musical drug of choice is later mainlined to the brain via earphones?

Research shows that cows listening to soothing music give richer milk. Those of us who are old enough remember ads for milk that came from "contented cows." On the human front, in order to encourage relaxation and sleep, we sing lullabies to our babies at bedtime rather than playing the *1812 Overture*. There's a reason for that.

If health is determined partly by what goes into our mouths, surely it's also affected by what goes into our ears. It's recently been determined that music exerts a profound effect on the immune system and that personal stereos can blast their sound at an intensity of 113 decibels, a level that quickly destroys fragile nerve cells within the inner ear. Applying a new variety of acceptable torture, law enforcement agencies sometimes play continuous loud music to force fugitives from their hideouts. Yes, music softens rocks, bends knotted oaks, and makes bad guys surrender.

I'm keenly aware of being affected by background music. The only time I appreciate raucous music is when I'm lifting weights in the gym. The loud and heavy beat pumps me up while I'm busy pumping up. And if the radio is tuned in to music while I'm driving, the tone and tempo of the piece affect the speedometer reading if I'm not extra careful. Does road rage ever erupt when someone is listening to a sonata? Or is that one sort of music that soothes the savage breast?

At any rate, we can accept as a given that different folks have different tastes in music, and we know that our choices affect us subliminally or otherwise.

My main gripe, however, is that it's harder to keep my air space free of other people's music than it is to avoid their cigarette smoke. As I run errands, cars waiting next to me at stoplights blast their music until my innards throb, and I wonder how people inside those vehicles survive the decibels with windows rolled up.

I enter an elevator and, for my supposed amusement, they are playing... well, elevator music. I use the telephone and am put on hold and held captive for several minutes of music, aimed right into my ear. When I seek the quiet of the beach, sunbathers bring radios along. In retail stores, music of the manager's choice pipes itself down his aisle and into my space.

Whatever happened to silence? How did we come to need constant background noise for our lives? The invasion prompts me to run from noise like others scramble from searing sun or heavy rain.

John Cage wrote a musical composition entitled, "Four Minutes and Thirty-Three Seconds." It's completely silent. I will consider buying tapes of this work for any retail store that agrees to play it all day long, in their store and on their phones. I will also consider not kicking sand on those at the beach who agree to shut off their radios.

There are important exceptions to my silence quest. Unaccompanied singing, alone or in groups, is welcome anytime, any place. So are lullabies and carousel tunes. Sounds of piano practice wafting from windows will not be prosecuted. And to be fair, I'd have to allow trumpet and accordion practice as well.

But as a general proposition, when I finally rule the world, music will be banned in elevators, retail stores, and restaurants, at public swimming pools, and on telephones. Posted announcements will explain: "This silence is sponsored by the Institute for the Preservation of Sanity." But since my coronation has been postponed indefinitely, I'll settle right now for organizing a National Day of Musical Silence. For that twenty-four-hour period, with the exceptions noted above, no one will generate any music that is audible to others. And at high noon, crowds will pause for one hushed minute as a memorial to silence itself.

Shhhhhh…

* * * * *

[28]

May I have your autograph, please?
November 11, 1999

One November evening several years ago, as featured speaker at a local PTA meeting, I arrived expecting one of those small but appreciative audiences. Instead, the hall was crowded. All available seats were occupied and latecomers settled for standing room only. I patted myself on the back, glowed modestly, and commented to one of the parents, "What a wonderful group!" "Oh yes," she explained, "we're all here for the turkey raffle."

Ah, fame.

I remember a once prominent gentleman being interviewed on television saying that he fully grasped the fleeting nature of fame when he witnessed his own statue being carried out of Madame Tussaud's Wax Museum to be melted down. And, as though to prove his point, I forget who he was.

It seems that, at best, we have mixed feelings about fame. Most of us can sneer and shrug at someone else's popularity and recite in unison the cliché that they still put their pants on like the rest of us do. We refer to fame as "ephemeral," "foolish," or as an "empty bubble." But it's harder to keep perspective when it's our own minute of glory and our own pants in question. We laugh about fame's superficiality and flitting nature, but are usually eager for the fifteen spotlight minutes during our lifetime that we're promised. And we hope the reason for that brief recognition is something we won't mind having screamed in headlines, since most of us would rather be famous than infamous.

The concept of fame poses a problem for me. I've never understood why people would crowd together in a public square, not to honor a person of renown nor to watch him perform his particular artistry, but just to catch a glimpse of him, implying they will somehow gain status themselves by having seen that famous hand waving from the car window or by having stepped on the street where his motorcade left tire tracks. In fact, we could probably develop a psychological test of sorts, just by asking for what famous person someone would brave sleet and cold – just to wave at the car. Or who is elevated so high in their opinion that they would stand in line for hours to get an autograph?

We find, however, that even the once simple diversion of collecting autographs has taken a new twist.

In grade school and high school, students used to exchange autographs along with clever little verses and wishes for good luck. One of my fastidious friends actually recopied our signatures in her book if our handwriting wasn't neat enough to suit her taste. I never did figure out what all that was about. But at any rate, we solicited those school day autographs out of friendship without harboring any illusion that the other was famous.

I've always wondered, however, why people would queue up just to get another person's signature. Why all the excitement that this person can write his name? The marketing of autographs has unquestionably taken any romanticism out of collecting them. And now that they've become a booming business, I have to question not only why people would pay for someone else's signature in the first place, but what elevates anyone in his own mind to believe his illegible scrawl is genuinely worth money. Well, I guess the fact that people are willing to pay him for it gives him the idea. In 1993, Wilt Chamberlain reportedly told a visitor he was a magician and asked, "Want to see me turn twenty dollars into a hundred dollars before your eyes?" According to wire reports, he whipped out a twenty bill, signed the front of it and handed it to a dealer who immediately put it up for sale at one hundred dollars.

Even children have graduated from hero worship to economics. One eight-year-old boy being interviewed on TV after getting the autograph of an outstanding high school basketball player was asked the reason for his excitement. He explained, with a huge grin, "Because his signature is going to be worth something when he is in the NBA." So much for hero worship.

I definitely don't want to knock free enterprise. In fact, I always planned to make a little money myself someday by writing a book and selling a few copies. But if people want to pay me just for signing my name instead, the line forms to the right! Or to the left! I don't care which. As a matter of fact, people already scramble for my autograph. But that's usually on checks or beneath paragraphs of fine print on the dotted line designated with a little x.

I guess I struggle with the question of fame because I don't think anyone deserves to be idolized; their laudable accomplishments admired and emulated, of course, but somehow without bestowing god-like status upon the person himself.

In spite of railing against the possible evils of renown, I stand ready to take my own comeuppance. As Pascal observed, "Even those who write against fame wish for the fame of having written well." Touché.

But fifteen minutes in the spotlight won't spoil any of us if we remember that most folks show up to win the turkey.

* * * * *

[29]

Merry Christmas?
December 9, 1999

Merry Christmas, everyone!

Well, not really everyone. 'Tis the season to be jolly, but 'tis also the season of assumptions. In the midst of holiday cheer we tend to forget that not everyone gets teary eyed over "Silent Night" or lines up at the mall to sit on Santa's lap.

Beginning in mid-September, signs appear in stores encouraging Christmas lay-away. Gradually, the season accelerates until it's now full speed ahead. Carols play in the shops, gift ads bombard us, wreathes hang on lampposts, and colored lights line the streets. Everyone but Christians better get out of the way! When Christians themselves complain about over-stimulation and commercial bulldozing at this time of year, what must those feel who don't participate in these festivities?

A young Jewish boy once confided to me that his teacher told everyone "Merry Christmas" when she dismissed school for the December break, but didn't ever mention his own religious holidays. His father advised him to "get used to it." I suggested that he not.

Assumptions. Somehow we're more comfortable assuming that everyone else is just like us. But even looking into the phone book business pages reminds us that we share our community not only with those of the Jewish faith, but with Muslims, Baha'i and Buddhists. Atheists and agnostics haven't purchased listings, and we don't know whether they are celebrating or bah-humbugging their way through December.

With all due respect to Walt Whitman, one wonders about the message when he wrote, "I celebrate myself and sing myself, and what I assume you shall assume."

Several years ago, I lived for three months in Salt Lake City and, for the first time in my life, experienced the world as a minority outsider. No one treated me unkindly nor disparaged my religion. Not at all. I was simply out of the cultural loop. I sensed instinctively that I was on the fringe and knew I would have to work harder to keep my fuzzy identity in focus.

When non-Christians occasionally bristle at being wished "Merry Christmas," it's easy to brush them aside as being "oversensitive." What's the big deal if we assume everyone else celebrates our holiday?

Well, let me use an analogy. What if we assumed that everyone in Kansas is a Democrat? (It's a stretch, but use your imagination.)

Operating with that as our assumption, we'd buy everyone donkey decals for their car windows, invite them to victory parties for national Democratic candidates, play Happy Days are Here Again over mall loudspeakers, and declare January 30 a national holiday in honor of FDR's birthday.

Now even if Republicans actually did constitute the minority party in Kansas (let me cling to that a while longer here), being ignored by Democrats would not destroy them. Nor will minority religions be devastated by Christmas greetings. After all, Christianity is an infant among world religions. But by disregarding and overlooking minority groups, we unintentionally demean them.

An awareness of other belief systems need not dampen our own celebration at all. We just need to remember that others don't get excited about the same holidays that we do.

Take note, however, that it's not only Christians who make unwarranted assumptions during this season. It's unrealistic for non-Christians to assume, for instance, that everyone spouting "Merry Christmas" is a missionary. Although this holiday is religious in origin, it has deteriorated in many quarters to a secular celebration – Santa Claus' birthday, perhaps. Many folks are lumped together into the Christian category by reason of heritage rather than belief and acknowledge those ties on only two holidays a year: the one with the colored boiled eggs and the one with the decorated fir trees. Their wishing "Merry Christmas" is often comparable to saying, "Have a nice day," or "Gee, I'm happy this time of year and hope you are, too." They certainly don't offer their Christmas salutation with the intention of winning converts.

I hope that during Christmas revelry, others don't consider Christians hostile or unkind. Some of us are ignorant. Teach us. Most of us are careless. We probably need to be reminded every year that Hanukkah isn't the "Jewish Christmas."

On a more practical level, we might be more careful about inviting children to birthday parties on dates of their own religious holy days. And maybe we could acknowledge that it's a bit presumptuous to ask every child we meet in December whether they are waiting for Santa Claus.

Actually, there's some good news about our oversights and assumptions. A multitude of religious groups in our community interacts day after day without serious conflict. It's a compliment to us all that we ordinarily live together peaceably, quietly accepting differences. But we don't want to forget that differences exist, since they are crucial to our identities.

The old melting pot concept suggests that we liquefy and blend into one. But it's not a pretty picture to visualize the meltdown product of Democrats, Buddhists, Christians, Jews, and Republicans. A better analogy for our rich diversity might be a patchwork quilt – a crazy quilt, even – with each group maintaining its unique and valuable character.

Perhaps this December we can greet strangers with more inclusive wishes for "Happy Holidays" or "Peace." Surely the message of peace is meant for us all. And somewhere, the one great God, Spirit, Yahweh, All-Knowing, First-Cause, Center of the Universe looks down and smiles.

John F. Kennedy urged us to "make the world safe for diversity."
Amen.
And peace.

* * * * *

[30]

Caution: Don't read this while driving
January 13, 2000

One sweltering day last summer, having parked my car in the sunshine, I put one of those large cardboard fans over the inside of the windshield to deflect heat while I was gone. Later, getting back into the car, I happened to read the warning printed on the back of the fan. It cautioned, "Remove before driving."

Now I'm no science whiz or automobile expert, but I'm also not entirely stupid and, even in my feistiest mood, had never contemplated driving the car with the shield blocking my vision.

Since then, I've collected such warnings – warnings that aim to protect companies from lawsuits more than protect the consumer. One hair dryer label warns, "Do not use while sleeping." On the label of an electric iron, "Do not iron clothes on body." (Well, they know we've all tried this at one time or another.) On a sleep aid, "Warning; this product may cause drowsiness." One consumer reports that cautions on a chain saw include, "Do not attempt to stop chain with your hands." And have you noticed?

Coffee from fast food shops is being labeled "hot" lest in a stupid moment we deliberately pour it in our lap. I recently enjoyed the tongue-in-cheek notice on a carryout cup of my iced coffee drink: "Caution, contents not hot."

Admittedly, such warnings have proved valuable to me, since I am a slow learner. After nearly suffocating three times when I pulled plastic bags over my head, I finally noticed the printed advisory: Warning – these bags are not toys.

And just this Christmas, as I prepared to sprinkle artificial snow on my cereal, I luckily noticed the warning that it was not edible.

Ah, yes. Our propensity to sue over our own ignorance and carelessness leaves its mark everywhere. But in spite of efforts to save us from our own bad judgment, we learn over and over that nothing is fool-proof to a talented fool. Jonathan Swift asked, "How is it possible to expect that mankind will take advice, when they will not so much as take warning?"

Bombarded by so many advisories we don't really need, I'm developing a list of warnings that we do need but don't get.

For instance, I've never bought a gun. So I don't know whether they come with warning labels. I suspect not, and I propose a label that says: "If this product comes in contact with bullets or unauthorized idiots, it could kill someone."

And we need several cautions posted on car dashboards. I suggest: "No, you can't still drive 50 miles after the gas gauge says empty." "This vehicle could be dangerous to the health of pedestrians." "Do not start engine without engaging brain." Or "Back seat might result in unwanted pregnancies."

On exercise equipment, for those deluded into thinking that the purchase itself is sufficient, I propose a label reminding: "This equipment works only if used regularly."

Bottles of alcohol should warn: "Imbibing will make you think you are funnier than you really are." Or, "Excessive drinking may leave you wondering where in the devil your family went."

Anyway, that's the idea. Here are some more:

On ice cream cartons and candy-bar wrappers: "This food can make you very fat."

On designer jeans: "The label on the rear-end of these jeans will not make you popular if you aren't already."

On large furniture items: "Buy this thing and you will have to polish it and pay to have it moved wherever you go."

On stylishly "in" clothes: "Even if we make this dress in a size twenty-four, don't buy it if you are over a size ten."

And how about this warning? "Caution – dates on the calendar are closer than they appear."

There are obviously lots of consequences that reasonable people don't need protection from, and we're bombarded with multiple reminders we could well do without. Besides, there are times we don't even want protection from ourselves. We can choose to lug around a grand piano if we want to, or buy exercise equipment just to impress our friends. We know what's in ice cream and decide to splurge on it anyway. And perhaps we enjoy wearing size twenty-four spandex in spite of the cautions. In that case, I say, go for it.

But in view of the superfluous warnings to which we're subjected, I challenged myself to create the one warning label I would propose if it were to be the only such label in the world. It would have to be a warning that protected us from a genuine danger, be universally applicable, not infringe on anyone's rights, and yet make a positive impact on our lives. The decision turned out to be an easy one.

A non-fading, prominently displayed label would be attached to every human being, ideally on our foreheads, quietly reminding us, "Fragile. Handle with care."

* * * * *

[31]

You aren't what you eat
February 17, 2000

I recently read that cucumber is the only food cockroaches won't eat. That's not something I've personally researched, but I'd like to believe it's true, since I'm a non-picky eater myself.

Admittedly, there are a few foods I enthusiastically avoid, but they don't belong to the primary food groups anyway. First, I don't understand why people rave about raw oysters when they swallow them whole to avoid tasting them. And second, I'll pass on the black olives, thank you. Tofu, in its many disguises, and snails (even masquerading as escargot) complete the list of personal rejects.

So what do I like to eat? Well, if I'm eating at home, a banana, bowl of cereal or bagel and peanut butter will do nicely – with ice cream as appetizer and/or dessert and/or entree. Once I even ate a green vegetable. If I consent to put on shoes to dine out, restaurants with pictures on the menus suffice. Better yet, I'd buy an apple or corn dog from a street vendor and keep on walking. You gotta admit, that's a cheap date.

Historically, I was the only student in our college dormitory who liked cafeteria fare (with the exception of the Cook's Revenge, prune whip).

While we're here in the confessional, I further admit I like airline food. And, no, I don't complain about hospital food either.

DON'T GET ME WRONG – I love to eat. When I'm sick, I can't remember whether to feed a cold or feed a fever, so I feed them both. My appetite will be the last thing to go.

In spite of these peculiarities, invitations to friends' homes for dinners are always a pleasure – whether the menu includes chicken under glass, soup and crackers, or pizza ordered in. Some of the most enjoyable meals I've eaten involved marshmallows burned black over a fire, hamburgers retrieved after falling through the grill, and an almost-failed pie that still tasted like peaches. I happily remember six people sharing a spread of nothing but laughter and leftovers.

So what's the issue? Well, depending upon how charitable my critics are, I am described either as one having an uneducated palate or, in fish tank lingo, of being a bottom feeder. Since we are supposedly what we eat, even my character gets maligned in the process.

Then I'm accused of "reverse snobbery" when I insist there is absolutely no reason for someone to know the names of eleven kinds of pasta unless he's a chef, nor reason to pay $80 for a meal unless it's our last one. And I emphatically reject the pronouncements of self-appointed, self-anointed gourmets who dictate which foods are "good" and which aren't. If some things are simply a matter of taste, it seems reasonable that taste itself is one of them.

I decided to do a little internet research about eating habits. The findings boosted my self-esteem for sure, since I learned that there are definitely different lunches for different bunches.

Of course, there was a site for vegetarianism, and one supporting the argument that Jesus was a vegetarian. Other pages offered tips for those interested in vegan or macrobiotic diets. Surprisingly, there's also a group called fruititarians – whose name speaks for itself. I also learned about raw foodists who ingest only those foods that have not been cooked. And descending that scary list even further, we find a group who dine exclusively on what they forage from the wild. You will just have to take my word for it that at the bottom of the list there were articles about cannibalism and even a page of cannibalism haiku that I was afraid to read.

The upshot of this research is that I no longer feel that my eating habits are peculiar. In fact, they are relatively efficient and reasonable. All of the alternative eating styles I discovered on the internet take too much work and time. Foraging in the woods, for heaven's sake, takes all day. I've climbed too high on the food chain to be interested in monkey brain delicacies or woodland roots.

When friends are totally honest about their own eating habits, interesting stories emerge. I know one otherwise normal fellow who eats black, overripe bananas and dry milk powder right out of the can. Another friend who prefers expensive restaurants and entrees with "gourmet" spelled out in parsley, sometimes eats canned spaghetti in the privacy of her own home. She doesn't like me to mention that.

Surely I've enjoyed delectable dinners and always appreciate the work and care that go into them. But ask me about the meal a week after it's been digested and I might not remember what I ate, no matter how appetizing the food. But I will describe in detail the smiles and laughter and conversation of those with whom I ate. Obviously, the way to my heart isn't through my stomach. One has to choose an alternate route – probably bypassing the love handles, coasting through the brain, and exiting at the funny bone.

It turns out that whether I'm eating in a restaurant or a home, and whether I'm dining on gourmet extravaganzas or spaghetti from a can, I'm reminded over and over again that it doesn't matter what's on the table. What's important is who's on the chairs.

* * * * *

[32]

More chicken feed at the casinos
March 9, 2000

I've been thinking lately about chickens. Not the common barnyard variety, but the educated ones who volunteer for psychological research.

This peculiar train of thought launched itself at the casino.

My mother is ninety and frequents casinos as often as possible ever since she hit a small beginners-luck jackpot ten years ago. When she recently paid me a visit, I accompanied her on a gambling trip one day to help shove coins in slots. We arrived at 8 a.m., lest our gambling money burn proverbial holes in our pockets, and we soon perched with busloads of other senior citizens at the slot machines.

Well, it happened quickly. Within the first hour I had disposed of the money I designated to lose, so pulled out pencil and paper to take notes instead. A poker table with green felt top beckoned me as a comfortable spot from which to work, but the dealer frowned upon my roosting there. So I wandered through the casino jotting down observations, apparently looking like an inspector from the Gaming Commission. A watchful employee, probably wanting me out of sight, soon offered me a corner table at which to write.

A Chinese proverb says that players are blind but that onlookers see clearly. Quickly demoted to status of fleeced onlooker, I had lots of time to see.

Casino hospitality is beyond reproach. Greeters open the door for new arrivals, the sign of pampering to come. Restaurants, snack bars and restrooms are just a few steps away. Employees circulate with free drinks and change so that customers don't have to abandon a promising machine when they get thirsty or run out of coins. The slot machines themselves make change for bills up to $100. And just when I celebrated the fact that they don't yet accept credit cards, I noticed an ATM machine within easy reach advertising "quick cash." Casinos don't lend themselves to writing or quiet meditation. Bells, whistles, and sirens scream from machines to announce that other players are winning in spite of one's own bad fortune. Loud music adds to the clamor, and superfluous television sets flash pictures in each corner of the room. Metal coins clank obnoxiously into metal bins for winners, a song of hope and frustration for nearby losers.

Slot machines sport creative names: Double Diamond, Wild Cherry, Go Bananas, River Gambler, Jurassic Jackpot, Hurricane, Money Storm, Sierra Silver. None was named Poor House, Fat Chance, or Down the Drain. My college degrees didn't help me understand the criteria for payoffs. I would have welcomed an orientation meeting or training seminar, but no. I overheard one resigned senior citizen admit, "It's like when Medicare pays. I just take what they give me." Everyone uses his own system to battle the odds. Some play five-dollar machines, hoping for speedy riches. Others play nickel machines to drag out the agony or increase playing time. Some stand up to play the machines... for hours. Some sit, plastic buckets full of coins in their laps. Some wander from machine to machine while others stay with the same one all morning, waiting for its harvest, whispering encouragement through lean times. Sometimes they give up on a stingy machine and abandon it, grimly fantasizing that it will surrender its jackpot to whichever undeserving person feeds it the next quarter. Eyes glaze over watching diamonds, cherries, and lucky 7's. Hope and superstition hypnotize players into momentarily forgetting that, in the long run, the casino isn't going to lose.

One image imprinted itself on my mind forever. In order to accumulate points for additional prizes, players can opt for a plastic card resembling a credit card that is attached to a long curly cord like those on telephones. One end is hooked to the player's lapel and the card end stays inserted in the slot machine. Those players sit plugged into the machine, literally tethered to the game.

I, of course, couldn't tell from looking whether customers were spending money they could afford to lose, or spending next week's groceries. But everyone seemed to be having fun, and I have to admit that I, too, can enjoy getting black patina on my fingers and pretending I'll soon be rich. If I don't donate more to the cause than I originally intended, and if I exchange forty dollars for forty dollars' worth of fun, then it's OK. Those who win for the day seem to have the most fun of all.

My mother, of course, came out ahead, so I made her buy me lunch. She tried not to rub it in, but I couldn't help but think of Coleridge's line, probably written when he took his own mother to a casino. "'The game is done! I've won, I've won!' quoth she, and whistles thrice."

Oh, the chickens! I nearly forgot! Well, in an actual psychological experiment, chickens were trained to peck a red button – a behavior for which they were rewarded each time with a kernel of corn that rolled down a chute. Once they mastered the button procedure, they pecked whenever they wanted a snack. When researchers stopped giving corn altogether, even the dumbest cluck, after a reasonable period of time, was smart enough to quit trying. If, however, the researchers sometimes gave the reward and sometimes didn't, following no predictable pattern, the chickens pecked until their feathered heads nearly dropped off, convinced that their jackpot would eventually come rolling down that chute.

"I'll try just one more time," they cackle, "one more time." I can almost hear those kernels plunking into slot machine bins.

* * * * *

[33]

Those little white lies
April 13, 2000

Lie to us. Please, lie to us. Whisper what we want to hear. Tell us fat is caused by a virus, that smoking won't hurt us, that chocolate is good for us. And with Mother's Day just around the corner, tell us that mothers spend as much time with their children as mothers did in the 1960s.

We all heard it on the news.

Is there any parent alive who really believes that?

Now I may not be an expert on the subject – but wait! I am! For thirty some years, from the '60s through most of the '90s, I counseled children and their parents.

In more recent years when the pressures of time gobbled families up, I'd recommend that parents consider spending fifteen private minutes daily with each child. That would require thirty minutes a day if there were two children, forty-five if – well, you know the math. The looks that often came over the parents' faces weren't looks of resistance or distaste, but sheer helplessness in terms of being able to carve those few minutes out of the schedule.

Once before, someone tried to salve our consciences by telling parents that the quantity of time spent with children wasn't important. It's the quality that counts, they said. Mothers were soothed at a time they were feeling guilty when many had begun working outside the home.

The saying lingers on, and I suggest that it's always been a seductive, attractive lie. Child rearing requires amazing amounts of time. We can't teach responsibility, communication, values, religion, academics, and have time for fun with children if we have only ten minutes of eye contact a day with them.

So now, just when we're feeling an intensification of the pressures of work and family, and dozens of outside projects vie for a slice of our twenty-four hours, the newest good news is flashed everywhere. Headlines proclaim we're with our children as much as parents were thirty-five years ago! How wonderful! These glad tidings made the front pages of newspapers and were featured on the national evening news. Phew! Thanks. We needed that.

Far be it from me to dispute the findings of this study. Someone apparently interviewed three hundred mothers to reach their happy conclusion. But I'm suggesting that we not accept these findings as a sign that we're doing just fine if our own gut feeling tells us otherwise. We're the ones who know if the pace is too fast to allow us to do what we'd like to do for and with our children.

I know that at the extreme, there are families in which youngsters have to arise as early as 4:30 a.m. to go to the babysitter's home. After another brief sleep there, they ride the bus to kindergarten, then take a bus to afternoon daycare, and are picked up by the parents at 5 or 6 p.m. School-age children frequently are involved in so many extracurricular activities that they have only one or two evenings a week at home. Parents spend their time taxiing children hither and yon, then prepare for the next morning's exodus.

I don't think parents have changed at all over the past thirty-some years in terms of what they want for their children. There is clear evidence that we care as deeply as parents ever did before, wrestle with many of the same child-rearing problems our grandparents did, and probably are more frightened than ever because of the pressures with which children have to deal every day. But do we really spend enough time with them?

What does time "with" a child mean? Do we count the hours when she's watching television in her bedroom and we're getting dinner ready? Do we count hours in the car when the child is wearing headphones listening to his own music? Do we count the hours we're on the phone and he's tugging at our pants leg? Most of us spend all day long doing things *for* our children. That's different than *with*.

And what is "quality time" anyway? I'd suggest it doesn't just mean reading to a child or playing baseball in the back yard. Sometimes it means hammering out family rules and imposing discipline when these are broken. Sometimes it means doing nothing together, simply being quietly available to one another. It means tolerating our child's anger when we won't allow what other parents allow even though this, too, saps our time and energy.

Guilt is a destructive force. Most mothers have it. Most mothers don't deserve it.

I've been consistently impressed with the efforts mothers make for their children, the sacrifices they make in their behalf, and their willingness to put their own careers and interests on the back burner. Many work outside the home because the family wouldn't eat regularly if they didn't. And eating's important. So the goal isn't to make anyone feel guilty. Nor do we really want to return to the '60s.

But we have to be cautious about research findings that are music to our ears. We don't want to let them lull us into satisfaction with the status quo, if deep inside we yearn for life to slow down.

Children are transients. We can't put them in storage until we have more time for them. One thing for sure hasn't changed since the '60s. Children grow up – with us or without us.

* * * * *

[34]

Identity crisis
May 11, 2000

I promised myself I wouldn't write about my purse being stolen.

Because if I did, I'd have to abandon my usually pleasant demeanor and describe the thief as a "jerk-or-worse" who pilfered from me in a church when I left the purse unprotected for about forty-five seconds.

Then, under cross-examination, I'd have to admit that I don't care whether he had a deprived childhood or even if he needed my money for his lunch.

And, although I quickly got on with my own life and will not long remain bitter nor require therapy to recover, I also don't intend to forgive the perpetrator since, according to the dictionary that Webster and I use, that means to excuse, or cease to blame, or absolve from payment. (Saints among us need not submit rebuttals.)

So as I write this, the thief is somewhere spending my money, perhaps trying to use my credit cards, and maybe even checking out library books under my name. (One could only hope.) Actually, the most personal loss is the punch card from my favorite coffee shop. I had already purchased the twelve required cappuccinos, and the thirteenth was to be free. He'd best not drink my freebie. And if he does, it would surely be too bad if he burns his tongue.

Unfortunately, having one's purse or billfold stolen isn't uncommon, and I heard many similar tales as I told my own. But like I said, I'm not even going to talk about losing my purse. I'm going to talk about trying to retrieve my identity.

Shakespeare said, "Who steals my purse steals trash." But he went on to emphasize that he strenuously objects to someone's filching his good name. In our contemporary plastic society, the good name is filched right along with the trash, and one had best be speedy in retrieving it.

So, after phoning the police department, credit card companies, insurance companies and (oh dear, I forgot the library), I went to the Department of Motor Vehicles to get a new license. I explained to the clerk that my purse had been stolen and that I needed a new driver's license issued for purposes of identification.

To which he replied, "OK, but to get it, you'll need some identification."

If the phrase "Catch-22" hadn't already been coined, I'd have coined it then and there.

Since the clerk had been through this procedure beaucoup times, he didn't exactly panic upon hearing my problem. I had carefully filed my old expired license away under some foolproof system that I haven't yet remembered, so that easiest and best remedy had to be scratched.

The DMV just happened to have a printed list of documents that can be used to establish one's identity in hardship cases like mine. I checked the list to see how I might qualify. Well, not having been in the military, I had no discharge papers. The Medicare identification card could have come to my rescue, except that it had been filched along with the purse. Alien registration documents would have been accepted, but I'm not technically considered an alien in spite of occasional suspicions to the contrary.

I laughed (sort of) to learn that my photograph from a school yearbook would suffice for identification – but only if the book was less than five years old. Hardly.

If only I hadn't been so law-abiding! I could have used a certificate issued by the Department of Corrections if I were an offender under their supervision.

When I was very young, I became fascinated with the case of my great-uncle, Bert, who had to go to court to prove who he was and, I was told, to prove that he had in fact been born. I remain fascinated, this time at closer range.

Happily, I was saved when I read that a birth certificate would be accepted as proof of who I am. So I drove across town to retrieve it – then wondered how in the world that would help since it bore no photograph and listed only my maiden name that I hadn't used for the past forty years or so. Just in case, in addition to the birth certificate, I gathered up other papers that verified my current name.

While sorting through identification documents in my safety deposit box, I talked with the banker who told me that during his career he had seen nearly everything. He told me that a female would-be customer once arrived at their bank drive-through facility and was asked for routine identification – at which point, she produced a wanted poster with her name and photograph on it. Regardless of her creativity, it didn't work at the bank and probably wouldn't have been accepted by the DMV either.

Oh, yes, I got my new driver's license and can whip it out now to prove that I exist. I deliberately frowned when they took the photo, just to document the day, so I'm not sure inquiring authorities will believe it's actually a photo of the smiling, cheerful me. And, no, none of my belongings was ever returned.

However, as I said at the outset, I promised myself not to dwell on the stolen purse. I'm just glad to have my identity back.

* * * * *

[35]

Late bloomers
June 8, 2000

Just when I relaxed and decided to shift into neutral for my ride through the next thirty years, some busybody researcher (probably under forty) compiled yet another annoying list. Rather than letting his elders coast in peace, he assembled a lengthy roster of people who accomplished amazing feats late in life.

Don't even bother with that young whippersnapper, Grandma Moses, who started painting at age eighty. We're talking nineties here. The list maker claimed, for instance, that some robust ninety-one-year-old woman climbed Mount Whitney, and her male counterpart completed his fourteenth marathon at age ninety-two.

We've been told that Dame Edith Anderson, at age ninety-three, gave a benefit performance, just about equaling George Burns' comedy appearances at ninety-four. George Bernard Shaw is said to have broken his leg when he fell out of a tree he was pruning. He happened to be ninety-six at the time. My personal unsung hero is a man from Tennessee who began learning to read at ninety-nine.

It's obvious that these overachievers disturb my internal poise. I'm reminded of the farmer who went into the hen house one morning carrying a huge ostrich egg. He announced to his chicken audience, "I do not mean to intimidate and I do not intend to criticize. I simply want to make you aware of what is being done elsewhere."

Well, I haven't taken the challenge lightly, and have been thinking about what the prerequisites for later-age accomplishments might be.

First of all, one has to live a really long time. That means we have to have come from a gene pool hardy enough to get us into our ninth or tenth decade. And it probably also means that we have to resist the temptation to bungee jump or race our motorcycles without wearing helmets.

I'm guessing that another prerequisite is having taken an active interest in life from the beginning. Life might begin at forty, if we stretch a point, but I've never heard anyone claim it begins at eighty. Many of the nonagenarians mentioned above didn't actually take up a new activity late in life, but simply had the energy and motivation to continue their life's work way beyond any reasonable definition of retirement.

But what about the others? What about the ninety-nine-year-old gentle warrior learning to read for the first time? What about the ninety-seven-year-old who began working full-time as a lobbyist for senior citizens? And let's do ask: what about Grandma Moses?

Somehow, these feisty role models retained a lively interest in the world and exuded courage – the courage to try something new and to keep on keeping on.

Poet Rainer Rilke says that if we imagine the individual "as a larger or smaller room, it is obvious that most people come to know only one corner of their room, one spot near the window, one narrow strip on which they keep walking back and forth."

What an accusation! And what a challenge!

Another adviser, trying to steer us off those worn paths, suggests that we write our own obituaries – that we include not only our previous accomplishments, but also those things we'd like to achieve before we die. The rest of the assignment is to work toward making the fantasy a reality.

Inserting a bit of that reality here, it might be a little late for me to include a ballet debut at Carnegie Hall on my personal list. But even though we can't all slay the biggest bears anymore, there are plenty of little bears in them woods.

So what is the greatest hindrance to leading a full life in our later years? Well, for one thing, maybe lots of inertia, a touch of apathy, and a dollop of laziness. It's all too easy to confine ourselves to those narrow strips of carpet in our room.

Of course, there are matters of health and money. But even confined to a chair by virtue of backache or bank account, maybe we could learn to hook rugs, play cribbage, write our memoirs or finally learn the names of those birds in our back yard.

And then there's fear of both the known and unknown – of small and larger dangers. We fear what other people will think and fear failure itself. A popular desk motto asks, "What would you attempt if you knew you could not fail?" What, indeed?

Rilke reminds us of the ancient myths and fairy tales about menacing dragons – those creatures that with one kiss are transformed into princes or princesses. He concludes, "Perhaps all the dragons in our lives are princesses who are only waiting to see us act, just once, with beauty and courage." Emerson adds, "This time, like all times, is a very good one, if we but know what to do with it."

A wise friend reminds me that not all worthwhile pursuits in our later years have to make the *Guinness Book of Records* or win public acclaim. And we shouldn't have to justify the paths we take. There are quiet adventures in gardens, in mountain retreats, in reading and solitude that satisfy us with peacefulness and grace. To many of us, these, too, are passions.

So I'm left with more questions than answers. What do I want to do with the next thirty years? What is my passion? What used to be my passion? And having seen the ostrich egg, what next?

* * * * *

[36]

Trains, planes, and bigots
July 13, 2000

When Abraham Lincoln was assassinated, an Indignation Train toured the country, stopping at each station to give citizens a chance to express their well-founded indignation.

Perhaps the time has come for another train. One with loud whistles to startle us from apathy, to send us running down the tracks, indignant.

Late last month, I read in the newspaper that Temple Beth Sholom, along with some other nearby buildings, was desecrated by hateful graffiti. I shook my head yet again, muttered something helpless and flipped the newspaper to the next page.

It took a friend, a non-Jewish friend, to blow the train whistle. Visiting me a few days later, she mentioned the article, and repeated with appropriate indignation, "They desecrated the temple!" How, she wanted to know, could we all sit so passively in the face of the hurtful and bigoted act, when the population should be up in arms.

I almost wish she hadn't said anything, because it's hot and humid and not the right season to think too much. I had a summer column full of fluff all written and ready to submit. But she did say something, and now I'm stuck with it. Stuck with thinking yet again about the answer, and trying to articulate concerns that go deeper than words.

Sydney J. Harris said that there are three great lessons to learn in life. The first is how to put up with things. The second is to refuse to put up with things. And the third is to be able to distinguish between the first two. Harris says that the hardest lesson is the third one, but I'm not so sure. I think maybe the hardest job is to refuse to put up with things.

First of all, we get used to them. Desecration of houses of worship, bigotry against races and blatant and veiled persecution of gays have become commonplace and sometimes not even considered newsworthy – at least not always front-page news.

On a recent trip that necessitated some travel in a propeller plane, I watched, fascinated, as the pilot brought the propellers to their maximum speed. At full pitch, the propellers revolved so fast that they became invisible, and I could see the scenery beyond as clearly as if the propellers didn't exist. Bigotry? Sometimes we look past it, right through it.

Besides our getting used to indignities, refusing to put up with things is genuinely hard work. Even with the best of intentions and hearts in the right places, we become overwhelmed and fatigued – tired of educating, mired in the pessimism of what a single person can do. We know that the journey requires just one step at a time, but feel deep down that in spite of our efforts bigots won't change their minds anyway.

How can an educated person be a bigot? What does educated mean if not to become aware of and accepting of differences? How can a truly educated person remain so fearful that human differences are interpreted as threats?

Most of us have at least learned to mouth what is appropriate and to avoid outright and hateful discrimination practices. But if we are honest with ourselves, we occasionally run into a prejudice of our own that cuts off the view. Sometimes it surprises us and brings us up short. It's a risk even to think about the issue because it requires courage to rethink our thoughts and suffer change. Or as Tom Robbins says, real courage is risking one's clichés.

It seems unreasonable to expect that we will love everyone, in spite of the ideal. And perhaps we can't even intellectually tolerate the ideas of certain groups. But we can always be kind. And kindness is enough – even if that's all there is. When we desecrate temples and act out prejudice against any group, we are desecrating not only buildings but also lives and souls of human beings.

Progress will be altogether too slow, and I guess I don't honestly believe bigotry will go away. But maybe we have to keep making our speeches even though there is simply nothing new to say. There have been some community steps in the right direction. Maybe each of us isn't crying alone in the wilderness anymore.

My friend was right. Sometimes the world bombards us with so many abominations that we stop being indignant. Sometimes, out of fatigue and hopelessness, we train ourselves to see right through it all, like the spinning propeller.

The danger is that if we don't stay alert, acceptance of bigotry sneaks up on us and grows stronger each time it goes unrecognized, each time we fail to be indignant. I've not validated the experiment myself. But I understand that if a frog is placed in a pan of cool water and set on the stove, and if the heat is turned up so gradually that the frog doesn't notice the increments, he will stay in the pan until he is cooked.

If we dare glance downward, we might see tiny bubbles forming at our feet.

* * * * *

[37]

Silver bells and cockleshells
August 10, 2000

I thought I knew all about flowers. I could create dolls from holly-hocks, make necklaces from clover and inflate sedum leaves into bulging frog bellies. I could even find two rabbits, two slippers, two earrings and one drumstick in a single bleeding heart blossom.

I had naively assumed, however, that those flowers emerged full bloom in florist shops and in other people's back yards. But having acquired my very own yard this year, I discovered that nurseries aren't always hospital rooms where newborn babies lie in baskets. I also learned that sometimes we learn things we didn't even want to know. Ogden Nash described himself as a horticultural ignoramus who couldn't tell a string bean from a soybean or a girl bean from a boy bean. He's not the only member of that club.

Wanting to achieve a flowering paradise from scratch, and being an impatient gardener, I started early by planting seeds indoors in tidy rows.

These reportedly would grow into healthy seedlings to be transplanted into my outdoor garden when spring finally arrived. After watching the tubs of dirt do nothing but lie there like tubs of dirt for several weeks, I dubbed this plot my Seed Burial Ground. It was an appropriate designation, because each barren row had been marked by a little headstone envelope with the deceased's picture, illustrating what it could have become in a more perfect world and in more competent hands. I decided to wait for further experimentation until spring.

Taking advantage of my enthusiasm, garden shops cheerfully sold me all the necessary equipment to plant flowers and take care of my lawn. It quickly became apparent that I could have bought a lot of bouquets for the price of the shovels and mulch. I developed new respect for dirt when I had to pay for it, and subsequently referred to it as soil.

Physical exercise would be an important fringe benefit to yard work, so I purchased a push mower. Or, as the young clerk at the discount store put it, "You mean it's a mower but it doesn't have a motor?" Friends raved about how much fun it would be to use one of those relics again, but no one actually showed up to mow. By early July, the relic had lost its charm and I found myself reading ads for power mower sales.

Eventually, the last probable frost date passed and knowledgeable friends told me it was safe to plant outdoors. Not to be undone again, I opted for actual plants this time rather than seeds. And predicting I might be less enthusiastic next year, opted for as many perennials as I could get away with. A nurseryman warned me that one particular flowering plant could take over my whole garden. I bought three of them. At least I didn't have to plant spearmint. It volunteered for duty in every bed.

Ever the psychologist, I gave my plants a motivational speech as I placed them in the ground. I suggested that they consider themselves on death row, their ultimate fate depending upon how well they performed this year. They shuddered and seemed to believe.

During the long waiting and watering period, I kept learning. I quickly learned that spearmint rules. Though we draw maps to plot our flower gardens, spearmint draws strategic maps of its own. It is impervious to threats and curses, thrives without water, plant food, sunshine or weeding. It digs defensive trenches for its roots far underground and lurks beneath the mulch, ready to ambush more legitimate plants after dark. Two sprouts arrived as replacements for each one that had been uprooted. Even if I used it in my tea there was enough to last lifetimes. Mine and that of all the tea drinkers in China.

I learned that if a weed was green and had blossoms, it deserved elevation to flower status. If it propagated, all the better. I learned that blossoming plants had to be dead-headed, which I consider rather violent terminology for a seemingly gentle pursuit like gardening. And I learned that even though weed-whackers trim efficiently, they are not appropriate for shaving one's legs.

I quickly discovered that nothing is simple. Among my garden purchases were four lovely plants with pictures on their cards illustrating bright yellow flowers that looked like poppies. I planted them as directed in full sun and they bloomed almost immediately and looked exactly like the picture. Unfortunately, the label failed to disclose the fact that these flowers bloom only at night. I felt obligated to go outside with a flashlight a couple times a week to acknowledge them, and considered having a midnight lawn party so my friends could enjoy them too. I'm sure that particular species was developed by some botanist who worked third shift.

So, Mary, Mary, quite contrary, how did your garden grow? Well, frankly, it grew very well in spite of myself. The shin healed from the weed whacker assault, a couple less heroic stems of spearmint raised their aromatic arms and surrendered, and most of my flowers bloomed during daylight hours.

But now, just when I thought the work was finished and I have time to smell the roses, I've heard rumors that it's nearly time to think about fall planting. As T. E. Brown observed, a garden is a lovesome thing.

Maybe I'll plant more spearmint.

* * * * *

[38]

Learning by heart
September 14, 2000

As a three-year-old, I stood one night on the platform before a Nazarene Church congregation and recited, complete with appropriate gestures:

"Though I am just a tiny tot, I can smile and bow as well as not."

Maybe the applause encouraged me. Or perhaps it was the back pew chorus of "Amen. Bless her little heart." Whatever the inspiration, that two-line ditty became the first of dozens of poems I memorized through the years, many of which I remember to this day.

My mother apparently took some criticism for making me learn lengthy verses, though I mostly remember practice sessions with my grandmother. I remember reciting strange poetry – about children being orphaned, about parents having to decide which child to give up during the Depression, and about the church closing because God went on vacation. It wasn't Keats or Byron, but in any case, no one forced me to learn.

My penchant for loving poetry and enjoying memorization relegated me to minority status in English classes. When teachers assigned verses to learn, I inwardly smiled amidst unabashed groans from the rest of the class.

Even now, I occasionally memorize a poem for my own pleasure, reciting it out loud to myself and, lacking a more substantial audience, to the air.

Lest someone label me a memorization freak, let me hasten to defend myself. I don't think memorization teaches discipline or strengthens the mind. And one has to decide what's worth remembering or making someone else remember. This distinction becomes increasingly important when, with advancing age, our brains become full. At that point, before any new tidbits can establish themselves in our memory, something else has to be ejected to make room. So although there are some things we absolutely have to memorize, such as the multiplication tables, there's no use cluttering our minds with nonessentials.

I recall that one junior high geography teacher made us learn the names of all eighty-eight counties in Ohio, but mercifully I've forgotten those. And once upon a time I knew the state capitals, but now am perfectly comfortable just looking them up.

My head still remembers the sixty-six books of the Bible in order, large chunks of the Gettysburg Address, the names of the four Japanese islands, and the preamble to the Constitution. I might forget friends' names, and occasionally my own, but I can't forget two verses (yes, two) of "The Star-Spangled Banner." Friends will sadly attest to the fact that I remember nearly every joke I've heard since childhood. Worst of all, I remember yet another song. In high school, our Latin class memorized and sang "There is a Tavern in the Town." In Latin. Over the years, there simply hasn't been much call for that performance, although whenever possible I try to work it into the conversation.

Obviously, if I could rid myself of these complex memories, my brain cells could be put to use recalling something useful – like my phone number or where I left my dictionary. Maybe some computer whiz will eventually devise a delete button for human memory that doesn't involve lobotomy.

But at any rate, in recalling my history of memorization, it dawned on me that teachers didn't even use the word memorize when speaking of poetry assignments. Instead, in what would now be considered quaint terminology, they instructed us to learn the poems by heart. Loving poetry, that's surely what I did. It's surely what I do.

I'm entirely convinced that it's essential to have minds with attractive and interesting pictures on the walls, and that poetry paints a multitude of murals. It waits on call to amuse, comfort, inspire, and sometimes to express feelings when our own words fail. What a pleasure to discover and learn a poem in which someone else shares our thoughts and feelings that had seemed deeper than articulation.

So my point is (and there is one) that with the onset of another school year, I find myself hoping that lots of teachers will risk temporary unpopularity by assigning poems to be learned by heart, and that teachers of the youngest students will introduce poetry early.

Preschoolers, even sophisticated ones in the twenty-first century, need to learn and remember exactly why Jack and Jill went up that hill and how they fared. Many older students will grumble and complain about learning poems, claiming they'd rather eat dirt and die. But even hardcore tough guys who consider poetry a sissy pursuit will perk up to the tale of "Casey at the Bat" or "The Charge of the Light Brigade." And who, at any age, could resist Shel Silverstein's "Glurpy Slurpy Skakagrall"?

Practical students will ask, as they always do, what purpose these poems will serve in the real world. We can only promise that they'll paint beautiful murals on the walls of their minds. A couple members of the class will understand.

A character in Janet Fitch's novel, *White Oleander*, advises, "Always learn poems by heart. They have to become the marrow in your bones. Like fluoride in the water, they'll make your soul impervious to the world's soft decay."

Hear, hear.

* * * * *

[39]

It rains on my parades
October 12, 2000

I've not been particularly fond of parades and usually don't clamor for space on the curb when one marches by. I've worked hard to understand the origin of this un-American attitude so I could more fully enjoy the festivities. But recently I had a decisive traumatic experience that threatens to undermine all my progress.

As Freud himself would tell us, the roots of the problem wind back through childhood to the few parade experiences I can remember.

As a Brownie and Girl Scout, I marched in Memorial Day parades through the downtown square en route to cemetery ceremonies. Our troop always rehearsed ahead of time so that we'd make a good impression. But parade organizers routinely lined us up behind a squadron of excited horses.

And since the horses regularly dropped smelly gifts ahead of us, we were always forced to abandon our practiced formation or get a foot-full.

As an observer, rather than participant, I recall childhood parades at the county fair. Actually, I recall just one unit of the parades. A band made up of orphans from the county children's home marched and played each year. Preceding their band, the youngest orphan of all rode in a pony-pulled wicker cart and pulled everyone's heartstrings along with her. The band played "Blue Skies" and made me cry.

We won't even talk about the fear of being run down on the curb by big men in funny hats who drive those tiny cars.

How and when did people decide that parades would be a good way to celebrate?

There could just as easily be a tradition of standing in groups and singing on street corners, or of juggling fruits and vegetables to express our excitement. I figure it all started when some lucky caveman killed a mastodon large enough to feed his community all winter. As he and friends dragged the carcass to his cave condo, hungry neighbors ran behind shouting and cheering. Wives banged on pots and pans, preparing for the cookout, and that's how it all began. Or something like that.

Now, after centuries of tradition, nothing will stop parade enthusiasts. I read that in one small community, the city council waxed vindictive and refused to allow a parade permit one Fourth of July. Not to be undone, all the parade participants stood stock still in parade formation along a neighborhood street, and the citizens walked by to see them! You gotta admire their creativity.

Genuine enthusiasts will watch any parade that rolls down the street. I still don't think that one small boy carrying a flag and pulling his dog in a wagon constitutes a parade — unless of course it's my little boy. Politicians waving from cars don't rightly qualify as a parade either, but I guess those parades celebrate the fact that we live in a country where politicians can wave from cars.

Nonetheless, through sheer grit and determination, the scars left by early parade experiences had begun to heal. But, as often is the case, a funny thing happened on the way to recovery.

One recent summer evening, I left a downtown parking garage after enjoying a dinner gala with friends. I had my parking ticket stamped by the attendant and coasted to the street for my exit. Lo and behold, right there in front of me was a nighttime parade. The noise was horrendous. Thirty or forty gigantic semi-truck cabs, lights flashing and air-horns blasting, streamed past to celebrate the opening of a truck show the next day.

Now these are the sorts of trucks that I try to avoid even on the highway. Not being able to spare five minutes in my busy life (apparently), I decided to bypass the parade and take an alternate route home. Parade lovers had chosen to park their cars and get out to watch the procession. And, yes, people sat on the curbs to cheer, even at bedtime.

I easily executed my detour and turned toward home. Details are messy.

But the punch line is that I found myself right in the middle of the truck parade, zipping along the designated route with them, surrounded by flashing lights and air-horns.

It wasn't long before a motorcycle cop pulled up beside my car, both of us still in motion, and he was mouthing something and scowling something. I indicated in pantomime that I couldn't hear him. In a voice that might have been audible all over the downtown area, he bellowed, "Open your window!" When I did, he continued at the same volume and with the same scowl. "Get out of this lane of traffic and let the trucks past!"

Well, I would have liked to oblige, but there was only one lane in the street at that particular juncture. But after another block or so, I found a dirt area off the shoulder of the road and pulled on to it to await the end of the parade.

As I think back on my adventure, I rather enjoy the spectacle of a little old lady in a cocky white hat whizzing down the highway in a semi-truck parade. It almost makes me wish for an air-horn. The ride was both scary and exhilarating, more so than marching behind the troupe of horses. I'm not sure, however, that I want to experience either one again.

It's easy to understand how that incident set me back in my efforts to overcome childhood parade trauma, but I haven't given up. Perhaps it's safer for me just to watch for a while. I'll continue attending my twelve-step program to get over the anxiety, and I'll show up at the next parade. Just save me a spot on the curb and promise to hold my hand if a big truck or black motorcycle goes by.

* * * * *

(Preparing for an Easter Bonnet Parade)

79

[40]

Pounds of prevention (and vice versa)
November 9, 2000

Dieting becomes a hot topic in November when we turn on the oven to prepare holiday feasts. We usually predict a weight gain and lament our fate even while stuffing the turkeys and baking the pies.

Realistically, weight problems aren't caused by what we eat between November and January but by what we eat between January and November. Nevertheless, I want to relieve everyone's mind through the holidays with some helpful scientific findings, plausible excuses and new motivations.

Eureka! Two years ago, researchers discovered that obesity might be caused, not by overeating, but by a virus. And they think it might even be contagious.

This virus discovery goes to the top of my own list of excuses for being heavier than the weight that the Surgeon General recommends. Earlier studies revealed that looking at goodies in bakery display cases could cause weight gain because of the body's chemical reaction to seeing food. We already knew in our hearts that was true. How else could eating a two-pound box of candy result in a five-pound weight gain?

Previously, I had blamed excess poundage on post-partum hormonal fluctuations, but that excuse expired when my youngest child turned thirty.

When all else failed, I accused ancestors. My mother willed me added fat cells when she overfed me as an infant. Grandma rewarded me for a clean plate when I gobbled up her mashed potatoes and gravy. Ancestors bequeathed me genes that will never fit into a size 6. And we all know it's harder to lose weight as we get older, since almost everything is harder when we get older.

The problem is such a tiresome one. Most of us realize that we should weigh less than our refrigerators, and we've struggled to lose the same ten or twenty pounds ten or twenty times.

We doggedly try all the diet clichés. We eat rapidly so that our stomachs won't compute how much is being consumed. We leave proverbial cherries off the walnut sundaes and eat alone or in the dark, where calories don't count. Waxing creative, I wrote to dress designers requesting that muumuus be reintroduced as fashionable.

I put pig magnets on the refrigerator and read a shelf full of books about healthful eating. In fact, I read so much about the evils of overeating that I eventually had to give up reading. Besides, I discovered that I could devour a whole plate of cookies in just two chapters.

Even in desperation, drastic treatments with liposuction and pills are just plain scary, and I'd prefer not having parts of my stomach removed. A little door in the side of my neck would be handy, though. Then I could graze all day long, enjoy the taste of food, and simply let it out the trap door before it does any damage. Never mind. That's an untidy fantasy.

As a supplementary safeguard, I considered patronizing only those physicians pudgier than I since they might tend overall to be less fanatical about weight issues than skinny doctors. The danger in seeing medical professionals at all is that they might pooh-pooh theories about metabolism or viruses and suggest that I develop a more active lifestyle and eat less.

I've actually tried exercising. Back in the '50s, (the decade, not the age,) I enrolled at a salon offering passive exercise. For a fistful of dollars, they allowed me to lie on a vibrating table like a motorized motel bed, and I was to lose weight in the process. It sounded too good to be true, and, indeed, it was. The only weight I lost was that fistful of dollars. Later, during a flight into sanity, I regularly visited a fitness center. That approach paid great dividends, as long as I exercised more than my jaw and used machines other than its coffee maker.

At other times, I've exercised by hiking along highways, dodging cars. And I once even considered jogging. I nipped that idea in the bud, however, when I read about some poor woman whose thighs rubbed together when she jogged, and her spandex shorts caught fire. (That's truly one of the saddest stories I've ever heard.)

Most of us have tried nearly everything. Luckily, one of the advantages of passing sixty is that one usually doesn't have to worry about being a size 6 anymore. I've long since learned that having a good shape doesn't mean being in good shape, and I frankly enjoy knowing that I could body slam some of those slender young model-types without straining a muscle.

My more modest goals are to remain healthy enough to live independently for a long time, and zestfully enough to embarrass my children.

In spite of lofty intentions, motivation occasionally sags and we find it difficult to keep dieting promises we make to ourselves. Recently, however, I solved my own motivation problem for all time and feel obligated to share the inspiration with others in the same cellulite boat at this holiday time.

Somewhere on the East Coast, a gigantic beached whale died on the sand in spite of heroic efforts to save her. Because of her size, she couldn't be buried. Instead, I tell you true, they had to blow her up. Blubber flew everywhere and even injured one of the bystanders.

Of course, my primary motivation is a long and healthy life, but I'm no fool. Virus or no virus, I'm returning immediately to a regime of healthful diet and workouts. Because, frankly, the idea of being blown up instead of buried rates right up there with having my shorts catch fire.

Happy Thanksgiving anyway.

* * * * *

[41]

When love isn't enough
December 14, 2000

Forty years ago, while chatting with a friend who had six children, I informed her that all children are alike at birth, their personalities being shaped through the years by how they are disciplined and nurtured. I, of course, had no children at the time, and to this day remain grateful that she allowed me to live in spite of my ignorance.

Most parents with even two children, let alone six, have first-hand proof that temperaments differ greatly from the moment of birth. While some babies lie peacefully in their hospital baskets, others squall a challenge, ready to twist the world's arm behind its back. Sometimes it's hard to believe that siblings share the same gene pool.

However it happens, through chemical quirks, gene pool lotteries or something even more mystical, children often display temperaments not only different from their siblings, but so different from that of their own parents that we suspect the stork dropped them by mistake on the way to their officially designated home. Nature toys with Nurture and often has its way. A quiet, unassuming couple find themselves parenting a boisterous scene-stealer, or a mystified conservative couple cohabit with a morose, asocial teenager with rings in his nose and other places.

We all know bright children who, in spite of adequate parenting, spend their academic lives sitting in the principal's office, failing classes, regularly saying the wrong thing at precisely the wrong time and spoiling even the happiest occasions with outlandish antics. And we know of the adolescents who dive without warning into deep depression or psychosis even though they've had the benefit of nurturing and reasonable discipline.

I feel a little less embarrassed about my wet-behind-the-ears tendency to hold parents fully accountable for the behavior and personalities of their children since at that time, seasoned mental health professionals also viewed parents as culprits, and frequently shook a blaming, unsympathetic finger.

Given the symptoms, we were told, the parents must not care enough about their child, or spend enough time with her, or discipline appropriately. Maybe they criticize her so severely that they undermine her self-esteem. Maybe mother hovers too closely or maybe she is emotionally unresponsive. Maybe father is absent, or perhaps authoritarian.

But, I'd also suggest, perhaps not. Bad things not only happen to good people. Bad things also happen to children of good parents.

We hear all too frequently about cases of blatant parental abuse and neglect – tragedies beyond comprehension that sadden us all. But the truth is, most mothers and fathers work hard at parenting. Most of us do the best we can every day with the capabilities we and our children have. And most parents expend the greater part of their time, energy and resources finding help when their child develops special needs. They spend hours keeping doctor appointments, attending teacher conferences and therapist consultations. In the process, they get good advice and bad advice. They get understanding and blame. Methods that work with every other child in the universe seem not to work with their own, and before long they have, indeed, tried everything.

Of course we should continually hone our parenting skills, because we have a tremendous impact on our children's lives. But the majority of seemingly successful parents are also just plain lucky – lucky to have healthy children, extended family support systems and money to provide for basic needs. If our children are fortunate enough to have been born on third base, we probably shouldn't feel too smug if they escape major difficulties and reach home plate safely. Besides, the game isn't over.

I've long since learned that no family can hang out a shingle proclaiming, "Everything is perfect in here." Eventually, even children from close-knit, stable families go out into the world with cars and friends and money to make their own decisions and make their own mistakes. Fearfully, we pray that those mistakes won't have lifelong consequences. Most of us don't take credit for our child's success and achievements. Perhaps we needn't be so quick to accept the blame for their problems and failures.

Frequently, when parents are faced with the frightening and formidable challenges presented by a mentally ill, physically handicapped or neurologically impaired child, their own self-esteem hits bottom. They tend to assume other families are picture-perfect and sense they are being looked down upon. I strongly suggest that if we ever run into a self-proclaimed perfect family we should keep running. If physicians, teachers, therapists, relatives and friends add to parental guilt, the burden becomes too heavy to bear.

I don't think God would mind if I clear up a couple misconceptions. First of all, I don't think he (she) decides to assign troubled children to certain parents in order to test their mettle. And, second, contrary to the popular cliché, sometimes parents are, indeed, given more burden than they are able to bear. I have seen them crash and burn. Marriages falter as husbands and wives blame themselves and each other, the demands of child-rearing leaving no energy to restore their relationship.

Since this is the season of generosity, let me offer some suggestions for holiday giving. Give parents the benefit of the doubt. Give encouragement and help whenever it's possible. Give struggling parents a break. And if you're a struggling parent, give yourself credit for the efforts you've made, and forgive the rest of us when we don't understand.

* * * * *

[42]

Just what the doctor ordered
January 11, 2001

It's time for a cleansing winter tonic and Grandmother isn't here to prescribe something. So I sought suggestions from my shelf of medical reference books. Apparently, my collection could use an update since the book that shoved itself toward me was the 1884 edition of *Dr. Chase's Last and Complete Work*. I literally wiped cobwebs from its edges.

Dr. Chase's volume reportedly sold 1.2 million copies. I have absolutely no idea where my own came from.

While medical treatments comprise one-third of the 865-page volume, the rest is a compendium of recipes, household hints and instructions for beekeeping, machinery repair and care of farm animals. Physicians of his era obviously didn't have to declare specialties.

I was surprised to learn that Dr. Chase advocated over one hundred years ago what is now considered alternative medicine. So I temporarily abandoned my search for a tonic to explore his cures for common ailments.

It was reassuring to learn that my cobwebs could serve some useful purpose. Dr. Chase recommends that when one is bleeding from cuts, one should bind the cut with cobwebs and brown sugar, then press it on the wound like lint. Or, "for either man or beast," use equal parts of wheat flour and salt, bound on the wound with a cloth.

If the patient suffers from a sore throat (and has a hardy disposition), place in a drinking glass two teaspoons of salt, a quarter teaspoon of black pepper and a teaspoon or two of pepper sauce. Then fill the glass with cider vinegar and water. Stir and gargle.

For an accompanying earache, alternate several slices of onion with some leaves of strong tobacco in a stack. Wrap the pile in a wet cloth and cover this package with hot embers until the onion is cooked. Press out the juice and drop it into the ear for instant relief.

(By the way, my attorney says to be sure to tell you not to try these at home. Or, as television ads caution, check first with your health care professional.)

To avoid the "stupefying action of drugs," Dr. Chase offers alternative remedies for insomnia. For example, just before retiring, one should eat two or three small raw onions, with a little bread, lightly spread with fresh butter. (One might as well sleep, since onion breath will probably preclude any better offers.)

My personal favorite is the "cure for the love of liquor," which is credited to a Dr. Hatfield. He claims, "Eat an orange every morning half an hour before breakfast. Take that and you will want neither liquor nor medicine." Dr. Chase himself offers one further admonition. "If in addition to eating the orange a day, you keep away from where liquor is sold, you will be safe."

I'll drink to that.

The list of cures goes on: for seasickness, canker sores, warts and freckles. Luckily, my tonic was there, too. To purify the blood, I am advised to eat a finely minced onion with breakfast, followed by a dose of charcoal or ground coffee.

If some not-too-close friend develops canker sores, I can offer Dr. Chase's prescribed cure, which, among other ingredients, includes gunpowder.

Smile though we may, Dr. Chase would be happy to know that natural remedies are coming full circle. Modern scientists are prowling rainforests to discover plants that could offer cures for old, seemingly unconquerable diseases. Nature again becomes the healer.

Jean Carper, in her book, *The Food Pharmacy*, advocates, as many other contemporary scientists do, that we try natural remedies before turning automatically to drugs – at least for minor ailments. Food has for centuries been regarded as a potent medicine. What used to be considered quackery is now fodder for serious study.

Reminiscent of Dr. Chase's work, Carper says that sugar almost always heals a wound when antibiotics fail; that yogurt boosts the immune system, cures diarrhea and contains agents that are stronger antibiotics than penicillin. Onions boost our good cholesterol, garlic prevents blood clots, and sugar at bedtime helps induce sleep. Red wine "knocks off bacteria about as well as penicillin," she says, and, I'd personally add, goes better with dinner.

Herbal therapy, massage therapy, vitamin therapy, yoga, acupuncture, healing touch... So many ailments, so many alternatives. Live leeches are again being put on wounds to suck out the infection. Saints preserve me from that one. The trick is not to run out from under our heads when making our choices.

Apparently running out from under his head in spite of my warning, Menelik II, the emperor of Ethiopia between 1889 and 1913, practiced one medical eccentricity. If he felt ill, he called for a Bible. Not to read, but to eat. He ordinarily had to eat just a few pages in order to feel better. But in 1913, while recovering from a stroke, he felt extremely ill and asked to have the entire book of Kings torn from the Bible and fed to him. Unfortunately, he died before having consumed it all. Ah, well.

The Edge newsletter recently outlined a short history of medical marketing practices that seems to suggest that what goes around comes around. In 2000 B.C, we were advised: "Here, eat this root." In 1000 A.D., "That root is heathen. Here, say this prayer." In 1850, "That prayer is superstition. Here, drink this potion." In 1940, "That potion is snake oil. Here, swallow this pill." In 1985, "That pill is ineffective. Here, take this antibiotic." And now in 2001, "That antibiotic is artificial. Here, eat this root."

One of my own favorite remedies, most recently recycled by Bennett Cerf, was promoted long ago by Lord Byron who advised, "Always laugh when you can. It's cheap medicine."

Fruits and vegetables. Laughter and Grandmother's chicken soup. We knew it all the time.

* * * * *

[43]

Don't expect others to hold your umbrella
February 8, 2001

Once upon a time, there was this good guy named Noah. Not a rich man nor a particularly influential man, but just a good guy. He tended to his own business and in a quiet way did what he could around home.

Now it seems that good guys were pretty hard to come by in those days. God himself had scouted the territory on numerous occasions but didn't come up with much. Public interest ran high in the brothels and taverns; violence was rampant on TV screens; skirts were high and morals were low. Something, somewhere, was missing.

God realized that a patch-up job would more than exhaust his supply of Band-Aids, so he decided to chuck the whole mess and start from scratch – or almost from scratch, anyway.

So while the bad guys were having all the fun, whom does God pick for the dirty work? The good guy. Now this was no small matter for Noah. He was just celebrating his 599th birthday when God announced,

"Son, I think it's gonna rain. In fact, I'm sure it's gonna rain. And I'll need a contractor for an ark."

Noah was flattered, but hesitant. "Look," he said, "I'd like to help out. But I'm already treasurer of the YMCA, librarian at the synagogue and coach for Little League." His long-suffering wife reminded him, "If you get involved in one more project, we won't have any family time left."

But God persisted. And the next thing Noah knew, he was building an ark on dry land and stopping periodically to question his sanity. God was pretty fussy about the specifications, and Noah wasn't one to slight details. Since the cause was a worthy one, he approached the lumberyards and Chamber of Commerce for a donation of materials, to no avail. His wife eventually volunteered to solicit funds through a door-to-door campaign in the city. Unfortunately, most people seemed to have contributed at the office. So Noah enlisted his sons to help him cut trees, and they, too, started from scratch.

The neighbors had been pretty tolerant all these years; but this time, Crazy Noah had really done it. They sat in the fields and taunted him – sarcastically waving umbrellas and citing the TV weatherman's predictions for dry weather. Noah tried calm persuasion at first, then angry argument. And finally he lapsed into a sullen, questioning silence. It was difficult anymore to be sure. He was tired of fighting the rest of the world and, lordy, how he wished it would rain.

Somehow, the ark got built. It was no small task gathering up the animals and birds and creepy-crawly things and getting them into their proper cabins on the ark. But it was even more of a challenge to entice his wife, sons and daughter-in-law to get on board. Helping the old man build the ship was one thing. Committing themselves to a ride on his fantasy was another. Fortunately, it began to sprinkle; a sprinkle that did wonders for their convictions.

So it rained – and rained – rained for forty solid days and nights. As cities and mountains and TV towers were covered by floodwaters, Noah gained confidence that he had done the right thing, even though there were no neighbors around to acknowledge this.

Being right didn't make it easier. With only one window in the ark, pollution was becoming a distinct problem. His wife missed her dishwasher, the boys grumbled about their chores and whined for their video games.

Noah calculated that they'd be off the ark at the end of the forty days. But it took 164 extra days for the waters to recede enough to let the creatures and people out. Noah was 600 years old by now. He had just taken his first real trip. He didn't know where he had been, and there was no one around to look at his slides. He lived to be 950 years old, and maybe he never did understand what it was all about. But he heard the call to build and he grabbed a hammer.

"So," a friend asked upon reading my Noah story, "what brought all that on?" Well, the inauguration's over and, excuse my politics, it's a bit scary out there. I first considered building another ark. But not being entirely sure of God's political affiliation, and remembering that the original passenger list included fleas as well as butterflies, I presumed I'd have to take on board two each of Democrats, Republicans, Independents, left-wingers, right-wingers, bright people, stupid people, and a couple dimpled chads. I just didn't feel neutral enough to carry that off.

Like Noah, our lives already seem overly busy, and we often feel powerless in the face of the enormity of the issues. Besides, Noah taught us that even in the relative safety of an ark we'd be in for the ride of our lives.

But I'm finally concerned enough about the ship of state that I've decided to get involved. It's too bad the water sometimes has to reach our knees before we notice. At least as a start, I'm going to stuff envelopes for worthy candidates and write letters on issues of concern. What is it that they've always said? The way for evil to prosper is for good men to do nothing.

Batten down the hatches. It's already starting to rain.

* * * * *

[44]

Show me the way to go home
March 8, 2001

Please do me a favor. If you happen to see me downtown or at one of the malls, take me gently by the shoulders and turn me around. Because, chances are, I'm headed in the wrong direction. As I am required to recite during Lost Anonymous meetings, "My name is Naomi, and I'm direction-ally impaired."

Many are afflicted with this invisible disease. Not long ago, on the streets of this very city, I found myself stopped at a traffic signal behind a car with a personalized license plate reading "LOST." This public confession served as fair notice not to follow, but the temptation was hard to resist, since she qualifies as soul mate. I haven't seen her since.

So many questions come to mind. Does she turn the wrong way leaving office buildings and stores? Can she find her car in a parking lot without assistance? Does she know which direction the front door of her house faces? Would she be able to find the meeting place if I invited her to Lost Anonymous?

The afflicted among us still can't find our way around malls and usually can't even find the color-coded store locator maps that are posted somewhere or another. We frequently have to ask clerks where to find the escalator. Why do they keep moving them, anyway?

Getting lost isn't usually life-threatening, because we can be found again. But it does prove inconvenient. On the brighter side, we meet lots of gas station attendants along the route when we stop to ask directions. As though reading from a script, each one ends his directions by telling us, "You can't miss it." Little do they know. Of course we can!

Unafflicted, well-meaning friends frequently offer advice. One of mine suggests that I head in the opposite direction of whatever my instincts tell me. Although that sounds a bit drastic, it might be an effective remedy, since my internal compass needle usually twirls at random instead of pointing north – wherever north is.

Aware of my own weakness, if people ask me for directions I usually tell them I'm a tourist myself. That's not exactly a lie and, whether they know it or not, it's a favor to them.

I've learned that although others value a sense of direction that points them always toward true north, they miss out on some interesting adventures.

My own confession at support group meetings includes the fact that I don't confine my disorientation to the local scene. One Saturday morning, headed for a shop in Kansas City, Kansas, I mistakenly crossed the river into Missouri and subsequently spent a full ninety minutes trying to find my way back across the bridge into Kansas. By the time I succeeded, the shop had closed, but the owner took pity on me and let me in.

On another occasion, I drifted by mistake off the interstate into a factory district of Kansas City on a Sunday morning and couldn't find my way back to the highway. The area was mostly deserted, but a tough looking loiterer gave me directions when I dared to stop and ask. As I thanked him, he requested a donation to buy his dinner. Having no confidence in my bargaining position, I gave him money for dinner and then got out of there. At least his directions took me directly to the interstate, and that's what I had unexpectedly paid for.

More recently at the Kansas City airport, after returning from a trip, I couldn't find my car in long-term parking. In spite of having the bus stop number correctly noted on my ticket, an attendant and I circled the lot for two and a half hours before finding the car. I thought perhaps it had been stolen, but aware of the model and year, the attendant said he doubted anyone would take it. I was so impressed with his persistence and patience that I proposed marriage.

Then finally, last summer, I toured most of Massachusetts while supposedly on a ten-minute drive to pick up a friend. But since it was vacation time, I choose to categorize that particular episode as a sightseeing road trip.

It helps a little to know that I'm not the only one suffering with this impairment, but sometimes the afflicted simply don't admit to their disability – particularly in writing. I had to dig deep to find literary references.

We've all sung my support group's theme song, "We are poor little lambs who've lost our way, Baa, Baa, Baa."

And I identify warmly with one of James Fields' characters from a poem included in the old McGuffy Reader. "We are lost, the captain shouted, as he staggered down the stairs." He's another potential member for our group, provided he's found his way to shore by now.

There's always a glimmer of hope as long as we're making progress. I'm proud to announce that I've not been lost inside my own house for a really long time. I figure that until electronic homing devices are invented for the likes of me, the worst that can happen is that our photos will end up on milk cartons.

I recently read that a certain Aborigine tribe speaks not of four directions, but of seven: North, South, East, West, Above, Below, and Within. I've pretty much mastered Above and Below and have given up on the usual four.

That leaves lots of time to concentrate on Within.

* * * * *

[45]

Democracy: only as strong as grass roots
April 12, 2001

It's early on Election Day. The rain predictably poured down between 7 and 8 a.m., vying to keep voter turnout as low as the ice and apathy did during the primaries. Poll workers, who could have napped through much of the primary election, will be kept busier today – perhaps.

But at 10 a.m., voter turnout still has reached only six percent, and it's already stopped raining. We can only hope for longer lines during the after-work hours.

It has always amazed me to watch television coverage of elections in emerging democracies. Eager to participate in their government for the first time, people stand in long queues in the street waiting their turn to vote while being protected from violence by military men with rifles. In spite of our own long tradition and good intentions, I wonder how many of us would brave sniper fire to cast our ballots.

Ordinarily, I'm no flag-waver. But regardless of who wins a particu- lar election, I've grown increasingly impressed with the way a democracy works – if we are willing to participate. I might even have to get a flag to wave.

Today, I vote without benefit of armed guard and am met, instead, by a group of pleasant women who ask my name, give me a ballot, and tolerate my jokes. As far as I can tell, there are no observers from Cuba, Russia, or Florida to watch for voting irregularities.

The ballot itself deserves applause, offering choices when others often have none. Ours is an election in which the outcome doesn't have to be a foregone conclusion.

During the campaign, candidates regaled constituents with letters, phone calls, flyers, speeches and personal visits, soliciting approval and votes. Their volunteers folded brochures, stuffed envelopes, licked stamps, raised money, made phone calls and planted signs in yards, some of them the first signs of spring.

Then, finally, in the privacy of the voting booth, the clamor fades, and we fill in the little ovals of our choice with black marker pen. What a comfort to realize that our own quiet mark has as much impact as that of the loudest zealot or most strident candidate.

But this year, something sprang from the ground besides tulips and yard signs. A dedicated cluster of citizens, plowing unfamiliar soil, nurtured a bumper crop of grass roots. To many of us, it was a new phenomenon.

In view of its significance, the very possibility of a grass-roots process should excite us all, regardless of the candidate for whom we choose to vote. How many places in the world do voters have the ballot option of "None of the above"? I wasn't the only one who learned something from that movement. Before the media and grassroots workers made more information available to the public, some registered voters believed write-in votes were illegal. Others squandered the blank ballot space to write in names like Mickey Mouse or Donald Duck.

Grass roots began to sprout when a dauntless few weren't satisfied with the options. And instead of just complaining about it, as many of us would, they talked with others who weren't satisfied either, who talked with still more others, and gained strength in numbers.

They empowered themselves.

Without the clout of political organization behind them, they, too, made phone calls and sent flyers to constituents. But they counted most on word-of-mouth and beat-of-heart; and the grass roots spread wider and deeper. Where else but here? Today, they, too, fill in an oval with black marker pen and then write in the name of their alternate choice. And their voice will count.

It's still early on Election Day. Surely everyone learned during the recent presidential election that every single vote counts. And since the rain has stopped, I'm sure the lines of voters are so long that election workers will demand an increase in pay next year. But I'm also afraid not.

Of course, those who don't vote forfeit any right to complain about what happens during the next four years, so we can justifiably ask about the complainant's voting record when the grumbling begins. We should have learned by now that every voter, as well as every elected official, exercises a public trust. Not just twenty percent or thirty percent of us.

Soon it will be all over but the shouting. Nothing left but ballot counting and election night watches.

As for the candidates, even some worthy ones will lose. When Abraham Lincoln lost his bid for the Illinois Senate, he said he felt like the boy who stubbed his toe; too big to cry and too badly hurt to laugh. But the worst risk of all is not to risk, and they gave it a shot.

So I'm applauding today. Applauding those with the guts to run for office, the citizens who care enough to vote, the grassroots organizers who remind us of possibilities, and the country where all of this is possible.

William James advised that we should seek incessantly, with fear and trembling, to vote in such a way as to bring about the largest possible universe of good.

So say we all.

* * * * *

[46]

You haven't changed a bit!
May 10, 2001

Remember that hyperactive go-getter in your high school graduating class? The one formally voted Busiest Senior and informally known as chummiest, all-around guy? Be forewarned that while the rest of us sag into spring, he's busy organizing this year's class reunion, and we can expect our invitations in the mail.

To attend or not to attend, that is the question.

Every television sit-com devotes at least one episode to the anxieties and antics surrounding reunion festivities. Returning graduates subject themselves to crash diets hoping to lose thirty pounds by June, maintaining the fantasy of fitting into that cheerleader outfit again. As things stand when the invitation arrives, only the pompons fit. Schemers lease a fancy car for reunion week, rent a girlfriend and lie about their credentials, while others shamelessly flaunt legitimate ones, or eagerly reunite with a long ago crush.

Anticipating an invitation, I began planning my own strategy, one I hoped wouldn't involve the sitcom extremes. I got out my old yearbook and reminisced as prelude to deciding whether to attend.

We stood like dutiful soldiers for the '50s photograph. Girls wore mid-calf skirts, blouses, sweaters, white ankle socks, and always a scarf around the neck or flowers at the top blouse button. Boys dressed casually in un-holey jeans and shirts, but no t-shirts with mottoes, and no earrings.

We actually looked like the kids we were. Worldly-wise, mature-looking high school students of 2001 would have intimidated us with a single glance, had they been disposed to look in our direction at all.

It's interesting to attend reunions to see how our classmates bridged the gap between then and now. And maybe a few of us well-adjusted people will attend simply to enjoy the company of old friends and catch up on the news.

But most of us have some pressing unspoken questions as well.

What happened to the Most Likely to Succeed? And what happened to the cheerleaders and football players after calls for cheers and touchdowns waned? Who deserves the prize for most changed and least changed over the years? Did the prettiest stay pretty, the most athletic stay in shape? Or is he working off a sagging belly even as we speak?

I wonder who among my own classmates will attend and who will send regrets. One advantage to staying home is that the only mental picture classmates will have of us is the yearbook photo taken when we were eighteen – a veritable fountain of youth. On the other hand, if we attend, we'll look each other right in the eye and lie in unison, "You haven't changed a bit!"

Going through the yearbook made me sad, maybe wistful. Not for those of us who graduated all those years ago, but for the young people in high school today. There are things I'd like them to know and perspectives I wish they could grasp right now instead of several years down the road. Most of us had to wait.

I'd like them to know about early bloomers and late bloomers. Some, in their reminiscing, might dub high school as the best years of their lives, but an equal number suffer through the social and academic stress, praying for escape into the real world as soon as possible. Some can't wait and leave school unfinished.

Given a choice during times of felt isolation, Most Likely to Succeed might wish to trade that title for a chance to be voted Most Popular Senior or Best Dancer. We can't expect her to take comfort in our advice to wait and see. Promises that better things lie ten years down the road ring hollow. Ten years is just too long to wait.

It's equally hard for early bloomers to realize they don't really have the world by the tail no matter how confident they feel. How do we applaud their achievements and yet fortify them against the inevitable obstacles to come?

I'd like all of them to realize that cliques don't last in an adult world. At least not in a civilized, truly adult world. Bullies usually stop bullying, the bullied don't get called out for fights, we stop name-calling, and we all speak to each other, civilly, in spite of differences.

If we're paying close attention, a reunion even ten years after graduation will show us how alike we really are, and how many different definitions there are of success and happiness. The grown-up world, we find, has room for all sorts of good people.

Sometimes we learn at a reunion that the Most Likely to Succeed didn't. The girl we most envied had died of cancer, much too young. And the star athlete's current involvement in sports consists of tossing a football to his children or grandchildren, just like his classmates.

So we're left to decide whether to attend this summer's reunion or stay home. Whether to visit the old haunts and see how everyone's doing, or be satisfied with our memories and let classmates picture us as we were at eighteen.

I'm leaning toward staying home. But an old high school boyfriend phoned me not long ago after a forty-five-year silence and began his conversation with, "Hi, honey! Whatcha' been doin'?"

* * * * *

[47]

Bravo? Encore? Maybe not.
June 14, 2001

As if there weren't already enough puzzlements to ponder, a reader writes to ask that I comment on what he calls "jumping-jack people" who act like "pop-up toasters run amuck."

He's referring to what he views as our indiscriminate use of the standing ovation.

In thinking about his observation, I have to admit that in retrospect, there are very few performances I've attended within the past ten years that didn't conclude with audience members standing to applaud. Then, as if that weren't quite expressive enough, we sometimes reach up with both hands and clap above our heads. It doesn't always seem to matter whether the musicians played on or off key, were brilliant or mediocre, were professional actors or third graders, lived up to audience expectations or did not. Savvy performers have learned to expect our ovations and arrive prepared with two or three requisite encores.

Now, I'm not at all averse to standing ovations and once even arranged one for myself. For the finale of my act for an amateur talent show, I played a tape of "The Star Spangled Banner," counting on audience patriotism to bring them to their feet. Desperate and pathetic as that move might be, it spotlights a fair question.

If we stand to applaud mediocrity or performances just one-cut-above, how will we offer the ultimate kudos when faced occasionally with pure genius or unparalleled talent? If standing isn't sufficient, and applauding with arms above our heads isn't sufficient, what next? Eventually, we could be driven to setting our hair on fire to express our appreciation.

Do audiences in New York City and other cultural centers reward every performance with a standing ovation? I don't know, and this isn't New York City, but John Gay, concerned about jumping-jack people as early as 1714, advised that, "Praising all alike is praising none."

Professional pop-up toasters filled half of the hall when President Bush addressed Congress last February. News reporters counted eighty-one standing ovations during his fifty-minute speech. One's political affiliation is simply irrelevant in this case, because nothing that flows from any human being's mouth deserves such vigorous calisthenics on the part of the audience.

I remember once coming to the aid of a child who fell and scraped his knee. Even though he didn't bleed, he screamed bloody murder. I told him I was sorry he fell, but suggested that he save his screams for the day he breaks a leg. Maybe, by the same token, we need to consider rationing our superlatives.

Lest readers jump to their feet at this point in something other than applause, let me hasten to add that I've often joined enthusiastically in standing ovations for both local and imported talent of undisputed excellence.

But at other times, I've participated in the ovation only because someone else started it and I didn't want to stay in my seat and be considered an unappreciative, impolite, unsophisticated doofus. It's sometimes hard to take ovations seriously when I've personally instigated vigorous applause dozens of times over the years. Frankly, I think pranksters could even pull it off among elevator passengers if they tried. Applauding is more contagious than yawns. We just hate to embarrass the instigator by leaving him to clap all by himself.

I'm wondering, though, if rather than being undiscriminating, we haven't simply extended the list of occasions that genuinely warrant a standing ovation. One person told me that she enjoys ovations simply because it's a relief to stand up after sitting so long. She'll forgive me if I don't include such base intentions in this list of more noble motivations.

Here's my own list:

• Ideally, a standing ovation still expresses our utmost appreciation for excellence.

• At other times, the ovation says "thanks for a pleasant evening" even if the show was less than spectacular. One secondary definition of ovation is "an ancient Roman victory ceremony of lesser importance than a triumph." We've all seen and applauded some of those.

• In a recent televised bid for yet another title, an international skating champion fell three times in an unglamorous heap on the ice. And, yet, at the conclusion of her piece, she received a rousing standing ovation. In this case, the ovation was meant to help the skater recover from her embarrassing performance.

• Stars of yesteryear sometimes give comeback concerts when retirement might have been the more prudent option. The audience stands to cheer, expressing gratitude for bygone years of pleasure. Could we actually stay seated and offer nothing but polite applause?

• When we applaud our own children, grandchildren and friends on stage, we jump to our feet out of sheer love, acknowledging their enthusiastic efforts, even if they tripped over the microphone cord, forgot their lines, or got lost in the wings.

Do those ovations brand us as undiscriminating or unsophisticated? I've decided for myself that they probably don't. It wouldn't be fair to dismiss these genuinely grateful audiences as pop-up toasters gone amuck.

But, on the other hand, and getting back to the reader's original concern, what if we do jump to our feet without any genuine feeling or thought at all, just following the lead of the habitual jumping-jack people? What if we've slowly surrendered to lower standards of performance? What if we've gradually lost our ability to distinguish excellence from the mediocre and thereby, in praising all alike, praise none?

Bravo? Encore?

Maybe. Maybe not.

* * * * *

[48]

Driving Miss Dora
July 12, 2001

I knew old dogs could learn new tricks, but until last summer I'd not seen one drive a car.

To preserve some well-deserved anonymity, let's call this old dog Dora. At sixty, she had never had a driver's license. She lived in New York City, where there's no place to park a car anyway, unless you have a particularly large family room. Cabs and buses rule the streets, every driver for herself and Devil take the hindmost.

Learning to drive in the Big Apple is a trial by fire and not recommended for the faint of heart, but a feisty spark of independence ignited itself and Dora got her beginner's permit and signed up for lessons at a New York City driving school.

Initially, a couple scoffers reared their ugly heads, but pity such lack of faith. They should have known her better. I felt perfectly safe in faraway Kansas, so jumped at the chance to assume the role of chief cheerleader.

But something seemed amiss when I spoke with her on the phone the evening of her first lesson. I inquired cheerfully, "How did you do with your first day on the driving simulator?"

"Not too good," she replied. "The instructor said I killed two people."

Fortunately, they were simulated people, and I presume that's what simulators are for. Nonetheless, I probably shouldn't have laughed.

While relaxing in the false security of distance, I learned that Dora planned to visit me and wanted to practice her lessons somewhere less threatening than New York City. I had no idea what privileges an out-of-state beginner's permit carried with it and set out to learn.

This was no easy task. By the time I found some sort of answer, I had checked with the Division of Motor Vehicles, the local police station, its state office and a city attorney, all of whom told me her license would be valid here, but none of whom would show me in writing where it said so. I wanted, frankly, to make sure if we were arrested that she'd be the one to go to jail.

Finally, I spoke with my insurance agent, who dared put into writing the fact that at least my insurance would cover her while driving my Dodge simulator.

I recalled long ago having spent many hours in the passenger seat while my teenagers learned to drive, but didn't know then that it was boot camp for adventures to come. I initially had allowed them to drive only in

cemeteries, hoping to minimize risks. But Dora and I took immediately to
the city streets.

Before she arrived, I had determined to remain stoic and patient
while she practiced, and to do so without benefit of tranquilizing medications. I already knew that Dora was a smart lady. But I trembled to think of
her distractibility. She was prone to remarkable scattered monologues like,
"Oh, look at that! Do you have a recipe for cornbread? Will you hand me
my sunglasses? Wow – what's that over there?" All that without even being
in a car.

In self-defense I took a vow of silence during her practices and
didn't draw her attention to roadside attractions other than yellow lines and
traffic signs.

During our daily outings, Dora also practiced turning corners and
maneuvering in and out of spaces in church parking lots. We looked for all
the world like two infidels unable to make up our minds about attending
services.

Always the determined student, she progressed quickly and, always
the stoic ride-along, I didn't scream or pass out. I did instinctively dodge
toward the center of the car when there were close calls on the right, but I
actually came to enjoy the scenic route when we carved wide curves to turn
at intersections.

Dora soon learned to put gasoline in the car and learned that one
doesn't necessarily have to call AAA when a tire needs air.

We experienced a couple genuine scares in our early miles together.
It doesn't take long to learn that it's not polite to pull out in front of semi-
trucks, and that particular incident was definitely a close call, complete with
raging air horn. The most frightening adventure, however, was her shift of
gears into reverse rather than drive – a maneuver that nearly sent us backwards down a ravine. I reviewed my notes on the subject of death wish,
concerned with both hers and mine, and developed a renewed appreciation
of the fact that even potty-trained adults sometimes have accidents.

I'm still concerned about the potentially hazardous combination of
Dora and distractibility, and sometimes when she was at the wheel, St.
Christopher and I contemplated jumping from the car. But, back home
again, Dora passed the driving test on her first try, bought a car, found a
place to park, apparently honed her skills, and already has hundreds of miles
of safe driving under her seat belt. I wish her well on her appointed rounds
and Godspeed to all of us who undertake the driving venture.

Dora, yet another old dog with new tricks, is rightly proud of her
derring-do and newfound freedom. Sure, there's a dent in the car's front

fender, one that curiously matches the one in her garage door frame, but it's become a badge of courage.

It's her medal for daring to change and grow – for seeing sixty as an access road, rather than a stop sign.

* * * * *

[49]

Coloring outside the lines
August 9, 2001

One of my all-time favorite gifts arrived in the mail several years ago from my brother. When I opened it in front of family and friends on Christmas morning, we literally gaped in amazement. The gift was hand-crafted – a sheet of hard, clear acrylic framed in wood, with four movable wooden arms and several tiny springs. It was beautifully, precisely constructed.

We continued gaping, because none of us could figure out what it was.

We took turns guessing, shaking our heads and exercising our imaginations while I puzzled over what to say in the thank-you note.

By afternoon, I surrendered to the riddle and phoned him. "Thanks, it's gorgeous. What is it?" His idea was extraordinary and was meant to solve a problem I encountered in crafting stained glass pieces. I could picture his mind working as he explained his intention and the inventive outcome. Such a gift! As it turned out, it was totally useless. But it hangs on my workshop wall as a symbol not only of his thoughtfulness, but also as a prime example of creativity.

What is creativity, anyway?

Sometimes we mistakenly limit its definition and err in thinking that creativity is something that can't be practiced and learned.

Certainly, creativity doesn't have to involve acrylic sheets with springs and wooden arms attached, and it doesn't even have to mean paintings painted or sweaters knitted. Although it would be nice to have invented the mousetrap or Velcro or have books on the bestseller list, there may not even be a visible product.

I like to think of creativity as looking at the world with fresh eyes. A matter of how we think, how we solve problems. And, particularly, how we approach our own.

Creativity requires letting our minds tilt on their axes so that we can view the world from a new perspective. It comes into play when we alter recipes, rearrange furniture, organize a pantry, or see humor in the world. It doesn't involve inborn talent as much as it involves attitude.

Perhaps we first need to quit thinking of ourselves as uncreative. A philosopher with the creative name of Coomaraswamy said, "The artist is not a special kind of person, but every person is a special kind of artist."

It's comforting to realize that we usually aren't competing for Nobel prizes or Oscars when we create. Judges don't perch on our doorsteps holding up signs, awarding Tens or Sixes or Twos for our efforts. And what if they did? What if we dared paint a picture, write a song, and construct a Taj Mahal replica with sucker sticks and yet get scores no higher than a Two? What if we just had fun trying?

In 1905, eleven-year-old Frank Epperson left a glass of lemonade with a spoon in it sitting on the windowsill and it froze overnight. Nearly twenty years later, he remembered this experience and patented the Popsicle. The rest of us might have said some naughty words at the time and tossed the idea into the sink forever.

Epperson's discovery reminds us that creativity requires dismissing preconceived ideas of what we're looking for. Because if we're too focused, we'll never see what we don't expect to find.

My favorite psychological experiment involves giving subjects a box holding nuts and bolts, tongue depressors, string, metal rods and other sundry pieces of equipment, then assigning a problem to be solved with the materials at hand. Of course there's a trick, and only the most flexible thinkers come up with the solution. Because the problem can't be solved without using the box itself. Those who fixated on the box simply as a container and couldn't see its greater possibilities failed.

Many inventions have resulted from someone's being flexible enough to see answers to questions that they weren't even asking. They cashed in on the unexpected when others might have discovered nothing but disappointment.

A chemist developing cheap antifreeze in 1923 stumbled on an ingredient now used for solid rocket fuel. Another researcher, trying to create synthetic rubber during World War II, discovered Silly Putty.

Serendipity. Technically it's defined as making happy and unexpected discoveries by accident. But maybe it's just a word for the pleasant surprises that wait in the wings for open-minded people.

When creative juices start flowing, we can do nearly anything we set our minds to if, at least temporarily, we dismiss from our house or our lives those people who are poised to tell us we don't know how. Anne Lamott suggests that we pick naysayers up by their tails like mice and confine them in a glass jar. I'd also suggest that we remember not to join the naysaying crowd when someone else is waxing creative, lest we get picked up by our own little tails.

Admittedly, creativity can carry us to wacky extremes. Consider the man who invented an armored suit for bear wrestling. He bankrupted his family in pursuit of the dream, persisting way beyond failure.

Years ago, I researched the subject of creativity and psychosis to explore what characteristics they might have in common. It turns out that, however we find our bursts of creative light, it's important to dip into the weird and wonderful at least occasionally, emerging with our creativity refreshed.

Only then can we give ourselves and everyone around us permission to color outside the lines.

* * * * *

[50]

The one that got away
September 13, 2001

Somewhere on a misty glen in Scotland, the fog lifts to reveal the idyllic village of Brigadoon – a village that comes into being for only one day each century.

When I first saw that movie years ago and fell in love with Van Johnson, I assumed that Brigadoon existed only in fantasy. Now I know that Brigadoons are for real, and I have one of my own.

Technically, mine is called the Atlantic Ocean. Or, to geography purists, Nantucket Sound.

Whatever the name, it exists for just two weeks once a year, then vanishes. Die-hard realists insist it's still there even when I leave, but believing that would be too much for a landlocked Aquarian to bear.

If you visit Brigadoon, you'll not find me among the beached sunbathers nor hiding out beneath an umbrella. I'll be in the water – whether high tide, low tide, feisty waves, no waves, cool mornings, hot afternoons, sunny days, or cloudy days. I call it "My Ocean" to distinguish it from the Pacific and other pretenders.

Ordinarily, the weeks on Brigadoon pass without remarkable incident, but this summer when it disappeared behind its veil of fog again, I came home with two stories to tell, and neither of them involves fins.

One August morning at about eight o'clock, I was sharing My Ocean with no one except one watchful sea gull. The water was still and smooth, like the unrippled surface of a lake. It was mid-tide, and not a wave in sight.

Swimming several yards from shore, I poked my head above the water and heard what sounded like clapping from an appreciative audience.

I didn't think my swimming merited applause and there was definitely no crowd on the beach. I looked to my left where the sound originated.

There I saw a huge school of fish, each fish eighteen to twenty-four inches long. They jumped several inches out of the water and back in again – over and over – the "clapping" being the slap of their tails as they reentered the water. Perpendicular to the shore, a line of them about sixty feet long and four feet wide was headed right toward me like a living wall. And they were fast! Instinctively, I swam for shore, quickly enough this time to deserve applause. I made it out before they reached the area where I had been swimming.

A lone observer on shore offered with droll understatement, "You thought you were alone out there, didn't you?"

From the safety of the beach, I watched the wall progress through the water, making its own surf in the otherwise still ocean. Dozens of seagulls flew over the fish, clapping and flapping their wings.

I hadn't been too frightened, because I didn't find out until later what the commotion was all about. What I learned is that I was sharing My Ocean with a school of bluefish that happened to be in the midst of a feeding frenzy. I also learned that they are vicious fish with sharp teeth. And rather than biting off a finger or an arm like the tidy shark, they prefer shredding their prey like cheese.

They were busy catching tiny breakfast fish, and, the natives wondered aloud, what larger critters lurked behind the bluefish looking for their own snack? Luckily, I didn't know.

One other early morning, again sharing the sea with only my companion gull, a woman walked down the beach with a large black unleashed dog. He spotted me in the water and made a dash in my direction. His owner called him back and tethered him before he could reach his prey. The woman explained pleasantly, "I'm really sorry about that. I'm sure he thought you were a duck."

Some people, upon hearing my stories, warned me not to go into the water alone. Why? To reduce the odds of my being chosen as the breakfast du jour? "Eat that young blond woman instead," I'd holler to the fish.

I love my Brigadoon, and we need an ocean here in the Midwest. I plan to petition local and state governments to get us one. It's actually quite workable. Consider the possibility of digging a deep trench for water flow from the Gulf of Mexico or the East Coast, with trenches paralleling the major interstate highways. All we would have to do is have the big hole dug somewhere on the outskirts of town for the water to flow into when it arrived. I figure the plan could easily be incorporated into the blueprint and budget for digging tunnels between state office buildings. So please do sign the ocean petition when it comes your way.

The tale of the bluefish feeding frenzy is the first real fish story I've ever had to tell. I work to keep the dimensions of the fish from growing as time passes, but, in truth, the story needs no embellishment. It's best told with gestures and facial expressions and I'd be glad to repeat it in person upon request.

Unlike its usual placid ways, Brigadoon held some surprises this summer. After all, not everyone's head has been mistaken for a duck. And that personal seagull companion – surely a guardian angel.

I plan to vacation again next summer when the Atlantic Ocean reappears, and I like to think that the bluefish will still be talking about their big breakfast that got away. "I swear," one of them will boast, "it was five feet long and a couple feet wide."

* * * * *

[51]

Collapse of the center
October 11, 2001

Asaharu, one-time guru of a Japanese religious cult, qualified himself as one of the most infamous criminals in Japan when, a few years ago, he directed his followers to release poison gas into the Tokyo subway system.

Several victims died. Hundreds of others required hospitalization and millions worldwide experienced fear and outrage.

Television coverage of that tragedy included on-the-street interviews with Tokyo citizens. If the translator is to be believed, one irate woman expressed herself as follows:

"What this man did was despicable, inhumane. The best punishment would be to crucify him. Put him in a public place and let everyone stick spears in him."

Today, as we clear the rubble of our own national disaster, interviewers again elicit the response of passers-by.

"We ought to blow them into oblivion."

"We should drop the bomb."

In the midst of coping with the terrorist attack, maybe we ought to pause long enough to figure out what's wrong with that picture.

The comments of the anonymous Japanese woman and those heard on our own streets today highlight a universal dilemma when we're forced to deal with terrorists, hate-mongers and murderers.

While we stand aghast at the monstrous behavior of the Japanese guru, bin Laden, and gaggles of their counterparts everywhere, how do we tame the beast within ourselves? Although abhorrent of violence, we experience a surge of feeling more vicious than we thought ourselves capable when we're faced with hate-mongers and terrorists. Monsters have a way of drawing us into their own pattern of hatred and retribution, setting loose our usually docile beasts.

In times of crises, this disastrous side effect of tragedies becomes apparent. Something emerges that, ordinarily, we'd prefer leaving dormant. The horror of the situation impels us to get out our spears to give the culprits what they deserve. In the case of a single villain, we compete for admission to watch his execution, calling it closure. We even consider televising the event so that no one has to miss it. Public lynching, seemingly so far in the past, clamors for a comeback. An "eye for an eye" bounds from the Old Testament to the lips of those who ordinarily don't quote scripture.

Don't think for a minute that this is going to be a treatise on the death penalty or a solution to the complexities of the recent terrorist attack. My head and heart still debate the issues. One day my head says, "An eye for an eye!" and my heart refuses to listen. Another day, my heart says, "You were right," and my head answers, "Forget it. I've changed my mind."

For years, we've seen the televised faces of terrorist victims in other countries, and now they look strangely like our own. No matter how indignant, I doubt I'd agree to pull the switch, or stick spears in Asaharu himself, or personally drop bombs on the citizens of Middle Eastern countries. Some have suggested bombarding that impoverished area with medicine and food. And yet...

But apart from all the legal or moral decisions for death and revenge, we need to be alert to what goes on inside of us when faced with the horrors of a vicious crime, prejudice or hate-mongering. What do we let it do to us? How do we take a stand and carry out effective action without being sucked into the cycle of violence that we claim to despise?

As a fairly imaginative person, I'm sometimes appalled at the creative retributions that come to mind for some of my own least favorite monsters. And now a new monster has earned his way on to the list. Of course I don't carry out my imaginary plots, and, luckily, I've never been able to believe the Sunday school teaching that thinking a thing is as bad as doing it.

But when we consider what that sort of creative revenge does to our own Center, does it mean that our old Sunday School teachers were right?

Well-meaning leaders are urging us to forgive. But the whole matter of forgiveness for the terrorist incident boggles my mind. And even if I totally understood the political, psychological and religious motivation behind it, I've never believed the old adage that to understand all is to forgive all. For now I've decided that I'll leave forgiveness to the Higher

Powers and the saints among us. My own job is to work toward releasing myself from the grip that hate and horror could have on me, lest my own Center be destroyed.

In the meantime, loved ones wander the streets of New York City holding photographs and dental records, stunned by the unreality of this human tragedy in our own front yard.

We've already lost one Center. In the name of peace, let's nurture and preserve our own.

* * * * *

[52]

Those early labor pains
November 8, 2001

Every weekday morning that summer, my mother combed my hair into pigtails so tight that they pulled my eyes farther apart on my face. Then, lunch in hand, I'd hop into the back of an open truck and ride several miles with other children and adults, some of whom spoke English, to spend the day picking strawberries or raspberries for pennies a gallon. It was my first real job.

While taking down my Labor Day decorations and reminiscing about that early employment, I decided to survey some friends of my generation, asking about their own first or worst job. As it turns out, first was often synonymous with worst.

Parents used to believe that the Devil himself found work for idle hands. Consequently, not many of us waited until we were sixteen to find employment, and our parents provided a helpful jump-start if our youthful ignitions failed.

We didn't often begin our careers in fast-food restaurants, and child labor laws weren't in place to dictate hours, pay or working conditions.

As a high school student, my brother worked in the bottom of railroad cars shoveling lime through holes onto a conveyor belt. OSHA hadn't prescribed masks or other protective measures. Another teenager spent hot summer days de-tasseling field corn and, in the dead of Minnesota winters, delivered bundles of newspapers to distributors.

A cohort who has maintained his work ethic through seven decades started out at age nine driving a tractor in front of a combine.

One respondent, as a seventh grader, worked for a small dairy. He washed cow udders with chlorinated water and then milked the cows twice a day. He balanced on a one-legged stool while performing this feat and received a total of five dollars a week for the combined milking and gymnastics.

At thirteen, a female respondent spent the summer topping onions in an onion field. She said it took most of the following winter to rid her body of the onion smell.

I heard some particularly pathetic tales. One respondent got his first job when he was only six years old. He followed behind a horse-drawn plow as the farmer turned up potato rows, and he was supposed to put the potatoes in a gunnysack. Since he was eager to fill lots of bags, he allowed some dried horse turds to sneak into the sacks, and his employment was short-lived. After a couple more false starts, he went on to have a successful adult career that had nothing whatsoever to do with either potatoes or horse turds.

Another worst job reported in my survey involved working on the trimming machine at a factory where phone books were printed. Employees informally called the machine the "finger chopper," and there was a multitude of close calls among the several accidents.

All of his fingers happily intact, that lucky laborer went on to play the guitar to entertain clients at a bordello. He claims that everyone else was arrested during a raid, but that he was excused because he just kept on playing and looking innocent. Knowing this fellow pretty well, I believe his entire story except for the part about looking innocent.

Others had more romantic, less controversial first jobs: sewing Renaissance costumes for theater productions, working as a soda jerk, filling bakery pastries with jelly, selling handkerchiefs (remember those?), working as a teenage dental assistant. Those who didn't pick up potatoes or play bordello guitar worked at fireworks stands and movie theaters, as day camp counselors, bartenders or babysitters. One respondent managed the primate house at a zoo, and another worked for the state, typing letters to revoke drivers' licenses. Another lucky high school girl candled eggs to determine the presence of chicken embryos.

Young people still sometimes land unusual first jobs.

I know one contemporary teenager who spent all summer sitting in his car counting how many people used the outhouses in highway rest areas.

Some early jobs we don't really want to hear much about. A young man of my acquaintance, while assisting with medical research, had the extraordinary assignment of harvesting sperm from elephants. Don't even ask.

How do we get from where we began to where we are – from tractor to teacher, from onions and lime to engineers, from berry picker to psychologist, from those first pangs of labor to artists, physicians, construction workers and truck drivers? And when today's youngsters grin and inquire, "Do you want fries with that?" do they even dream of what's to come?

It's amazing that somehow we each find a spot as adults, following a zigzag trail from those first jobs to an intersection where our talents meet the world's needs.

So, while belatedly taking down those decorations and prematurely counting my blessings for Thanksgiving, I offer thanks to those who clean up other people's necessary and unnecessary messes; to those who climb poles and dig holes, work under the earth or high above it; who get shot at or risk fire and weather; who test my deodorant, write instructions for the microwave oven, and milk the cows.

And special cheers for those settling into their very first job on the zigzag trail.

* * * * *

[53]

Flour in the desert
December 13, 2001

It's happening again, and I still can't figure it out.

Television news reports show haunting pictures of starving refugees in war-torn countries. They've lost all their possessions and are struggling to survive with or without flimsy tents on arid land. Finally, after endless days of planning, promising and bargaining, international relief trucks arrive at the camp. Refugees fight their way toward the trucks and compete for supplies they so desperately need.

The tragedy is unquestionably compelling. The dilemma for me is that in nearly every televised instance, relief workers are handing out gigantic bags of flour. Although the recipients appear grateful and relieved as they return to their tents, there's something I simply don't understand.

In trying to imagine myself in that catastrophic predicament, I picture leaving the truck with my hard-won sack of flour while wondering what in the name of Julia Child I'm supposed to do next. Without some further illumination, all I could do is sit on it or use it as a pillow.

I've definitely never won prizes for baking, and flour doesn't qualify as a staple in my kitchen. But I've watched other people make bread and I know it involves more than flour. If my benefactors also handed out eggs, milk, sugar and chocolate chips, I think I could make some brownies. If I had an oven. Or if they air-dropped pork chops, I could coat them before frying. If I had a frying pan. And a fire. I could even make paste – and eat it if I had to – if I had some water. But with flour alone, I know I'd be running to the neighboring tent for instructions. Or perhaps they'd lend me their phone to contact the county extension course service.

It concerns me that we assume all these refugees know what to do with the flour while I'm totally in the dark. Might some of those bags hold rice? Maybe so, but without fire and water, I'd still miss dinner. If for some tragic reason I find myself in a refugee camp before I get smarter, that truck had better bring canned goods and a can opener instead.

Years ago, a native of Switzerland told me that if disaster struck, America would be in good shape because of our vast supply of resources and well-advertised know-how. Quite to the contrary, I worried then and worry still, that we'd be in big trouble. Because most of us are privileged and spoiled. Most of us don't know how to be destitute and aren't prepared to make fire by rubbing sticks together or to walk three miles for that bag of flour.

News reports don't show us what happens after flour is delivered to refugees, so perhaps some of them are puzzled as well. Maybe the powers that be got wind of that fact, since during the most recent crisis, our government dropped packages of more practical, pre-prepared meals. If those plastic bags are as hard to get open as the ones I find on supermarket shelves, I hope the authorities also included scissors.

Realistically, how would we do as a nation in desperate trouble? Do most Americans know that raw potatoes are edible? How many of us could grow a potato or know to look underground for them? Could we catch and skin a rabbit or tell directions by the stars?

I certainly haven't volunteered to compete on television's "Survivor" show and would quickly be voted off the island for toting a cell phone. I do know how to cook dandelion greens. And I have eaten my share of squirrel, but I've never had to catch one. As a child, I sat on the creek bank and marinated my fishing line in the water, but nothing edible ever found itself hooked. I can't distinguish poison mushrooms from safe ones and would have to send wild berries to a lab for identification. I haven't constructed shelter for myself since childhood when I draped blankets over the backs of kitchen chairs.

It's just plain difficult to imagine life without Charmin and Puffs. And, sad to say, my survival skills rely heavily on electricity, cars, supermarkets, telephones and the expertise of other people.

Ralph Waldo Emerson was one of my college heroes. I marked and re-marked his essay on self-reliance with underlines and asterisks way back then, and read it again just recently.

"Society never advances," he says. "The civilized man has built a coach, but has lost the use of his feet. He is supported on crutches, but lacks so much support of muscle. He has a fine Geneva watch, but he fails the skill to tell the hour by the sun. A Greenwich nautical almanac he has, and so being sure of the information when he wants it, the man in the street does not know a star in the sky."

When Napoleon conquered Europe, he said that in order to have a perfect army they should get rid of all weaponry until each soldier could take his own supply of corn, grind it in his hand-mill, and bake his own bread.

With that in mind, and since there are still several shopping days before Christmas, perhaps some of us should add the "Survival Guide for Dummies" to our wish lists.

Better yet, how about wishing for the kind of world in which we don't need one?

* * * * *

[54]

Put on a happy face
January 12, 2002

Never once, in all my trips to the mall, has a cosmetic saleswoman stopped me to ask if I'd like a total makeover. I hear them offer to transform other customers, so I know the service is available. But as I approach the cosmetic counter, employees turn away and busy themselves straightening lipstick cases or rearranging perfumes.

It happens every single time, and I figure it means one of two things.

More than likely, I tell myself, the salesladies hesitate to mess with perfection. There's nothing that Oil of Olay and I together can't handle, and my natural glow shines like a beacon as I float down department store aisles.

Or, it's possible, instead, that I'm considered a hopeless case. Maybe in my jeans and sweatshirt I look like I don't particularly care, or that I'm happy with the way I am. Or maybe they think at my age the transformation job would require spackle and grout.

Regardless of the reason, I'm threatening this year to climb up barefaced on one of those cosmetic counter stools and see what happens.

Several years ago, an amateur cosmetologist gave me a test to discover which season best reflected my personality and then plastered me with makeup consistent with that season. I don't remember which of the four seasons best defined me, but it resulted in purple eyelids and orangeish cheeks. Ever since then, what you see is what I got.

National Geographic Magazine often treats us to photographs of primitive tribe members. They sport paint on their faces, rings in their noses, loops in their ears, tattoos on their bodies and disks in their lips. We grin and say, how peculiar! Rings, piercing, face paint and tattoos? But wait a minute. Where have we seen that before?

In our own semi-civilized country, we spend billions of dollars a year for cosmetics, and yet, if properly applied, they say, no one notices we are wearing it. Go figure.

Long before the advent of shopping centers, Cicero concluded that the very lack of adornment is an ornament in itself and actually becomes some women. I was almost in the cosmetic loop for a while when our own generation went through a decade of that natural look. But now, *au naturel* has reverted to its old meaning. In the meantime, I haven't bought nearly enough anti-sag cream for any cosmetic saleslady to earn the use of that pink Cadillac.

Apparently someone always thinks there's room for improvement, no matter how hard a woman tries. A magazine anecdote tells of one woman who, when asked by a mall salesperson if she'd like a total make-over, agreed to accept the full treatment. Twenty minutes later, wearing the completely renovated face, she entered a second department store where she was immediately offered another total makeover. Sometimes it's hard to keep up.

I remember the exact moment that JFK was shot, and I remember with equal disbelief the moment I learned that some of my peers routinely spent more than an hour just preparing their face and hair every morning. We natural beauties and/or hopeless cases were dashing from bed to the outside world in twenty minutes, including breakfast.

Five thirtyish women recently appeared on the Oprah show because of their genuine fear of being seen without makeup. One of the women, married for eight years, claimed that even her husband had never seen her bare face. Oprah challenged them to a week without cosmetics, and their anxiety was pathetic to behold. They apparently kept their self-esteem on the bathroom shelf among the lipsticks, paints and powders. In a similar mode, many women prefer not being seen in the morning before they put on their face, and some might not even be recognizable to their friends at that hour.

Although cosmetics have long ago become the norm, even considered a necessity in many quarters, the practice hasn't been without its critics. Shakespeare chided, "God has given you one face, and you make yourselves another." And in the seventeenth century, Thomas Fuller was less kind, asserting that she who paints her face would doubtless be a whore.

Critics remain in the minority and haven't had any negative impact on cosmetic sales. Most of us know, like Keats, that to be born a woman is to know that we must labor to be beautiful. And now that all those baby boomers are reaching middle age, cosmetic sales are expected to reach new highs.

All this reminds me that among my childhood souvenirs is an autograph book, and that among the entries is a particularly short one written by my father. It says simply, "Pretty is as pretty does." And, sure enough, I've generally observed that smiles, deep laugh lines and a twinkle in the eye do more than cosmetics for the complexion. Artificial beauty is only skin deep, but ugly disposition goes to the bone. Are we aging debutantes really obligated to spend our time, energy, and money trying to look young again?

I personally subscribe to the theory that if a woman isn't beautiful at seventeen, it probably can't be helped. But if she isn't beautiful at seventy, it's her own fault.

* * * * *

[55]

Exercise in futility
February 14, 2002

It's not a pretty sight. Wearing my purple spandex tights, halter-top, and fluffy white sweatbands, I pour myself into the recliner to watch Richard Simmons sweat to some oldies on TV. If I point my feet into a V shape on the footrest, I can see the screen without lifting my head. During commercials, I stay in position and study my brand new, white athletic shoes. They are, after all, the root of this predicament.

Having worn my pair of college tennies for the past thirty years, I decided last week it was time to shop for new ones.

But nothing is simple anymore. The clerk led me through a litany of possibilities: jogging, racquetball, aerobics, basketball, track, cross-training, soccer or power walking. There were no designer shoes for reading, resting or snacking, so I chose "aerobics" as the least formidable alternative. As the clerk rang up my purchase, she praised the shoes so highly that I imagined them executing the dance routines without me. I would hope so. They cost about thirty-five dollars a foot.

I was nearly out the door when racks of garish athletic apparel caught my eye. The clerk mistook my shuddering for excitement and quickly helped me choose the purple tights and halter that, even as we speak, are cutting off my circulation. The sweatbands were free that day to any athlete or impostor spending over a hundred dollars.

The whole affair creates an annoying predicament. Vigorous exercise simply doesn't fit into either my short- or long-range plans. Like it or not, I am going to die someday. So I'm bullheaded about wanting to spend any remaining days in pursuits that I've chosen myself. Daily exercise might extend by a couple years the lives of my energetic friends, but those friends could also be hit by my pizza delivery truck while they're loping down the highway. Besides, someone has to stay rested to give those folk mouth-to-mouth resuscitation when they collapse.

An ancient Asian philosopher once told me that, "Nothing beautiful ever hurries." Or maybe I made that up. At any rate, that bit of wisdom allows me to move about less frantically than others, if, indeed, I choose to move about at all. Runners argue that exercise stimulates endorphins that result in a sense of wellbeing. So do meditation and a nap. They also boast that when they exercise, they don't perspire – they glow. I've got news for them. It's sweat and it stinks.

My friends would probably deny that they put any pressure on me to exercise. But they've made inertia such a dirty word that I was forced last year to buy an exercise bicycle. Now, every week, I have to jack up the mileage indicator to impress them. And even though they delight in thinking of entertainment possibilities for my muscles and tendons, I studiously avoid imposing my own views on them. Do I try to make them watch three hours of television a day or take naps after lunch? Do I shame them when they refuse to eat more than two doughnuts at breakfast? Sure, that slender athletic person inside me struggles to escape, but she can ordinarily be subdued with a bowl of butter pecan ice cream.

Athletes and slackers are all going to die some day – fat or thin, in or out of shape. If I thought St. Peter would weigh us at the Pearly Gates or require the four-minute mile as a final entrance exam, I'd pump some serious sweat into this spandex. For now, I plan to enjoy a salami and cheese sandwich with mayonnaise and watch the Simmons wannabes stretch and glow.

* * * * *

(1988 Assistant Ice Cream Taster, Dreyer's & Edy's Grand Ice Cream)

[56]

Gold medal in skipping
March 14, 2002

Weeks after they extinguished the Olympic flame, we're still applauding the quality of performance, the effort and heart, and the competitive drive that sparks it all. The athletes deserve our accolades.

But unfortunately for losers, the world not only loves success but also often insists upon it. And the evidence is everywhere.

In our desperation to create heroes, television programs laud those who eat the grossest worm or allow rats to climb on their bodies for the longest period of time. Grown men vie to build the tallest building in the world or have their mules pull the heaviest load. Whatever we sacrifice to achieve it, we clamor for our fifteen minutes of fame and don't want ourselves or our children selected for those "agony of defeat" commercials.

Let me suggest that success is badly overrated and that a good folly is often worth what one pays for it.

It is likely that most people haven't heard about my dancing career. That's partly because it ended quicker than you can say "choreography." I was edging toward thirty when a friend talked me into taking modern dance lessons. I have good reason to suspect that I lurched instead of leaped and didn't do the black leotards justice, but I don't know of any undertaking I have enjoyed more. That fiasco proved beyond any doubt that one can fail miserably and yet experience joy in the process.

Pressure to succeed and excel begins early. And by the time children are twelve years old, they often have no activity left that they engage in strictly for fun.

From the first day of kindergarten they hear their parents' litany. "Just do your best in whatever you undertake."

Impossible!

A talented child might have all it takes to excel in several different areas, but she can't possibly do her best in them all. Like the rest of us, children have to emphasize what is most important to them and be allowed to be less than spectacular in the other pursuits. Or, heaven forbid, maybe just have fun. The necessity of accepting our stumbling selves has somehow become a luxury.

Even in our chosen area of focus, we are probably wise to set the sights a bit lower than perfection. Neil Steinberg says that when we pursue her, Perfection places her hands on her slim hips and laughs.

He's right. I know, because I've heard her.

Of course, I'm not advocating a society in which no one strives to do well. But we also need a perspective that allows us to accept our imperfect selves and to de-emphasize failure. Most children want to please the adults who are important to them whether the adult expectations are reasonable or otherwise. And they will try, regardless of the personal expense.

Years ago, I heard one of those stories that stick to the inside of the heart. An award-winning actor being interviewed for television said that when he was eight years old he came in second in his class spelling bee. He recalls being so excited about his accomplishment that he skipped all the way home.

When he reached the house, he ran to his father and told him the news. His father asked, "Second? If you had studied just a little harder, you could have come in first."

The actor continued in the interview, "It was the last time I was satisfied with second place."

Then, as theme music began to introduce a station break, I heard the actor say, almost under his breath, "It was also the last time I ever skipped home."

At one time or another, we've all been runners-up and also-rans. And most of us don't get to stand on the podium to accept medals and flowers.

But the luckiest among us are still skipping home.

* * * * *

[57]

Recipe for boiled frog
April 11, 2002

If you place a frog in a pan of cool water and set it on the stove, then turn the heat up just a few degrees at a time, the frog will sit there and allow himself to be boiled.

At least that is what I have heard. And I believe it.

The poor creature simply accommodates to his gradually changing environment and fails to realize that he is in dangerously hot water.

That is a distressing state of affairs for the frog. But we will worry less about him when we consider the fact that we often find ourselves in an identical predicament. Not by choice, but just like the frog, we drift into it – ever so slowly, ever so gradually, until our goose is nearly cooked.

It happens to individuals, to communities, even entire nations.

We have all known at least one wife/mother who carries the entire burden for a family. She feeds the cat, finds lost schoolbooks, picks up dirty socks, turns off forgotten lights and runs everyone's errands. She has assumed these duties one by one until they become for her a way of life – a stifling way of life that comes to be accepted, and even expected, by those around her.

We have known at least one businessman who day by day drifts into compromises with his work and wakes up to discover he has become the office flunky when he is infinitely capable of more than that. Capable of more than being used.

In our communities? Sure, there are some robberies and a few homicides, but that is in someone else's neighborhood, and we don't have to worry about it now. Tensions rise a few degrees at a time, so slowly that we don't notice. Then, as though it happened over night, the city is draped in yellow crime-scene tape.

Admittedly, it takes a pretty big kettle to boil an entire nation, but it can be done. It has been done before.

Few citizens will object if the government exerts a little authority, so why not turn up the heat a few degrees? If no one reacts when they take over the airports, why not control industry? And if there is still no reaction, how about the schools? And why not the churches?

And then one day, the horror of what we have allowed to happen dawns upon us.

We simply drifted. It is a seemingly harmless pattern at first. But bit by bit, we came to accept greater and greater compromises until it became the easy way, the natural way, to do things.

If we are lucky enough to be jarred awake, we realize, "By golly, it's getting warm in here!" And, indeed, when we take a good look, we find that we are in uncomfortably hot water up to our chins.

Unfortunately, we can't simply drift out of this predicament the same way we drifted into it. Change requires guts and determination. We may have to make one grand move. Or it may mean, instead, that we make a series of small, quiet resolutions.

But either way, we are letting the world know that we are turning off the heat. And that we have stopped drifting.

In Mary Oliver's poem "The Journey," she writes, "One day you finally knew what you had to do, and began, though the voices around you kept shouting their bad advice – though the whole house began to tremble and you felt the old tug at your ankles."

If we aren't convinced that this can happen to us, as individuals, communities, or nations, we probably could catch a frog and carry out that simple experiment. But better yet, we might periodically check the water in our own kettle.

See the bubbles forming at the edges of the pan? Jump!

* * * * *

[58]

Lessons learned at springtime's knee
May 9, 2002

Mother Nature behaved so erratically this year that I declared spring four times before it actually arrived. The fact that my tulips were similarly hoodwinked makes me feel a little less gullible.

But recently, Mother N. sobered up and spring sprang for real.

Miracles abound every year when we turn our clocks ahead in deference to daylight saving time. Somehow, that seemingly simple clock adjustment resets the entire universe. I learn what I can from the lessons it teaches.

I always notice first of all that my spring clothes shrank during their winter respite in the closet. As sure as dandelions freckle grass, I'm off again, to shop for something stretchy that might last through the season. The lesson to be learned from this curiosity escapes me so far, but perhaps I don't have to learn everything at once.

The most gratifying sign of spring is that neighbors come out of hibernation, grateful, for at least a little while, to be mowing rather than shoveling. One neighbor emerges as soon as buds appear on the trees and stays outside like yard art until the first snowfall covers her flower garden. She's the legendary Jones that the rest of us can't keep up with.

Even the black thumbs among us make trips to local nurseries and come home with car trunks full of mulch and budding promise. I've learned one springtime lesson the hard way. There's never enough mulch.

Tulips and daffodils poke their way out of hiding and group themselves in bouquets. Not remembering from year to year where I plant them, I can be perpetually surprised when they pop up. In fact, there was yet another advantage to my pathetic memory this spring. I was actually able to hide my own Easter eggs! This experience probably taught me something, too, but, if it did, I forget what it is.

I've learned to invest time and energy in long walks, and, begrudgingly, have learned to detour around cars parked stupidly across the sidewalk. If a household has more vehicles than will fit legally in its own driveway or on the public street, perhaps there's a lesson there, too. (Whoops! Did I digress from my Gentle Ode to Spring?)

Meanwhile, back in the neighborhood, children quickly reappear on the scene. They marvel at the roly-polys and search for ants to feed the doodlebugs that take up residence in the dirt beneath my backyard deck. These devious creatures (the doodlebugs, not the children) rout out funnel-shaped holes and wait for unwary ants to slide down the slope into their trap.

Slow learners that they are, ants continue to build their hills in close proximity to the doodlebug traps. I absorb this particular lesson without much difficulty.

One vanishing cult of Kansas women participates in an ancient May ritual called spring cleaning. I once witnessed this ceremony but fortunately am among those who have been deprogrammed. I've already learned all I want to know about scrubbing and shining.

Storms keep us on our toes and sometimes in our basements. Winds live up to their Kansas reputation and occasionally funnel themselves into more ominous form. I've learned not to climb up on my roof to watch. After the tempest, I harvest a fresh crop of shingles from the yard and return wayward lawn chairs to the porch.

During one of our most ferocious storms, when shingles and trashcans sailed through the neighborhood, I worried about my tulips, already in full bloom. But, as I discovered the next morning, they had turned their faces away from the wind, pulled their red caps over their heads, swayed with the breeze and didn't lose a single petal.

I'm betting there's a lesson in there somewhere.

* * * * *

[59]

Awash in daytime suds
June 13, 2002

When the innocent young heroine opened her bedroom closet door, devils grabbed her arms and pulled her into the fires of Hell. Don't you just hate it when that happens?

I'm new to this soap opera business and happened upon one of the most outlandish by accident several months ago. In surfing through channels, I saw a handsome young man poised to kiss a pretty young woman and, like some pathetic voyeur, tuned in the next day to watch the kiss. I became suspicious when, two weeks later, their lips were still parted in anticipation but hadn't met.

Since then, someone's entire house sank into Hell after blood ran down its interior walls. A bewitched doll turned into a real boy, and our heroine was encased in a cone of ice by her evil clone.

Another leading lady in that drama has been assumed dead several times, but is always rescued by her lover, who, I'd think, would by now have tired of the chore. She has amnesia so often that even I forget who she is. Two lovers, once thought dead, float back and forth through time and space, thanks to mysterious powers of the Bermuda Triangle.

Please (double-please!) believe me when I say that I don't arrange my schedule around this horrible show, but if I'm unoccupied at the time, I sometimes tune in to see who is currently dying, amnesiac or illegitimate. For science's sake, I surfed through several other soapy episodes one afternoon only to discover that they have much in common.

I've learned, for instance, that television stretches one day of real life across weeks of programs. Hence, my long wait for that kiss and a plot that never ends.

Characters, all of them, stay dressed up, party-ready, twenty-four hours a day.

They can do that because no one has a job or cleans house. They spend their lives talking, lying, drinking, and making phone calls and whoopee.

Everyone has taken at least one DNA test to settle a child's paternity.

Children are briefly seen and rarely heard, entering the picture just long enough to say good night or to get that DNA test.

Substitute actors take over another actor's role for one day or indefinitely, hoping fans won't notice the switch.

I'm told that prominent actors have sometimes made their professional debuts on soap operas (euphemistically called "daytime dramas"), and, in the industry's defense, I admit I'm not monitoring the most respected among them.

Some years ago I read that a female marine biologist quit her profession to write and publish soap opera summaries. Reportedly, she sat in front of seven different television sets, keeping track of plots for those who missed their daily fix. With the advent of such magazine summaries and VCRs, no one has to know of our addiction to "As the Stomach Turns." In spite of their denials, I have a sneaking suspicion that many soap opera enthusiasts among us remain closeted.

Inquiring minds have to wonder why these programs are so popular. Surely most of us can't identify with the convoluted, tragic lives those sagas portray.

Do soaps take our minds off greater crises of the real world? Have we adopted someone else's dysfunctional family as respite from our own? Do we vicariously enjoy the elegant, leisurely, sensuous life styles? Are our lives so boring that we need to spice them up with outlandish fantasy? Do we need a hobby?

Maybe daytime dramas really do teach us lessons for life. Since being alerted to the dire possibilities, I'm prepared to outsmart any devils who dare lurk behind my bedroom closet doors.

But plots are unpredictable, so tune in again tomorrow.

Same time. Same suds.

[60]

Whose job is it anyway?
July 11, 2002

Friends sent me a photograph of a dead armadillo lying stretched out in the middle of an Arizona highway. A highway maintenance worker, traveling his appointed paint-machine route, had painted two yellow stripes right over the top of the carcass. Beneath the photograph was the caption, "It's not my job."

Where in his job description did it say to remove dead armadillos before painting the highway stripes? Apparently nowhere.

Does that guy pick up his own dirty clothes at home or roll up the neighbor's car window when it rains? Or aren't those specified in the manual either?

Employee lounges often sport a sign above the sink saying: "Your mother doesn't work here. Please clean up your own mess." What a tragedy to have to be reminded. Heaven only knows what would happen if some slothful employee discovered a dead armadillo on the counter. Well, maybe nothing would happen – and thereby hangs the problem.

Who are those people who toss candy wrappers and fast food cartons out the car window and leave doggie-do on the sidewalk? Who is it who knocks boxes off grocery store shelves and leaves them laying in the aisle? Or changes her mind about buying a bag of frozen peas and stashes it on the bread shelf?

It takes a shopping cart full of gall to assume that someone else will clean up the mess and lots of egotism to demand that kind of service from the rest of the world.

Gilbert and Sullivan tell us in song that they've "got a little list, got a little list, of society's offenders who never would be missed." Lazy prima donnas are definitely on my own little list.

There is, indeed, a hardy cadre of conscientious, responsible people who clean up what needs cleaned up. I forget how one gets assigned to this elite regiment. But we pick up the box of cereal that someone knocked from the grocery shelf, we capture trash that's blowing down the street in our neighborhood, and we install the new roll of toilet paper in public restroom holders. And while we're there, we might as well re-hook the tank chain on a toilet that won't flush.

Do we need to join a support group for the demented, or are we on to something important?

Could it possibly be that each of us is responsible not only for ourselves but for the larger world? Tell me once again. The buck stops where?

Walter Anderson, writer and editor, made of list of seven rules to live by. Number One on his list is: "Know who is responsible." We have only to look in the mirror to find out. Anderson believes that when our personal creed begins with the words, "I am responsible," we can build a new life – and maybe even a new world.

Someone else composed a commendable little piece called "Golden Rules for Easier Living." We probably should tack his list in our places of business and tape it to our refrigerators. And for posterity's sake, teach it to children along with their nursery rhymes. Gentle training begins by age three and the list reads, in part:

> If you open it, close it.
> If you turn it on, turn it off.
> If you unlock it, lock it up.
> If you break it, admit it.
> If you can't fix it, call in someone who can.
> If you borrow it, return it.
> If you value it, take care of it.
> If you make a mess, clean it up.
> If you move it, put it back.

And, I would personally add, in deference to caring for the wider world: Move the danged armadillo off the kitchen counter even if you didn't put it there.

* * * * *

[61]

Goodbye again, cruel world
August 8, 2002

The sky is falling! The sky is falling! Chicken Little is loose again.

What now, you ask? Well, an asteroid expert in England recently warned that a massive asteroid was on a collision course with Earth, destined to destroy life as we know it on February 1, 2019. I marked my calendar because, in the worst-case scenario, he predicted that we'd be reduced to conditions of the dark ages.

Other scientists, the ones sporting rose-colored glasses, argued that the collision might not happen at all. They counted on a lucky swerve or perhaps divine intervention, and designated February 1, 2060, as the earliest possible collision date. But in spite of this optimism, they still unanimously recommended that the world prepare for an eventual asteroid crash.

Does anyone really know how to prepare for a return to the dark ages? I still have six jugs of distilled water, twenty-four rolls of toilet tissue and three flashlights left over from the Y2K scare. And I have empty notebooks and sharpened pencils to record details of an asteroid crash in case I get to write a column in the Dark Ages Daily.

Perhaps I take the scientists' dire cosmic predictions more lightly than some because I'm no newcomer to this end-of-the-world-as-we-know-it business.

When a self-proclaimed guru from Cleveland predicted that the world would end on a designated day in September 1945, I personally helped spread the doomsday message, alarming everyone on the school playground with my horrifying announcement. The teachers, jaded creatures that they were, appeared less than grateful.

I wasn't around to promote some of the earlier ends of the world, those that Nostradamus predicted for 1666, 1734 and 1886. And lest we forget, the world should also have ended twice in July 1960. Obviously, forecasts of Earth's demise have been routinely exaggerated.

Even more recently, citizens of India and Nepal who believed deeply in astrology determined through their studies that the world would end on February 3, 1962. What they observed in the lineup of planets couldn't have been more catastrophic for the world. Business on the New Delhi stock exchange reportedly went into a slump. Memorable philosophical sayings came to the fore like, "Bandh kay toe sath nahi lay jai gai," which I've been told means, "You can't take it with you."

Hundreds of California believers fled into the Arizona desert to await their doom, and, as ends of the world go, that one had real flair.

Then there are those biblical predictions in the Book of Horrors that make the toughest among us wince – what with the scorpions, locusts, thunder and bottomless pits. I read so much about the apocalyptic possibilities that I finally gave up reading.

Robert Frost once tried to weigh the relative merits of annihilation by fire or ice, but gave up and concluded that either would suffice. T.S. Eliot took the laid-back position that the world will end without much fanfare at all. Specifically, not with a bang, but a whimper.

Anyway, the question isn't yet answered definitively. Unless some new prognosticator sets the dooms day clock ahead another notch, we have several more years until the asteroid lands in our back yards.

In the interim, we probably should keep weeding our lawns and balancing our checkbooks. But should believers move to the Arizona desert? And where do we find out what to put in our dark ages shelter? Is the new Homeland Security department in charge?

For now, I'm siding with the nonbelievers and expect to prevail through a continuing list of dire predictions.

Robert Frost said that everything he learned in life can be summed up in three words.

It goes on.

* * * * *

[62]

Nothing but the naked truth
September 12, 2002

The Best Summer News Story award goes not to the stock market roller-coaster saga, the preposterous heat index, the sleazy white-collar crooks, nor to political intrigue in all its guises.

First prize goes to the story of a group of creative, feisty women in Africa.

According to the Associated Press, six hundred unarmed Nigerian women held seven hundred Chevron-Texaco workers hostage inside a Nigerian oil terminal, demanding jobs for the villagers and electricity for their remote, run-down villages. The women ranged in age from thirty to ninety, the core group being married women, aged forty-plus.

After a weeklong standoff, the women agreed to end their siege when the company offered to hire some villagers, build schools and develop electrical and water systems. The women sang and danced in celebration of their success but were smart enough not to leave the facility until the agreement was put into writing.

Shortly after the signing, lightning struck the plant and a significant amount of crude oil was lost. Some theorized that God was punishing the company.

But what makes this story so special is that the women's successful protest was entirely peaceful. Their weapon? They threatened a traditional and powerful shaming gesture if their hostages tried to leave. The women would simply remove their own clothes.

Interestingly, in that culture, unwanted displays of female nudity place the shame not upon the women, but upon those at whom the action is directed.

I'm deeply impressed.

In our own culture, women would consider themselves insulted if someone paid them not to remove their clothes. But perhaps we need to consider whether the full monty could realistically become another weapon in the world's ever-growing military repertoire.

Women have always considered creative strategies and frequently proved that we don't have to kill one another to settle disagreements.

Remember Lysistrata? Frustrated by the relative weakness of the women in ancient Greece, she convinced the women of Sparta and Thebes to refuse sex with their husbands until a treaty of peace was signed between Sparta and Athens. The wives swore an oath to do so. After scenes of the husbands' painful frustration, the play ends with the treaty being signed, the men reunited with their wives, and the end of the Peloponnesian War.

And, of course, Lady Godiva rode naked on a white horse through the city of Coventry to extract a promise from her nobleman husband to reduce taxation.

Someone in our own century (probably a woman) suggested that soldiers go to battle naked. From a physical standpoint, they would soon be footsore from the rough terrain and mosquito-bitten where mosquitoes previously feared to buzz. Psychologically, they would feel so foolish that they wouldn't fight. Besides, nudity might well serve as a reminder that they and their enemies are more alike than different. How does one identify the enemy if no one wears a uniform or hat?

One wonders about smaller battles waged in bedrooms and what silent victories have been won nonviolently with negligees or less. The weaker sex? I think not.

Of course women also wield influence and power when fully clothed. Some of us do, indeed, fly planes, drive tanks and fire guns. But our arsenal also includes brains and creativity, courage, laughter, votes, a dash of the outlandish and giant hearts. We are women, hear us roar!

I plan to petition world governments to appoint an international Mothers War Board. If conflicts arise among nations, battles cannot be waged unless this board of moms unanimously approves. Members will weigh the necessity for war against the possible loss of sons and daughters and will charge themselves with designing nonviolent solutions.

Au naturel, if necessary.

* * * * *

[63]

Who let the dogs out?
September 19, 2002

When I was in high school, I knew everything there was to know. Not about chemistry, since I set the record in that class for breaking test tubes and beakers. And not about algebra, even though the teacher sat me unceremoniously in the front row.

My particular specialty was religion. I could recite all the books of the Bible in order, had memorized every verse of dozens of hymns, and I sometimes gave the sermon when the minister vacationed. I sang in the choir, taught Sunday school classes and slowly metamorphosed into a ball of accumulated virtue. Because I had the Truth.

Armed with unshakable convictions, I enrolled in college to become a minister.

But a funny thing happened on the way to the pulpit. I guess it's called education.

My first comparative religion class was both an eye-opener and a heartbreaker. If my own religion had dibs on the truth, what could I do with other belief systems that also claimed ownership of the truth? Not just the truth of major religions but the truth of those who worshipped peacock angels and other deities I'd not heard about. I well remember mourning the loss of my longstanding certainty.

Something had reached inside my head and stretched its narrow passages, and the operation was painful. Other students and I spent hours discussing issues that had been discussed since the world's first philosopher got the first big headache from thinking.

But amidst all this wonderment and discovery, the thing that amazed me most was this: how could those who held their beliefs tightly and with great certainty not realize that others held their own beliefs just as tightly and with the same certainty? How could it not enter their minds that there might be many truths – or that perhaps we all share the truth but can't claim exclusive ownership?

Let me be quick to say that I think a belief system is crucial to spiritual wellbeing. And many of us choose to express these beliefs within the structure of an organized religion. We are also free to foster growth and change in our spiritual lives or free to cling to what we learned as a child. Those are personal decisions.

I tell you true, it was lots easier when I knew everything and had Truth in my pocket. Because then, as they say, I had only one bulldog and could send it out to bark at every issue. I knew not only what was right for me but also what was right for everyone else. Of course, God spoke to others but most frequently through me.

Recently, many of us have had our heels nipped by other people's bulldogs. They know what everyone should believe and how everyone should act. God has told them who will go to heaven and who will end up in hell, and they're keeping a list.

Frankly, I'm tired of wearing Band-Aids on my ankles.

You wouldn't have liked me much when I knew everything. And I might not have liked you much either. I can still recite the books of the Bible in order and could hold up my own end of theology exchanges if

I had to. But now I know there's more to faith and life than arm wrestling over the truth.

No, I'd never really want to interfere with anyone's freedom of speech. But I have to admit that sometimes after exposure to loud religious rhetoric, I fantasize tougher leash laws for the city – something that would make people leash their bulldogs and keep them out of other people's yards – and out of city hall.

But, wait! Isn't there already a law about that?

* * * * *

[64]

You've got mail! Maybe ...
October 10, 2002

My mother claims that since early childhood I've had this "thing" about mail and mailmen. Long before I was old enough to write letters or be on anyone's junk mail list, I perched myself on the porch railing twice a day to greet the mailman to see what he'd bring.

That's the love aspect of the relationship. The fact that I held him personally responsible for any disappointments anchored the other end of the love-hate conflict.

As a slow learner or hardcore correspondence junkie, I continued waiting twice a day even after mail-less weeks and months.

Eventually, I learned not to blame the postman when my mailbox was bypassed, and adulthood cut down drastically on porch perching. So unless I mention it in a careless moment, neighbors usually aren't aware of my fanatic preoccupation. But I've never gotten over the thrill of anticipation.

Unfortunately, there has been some adventure along this addictive route, and I've learned that it takes a tough breed of mailman to deal with a mail junkie. Some of them, even those who make it through rain, sleet and dark of night, don't survive my enthusiasm.

One of my late, lamented mail carriers in Colorado was a particularly shy, ill-at-ease man of incredibly few, if any, words. Since he arrived at a regular time each afternoon, I learned to wait and watch from inside the house (a variation of the original porch perch) until he approached our driveway. Then routinely, I'd meet him at the door, reach for the handful of mail he offered and quietly tell him, "Thank you." He didn't ever respond.

One afternoon, my flair for drama created an unexpected complication. As usual, I opened the screen door just as the carrier reached into his bag to gather up my mail. But instead of following the usual script, I ad libbed a sultry, "We've got to quit meeting like this."

The poor fellow panicked. He grabbed a bunch of mail, shoved it into my hand and took off across the lawn faster than either of us knew he could travel. Half amused and half regretful, I began sorting through the letters to see if my harvest was worth the poor fellow's trauma. But I was never to learn what was inside those envelopes. In his nervous haste, he had given me the batch of mail for the rest of our block and was heading full speed down the street with my own mail still in his hand.

Adding insult to injury, and striking the fear of God into him for certain, I had to run after him and convince him to stop to make the exchange.

He wasn't with us long after that. I like to think he was going to change routes anyway.

Sadly, mail delivery systems changed drastically over the past few years. Instead of a mailman coming to my door where I can ambush him, I have to walk a block down the street to retrieve my mail from a fleet of locked boxes. The mail carrier works from the safety of an armored truck. I'd like to think that these innovations aren't the result of my Colorado episode, because I haven't terrorized a mailman since.

There's still something special about envelopes, stamps and personal signatures, but e-mail fills the void when I need a correspondence fix. Since the computer makes unlimited deliveries, I can check for mail every hour if I choose and can even take a peek in my computer mailbox at midnight if sleep eludes me. I guess it's become the 21st-century equivalent of porch perching.

Obviously, my mail fetish is well under control.

Nonetheless, if you get a minute, write.

* * * * *

[65]

Where there's smoke, there's ire
November 14, 2002

Last summer, while vacationing on the East Coast, I escaped bluefish during their feeding frenzy. This summer, I survived another lethal species: puffing swarms of smokers. And it turns out that the female of the species is much deadlier than the male.

Let me admit from the outset that the word fanatic aptly fits my stance against smoking. Twenty-five years ago, and I remember the exact moment, I vowed never to subject myself to second-hand smoke again.

As a result, I've missed half of several meetings, changed seats in numerous restaurants and had to construct a smoke-free bubble around myself.

But as a result, my lungs blush a pretty pink and I don't hack all over anyone's breakfast.

One statistic of the East Coast species particularly astounded me. During my two-week stay, I was introduced to fifteen women and the husbands of those who were married. Of the fifteen women, thirteen of them smoke. Of the husbands, none. Absolutely none.

Why in the world is that? One of the women said they were driven to smoking by their husbands, and that's the only feasible reason anyone offered. The actual reason obviously has nothing to do with differences in culture or social status; these partners live in the same houses and write checks from the same checkbooks.

Why just the women? Do they have an unspoken suicide pact? Do they live in a 1950s time warp? Do they fear gaining weight if they quit? And if it's simply a case of birds of a feather flocking together, to what flock do they belong? What do they have in common?

It isn't that those matronly smokers have tried to give up the habit and failed. That would be entirely different, and I understand that women have more trouble overcoming the addiction than men. The truth is that in spite of documented, well-advertised consequences, these otherwise intelligent women enjoy the habit and aren't the least bit interested in rehab.

This year, smoking presents its devotees with an additional challenge. Because of recent tax increases on tobacco products, cigarettes cost nearly fifty dollars a carton in New York, with prices in other states creeping toward that level. Since few can afford the exorbitant cost, the smokers I ran into were constantly bumming smokes from one another.

I fantasized about the day that everyone's last pack empties, and there's no one left to bum from. But, of course, when they run out of money, they can always sue tobacco companies for not warning them that they were killing themselves. (Whoops, sorry! A puff of sarcasm there.)

Since I'm complaining about other people's bad habits, I'll confess to an ice cream addiction, and I'm aware that an excess could kill me. Until I've conquered that delicious vice, however, I promise not to make other people fat and sticky by dripping my Rocky Road all over them.

So instead of escaping bluefish this summer, I got my exercise moving upwind of smoke, moving from chair to chair, or room to room, like some Nervous Nelly. I waited alone in restaurants twice each meal while erstwhile companions went outside for cigarette breaks – a ritual that struck me as inhospitable and less than entertaining.

Frankly, I'm glad to be back home where only a couple women in my wide circle of friends smoke. I probably will never know the reason for the difference in geography.

Those East Coast smoking matrons showed me that peer pressure is alive and well. Even as adults, we can suddenly become the identified misfit just when we thought we had adapted to life with reasonable grace. And since I don't drink, either – well, you can imagine.

* * * * *

[66]

In search of heroes
December 12, 2002

My friend Sam makes me think.

Recently, he and I talked about heroes and those whom we thought best deserve the title. We generally agreed that heroes are folks who show courage in the face of danger – being afraid, but acting anyway; setting aside self-interest in order to save another person or to serve a greater cause.

Of course we listed military, police, and firefighter heroes who rightly deserve medals and accolades. But during that discussion, we also considered other contenders who would or would not qualify as heroic according to our guidelines.

My own list would not include Wonder Woman or Superman of comic book fame, whose powers give them such an advantage that they have little to fear in the first place.

Not Bruce Willis nor Arnold Schwarzenegger, who escape the bad guys when the director yells, "Cut!" or use stand-ins when real dangers threaten.

Not Gilligan, who laughed his way through crises but caused most of them himself in the first place.

Not sports legends who get big bucks for doing spectacular things with balls, bats, or golf clubs.

Not military bigwigs who shout, "Charge!" from behind their mahogany desks.

Not thrill-seekers who risk their lives to perform bizarre feats.

And maybe not even someone who finds a cure for dread diseases from the comfort and safety of the lab.

Sam and I shared stories of our own nominations for heroes.

I chose citizens of third-world countries who stand in line to vote even at the risk of being shot at in the process. I voted for whistle-blowers who risk their jobs, reputations, and their lives to expose danger or uncover criminal wrongdoing.

Sam spoke emotionally about last year's television coverage of a white man being dragged from his big-rig truck, and being repeatedly kicked and hit with bricks by rioters. A black man, seeing the white man's plight, drove to the rescue. His wife and daughter were with him in the car. He covered his child with a blanket on the floor of the back seat, stopped the mayhem in the street, helped the trucker into his cab, and drove the big rig to a hospital to get medical help for the victim.

I spoke just as emotionally about a young boy who, after thinking it over for an evening, agreed to donate a kidney to his older brother. The family had struggled with this decision, and, after making sure he knew what the procedure involved, his parents decided to leave the final word up to him. He made his announcement at breakfast the next morning. Yes, he would do it. Later, waking from surgery in the recovery room, he asked his mother, "Now, when do I die?"

I'm convinced that events don't create heroes. Instead, when faced with a crisis, we simply learn what we have already become. A maxim as early as the seventeenth century teaches that, "heroes are made of the same stuff as common man." Fortunately, most of us have never been called upon to do anything heroic. Or perhaps we close our eyes to the opportunity. It's interesting and humbling to wonder how we'd measure up.

In the meantime, Sam and I continue refining our definition of heroes.

Also in the meantime, he contends with a neurological problem that confounds medical experts and would leave a lesser man angry and debilitated. But Sam spends his time making people laugh and dedicating his time and energy to causes bigger than both of us.

It's not always easy to recognize heroes since not all of them wear medals.

Like I said, my friend Sam makes me think.

* * * * *

[67]

There's good news and bad news
January 9, 2003

If you missed the beginning of the performance of John Cage's avant-garde organ piece in Frankfurt, Germany, you still have time to get there before it's over.

The composer's instructions dictate that the composition be played as slowly as possible and, if musicians do it right, the performance will last 639 years. It opened with sixteen months of silence (time being marked by the sound of air rushing through the bellows), and the first three actual notes were played on Sunday, January 5th.

Organizers of this Cage tribute trust future generations to continue the project since they won't be around for the finale themselves.

Numbed by horrific front-page newspaper headlines, I resolved last year to focus on more obscure stories on the inside pages. That Cage story and these other pieces from my collection remind us of our human absurdity and cushion the blow from hardcore news. Perhaps.

• A religious group in Garland, Texas, announced that, after taking the form of a Taiwanese UFO cult leader, God would broadcast live at midnight on March 31, 2002, on Channel 18. He would be heard, rather than seen, and his message would be broadcast into every home in all the Americas whether or not the television sets were turned on. The designated time passed without God's breaking into the programming. The group's leader published a simple explanation the following day: he had been wrong.

• Then there's the Tennessee lawsuit filed by Veronica M. against a fast-food restaurant. Veronica claimed she suffered a second-degree burn on her chin after an extremely hot pickle fell from one of the burgers she bought at their establishment. The pickle was said to be defective and unreasonably dangerous to the customer. Not only did she ask for a large sum of money for the permanent scarring, but her husband sought a lesser amount for losing the services and consortium of his wife.

• The Museum of Fashion and Textiles in Santiago, Chile, added an outrageous treasure to its collection with a purchase at Christie's auction. It spent $21,150 for a conical bra that Madonna wore on her Blonde Ambition Tour. And an anonymous bidder recently purchased a wad of Elvis Presley's hair for $115,120. Presley's opportunistic hairstylist had collected the hair in a plastic bag.

• A cat lover in Wichita couldn't bear to bury her dead cat. In fact, she couldn't bear to bury any dead cat – whether one of her own or those she found in the street. So she wrapped them up and put them in her freezer. Forty or sixty cats. Apparently her hobby broke no laws, and when last reported, the cats were still on ice.

• And, definitely stranger than fiction, divers are searching for Babe Ruth's piano, which he supposedly tossed into Willis Pond in 1918, thereby placing a curse on the Red Sox who haven't won a World Series since 1919. Retrieving the piano will end the curse.

• My favorite story accompanied the news photo of a group of Chilean poets standing in a wire cage, reading their poetry to zoo monkeys that they considered to be sensitive, intimate and emotional beings. Maybe they conceded that, poetry markets being what they are, sometimes you just gotta do what you gotta do.

None of these lesser stories made front-page headlines. But they're worth searching for. They make us laugh, make us cry, make us shake our heads in wonder, make us tremble with fear and let us feel superior until we do something relatively stupid ourselves.

No moral here. Just a reminder that in spite of evolution, all the monkeys aren't in the zoo.

* * * * *

[68]

Taking the double-dog dare
February 13, 2003

When I was very young, I sat under a tree in our yard and sang songs for the neighbor lady as she stood at her kitchen window washing dishes. I invented stories for my brothers about being kidnapped on Monkey Island. A friend and I danced to the music of Edison records, acting out melodramatic fantasies.

Most of us recall similar childhood scenes.

But, eventually, we encountered at least one person who reminded us that it was time to grow up. Besides, they implied, you're not a dancer, writer or a singer. And, of course, if you can't do something with a certain degree of expertise, you shouldn't mess with it at all.

Some of us were asked during chorus class just to mouth the words. In art class, teachers reminded us to stay inside the lines and warned us not to color oranges blue. Maybe they laughed at our writing or sarcastically called us "Grace" when we tried to dance. Who told us to stop whistling?

Gradually, the joy wardens taught us how proper adults should behave. We have to work, they said, and for most of us, those serious responsibilities don't involve the arts.

A graduate school professor gave me that discouraging word loudly and clearly. In my twenties, I somehow lost all of the prose and poetry I had written since childhood. When I told him of my loss, he commented tersely: "Good. That means you've grown up."

Well, he was wrong. And if he wasn't dead, there are some things I'd like to tell him.

Sure, we have to grow up, I'd say. And, of course, we're not to act like ten-year-olds again. But somewhere deep inside is a primitive drive to express ourselves, and it wants out. Cavemen drew pictures on the walls, just as toddlers do. They drummed on rocks and molded figures out of clay, just as children bang on pans and make mud pies.

131

Primitives who fashioned their own clothing weren't content just to weave the material, but added intricate, brilliant designs.

But in our current culture, while we're encouraged to develop physical and mental abilities as we approach adulthood, that isn't usually the case in terms of artistic skills. Those who choose the creative path sometimes walk the path alone and risk starving in that cold proverbial attic.

How did the metamorphosis from spontaneous, creative child to inhibited adult come about for each of us? When did we lose the joy? Sadly, under the pressure, some of us crawled into the adult box assigned to us, packing ourselves away with the modeling clay, harmonica, tap shoes and sketchpads.

One poet, who refused to be dissuaded from the craft, describes it in these words:

"We danced with shirttails flying, /pigtails swirling, arms stretched out/ to catch the wind, feet alive to music/ that grownups didn't hear. Wielding chunky sidewalk chalk/ we sketched the world on driveways:/ flowers, families, sunshine stars. Held rainbows in our hands./ Tuneless songs with endless chorus/ bubbled from an inner spring./ We rhymed and chimed and mimed/ our words, singing poetry./ What dictum stilled our dancing feet,/ suppressed our songs, re-wrote our script/ in pallid prose, and bleached our life/ to black and white?/ And why?"

Today I dare us, double-dog dare us all, to dance in the kitchen, sing off key, rhyme some lines. Whittle and sculpt. Paint pictures for children to hang on their refrigerators. Get out the old trombone and frighten the neighbors. Or just whistle.

As one philosopher explained, "An artist is not a special kind of person. But every person is a special kind of artist."

Reclaim the joy.

* * * * *

[69]

Seasick on the shore
March 13, 2003

Two summers ago, while I was vacationing on the East Coast, friends and brochures enticed me into an afternoon of whale-watching. Ordinarily, I preferred the beach and shallow water. But having already mastered bathtubs, swimming pools and tourist boat rides near shore, I agreed to go.

The weather was perfect. I quickly squeezed myself into a spot on the prow of the boat to enjoy the wind and sea spray and to be among the first people sighted if any whales were out people-watching that day. The first two hours delivered everything friends and brochures had promised, except whales, and I definitely got my money's worth in sea spray.

Then, quite suddenly, the ocean turned rough, with waves so high the boat left the water and crashed down again with each wave. As snowboarders would say, we got lots of airtime – an added attraction that definitely wasn't in the brochure.

When conditions didn't improve, our captains ordered everyone away from the prow to the sides of the boat for safety. Still later, they ordered everyone into the glass-enclosed cabin.

We crowded inside to sit on wooden benches, very much like captives in a pirate ship's hold.

Without fresh air and readily visible horizon, an epidemic of sea-sickness broke out among all but the most hardy – of which I was not one. Happily, I didn't lose my lunch but quickly decided that the best definition of Hell on earth would be perpetual seasickness. I remembered from my Girl Scout manual or some television documentary to search out a horizon and keep my eyes focused there. That helped.

Some of the other passengers closed their eyes and bowed their heads, probably praying between bouts of nausea.

A crying child sitting behind me called out, "Mommy, are we going to die?" I sighed with relief when her answer was, "No."

Helpless and frightened, our gyroscopes no longer working, we were at the mercy of those running the ship and at the mercy of the ocean itself. Of course the problem was that no matter how sick everyone was or how much the waters calmed, the boat would still take two hours to reach shore again.

Before finally turning the boat around, our captains stood near the prow, occasionally shouting: "Whale! Whale!" We didn't get to see them, of course, but didn't get refunds either, since whales allegedly had shown up.

Until recently, I hadn't thought about this fiasco of an adventure for a long time. But the world is topsy-turvy again and my stomach is churning. We're in the hold of another speeding boat hell-bent on taking us into rough waters. Remembering other stormy rides and thousands lost at sea, many of us beg and pray they turn this boat around. There aren't enough life preservers for everyone on board and the child within us all is asking, "Mommy, are we going to die?"

I strain to read the logo on the side of our boat, but turbulent waves have blurred the paint. Does it say Ship of State or Ship of Fools?

Whichever it is, we're headed out to sea, invading whale territory, paying dearly to see them perform for us. There will be no refunds and, believe me, the trip back will seem endless. Did we actually buy tickets for this venture or were we kidnapped from the shore?

I'd like to shut my eyes and make it all go away. I'd like to click my heels and find myself back on the beach. Instead, I'll try to find some spot to anchor myself, some steadying horizon. It's going to be another rough ride.

* * * * *

[70]

Strike while the bug is close
April 10, 2003

A bird in the hand... is a real mess.

The squeaking wheel... gets annoying.

A penny saved is... not much.

If you have school-age children close at hand, corral a couple and see if they can do better on a proverb test than those whose responses were gathered by teachers. Students were given the first half of classic proverbs and asked to complete them. Here are some other attempts:

You can lead a horse to water, but... why?

If at first you don't succeed... get new batteries.

Two's company, three's... the Musketeers.

Where there's smoke, there's... pollution.

There's no fool like... Uncle Eddie.

Stories, proverbs and classic fictional characters comprise our collective imaginations. How and when do we learn about them? Would high school students do significantly better on the test than grade school children, or have these treasures been lost?

I hope, too, that three- and four-year-olds still learn nursery rhymes so they'll know why Jack and Jill went up the hill and how that escapade ended. On an early television episode of "Who Wants to Be a Millionaire," one embarrassed contestant went down in flames after missing the very first question. Asked to choose from among four choices what Jack Horner pulled out of the pie with his thumb, he said "blackbird." I like to think we can chalk it up to nervousness.

While the children are still corralled, ask them to tell the story of Noah or Jonah. Even if one embraces no religion at all, these stories are cultural references and have crept into our daily language usage. At a minimum, we have to know that when someone calls us a Jezebel, it isn't exactly a compliment.

The same holds true for stories from Greek and Roman mythology. These tales are more creative and exciting than any television series, yet it's the lucky child who is introduced to them early and retains them in their repertoire. I'll omit examples, not having been among the lucky ones. Do children know Aesop's stories of the fox and the grapes, the dog in the manger or the hare and the tortoise?

I'd make the case for classical poems being central to our culture as well, whether we appreciate poetry or not. Perhaps upon reaching adulthood, our test could require completing lines such as:

A thing of beauty is...

By the shores of...

There is no joy in Mudville...

How do I love thee...

Maybe I'm making too much of these oversights in learning. Maybe younger generations will develop their own points of reference and not need ours. Maybe their folk heroes will be Xena the Warrior Princess, Homer Simpson and SpongeBob SquarePants. But one can hope not.

While respecting the old, we should keep up with the addition of stories, characters and sayings that will be part of our shared consciousness in the future, though which ones will last is hard to predict. Surely, the Cat in the Hat, Harry Potter and the Grinch will endure. If we've kept reasonably in touch, we'll also be able to complete such phrases as "May the force... " and "Go ahead, make my... "

While experts revise the curriculum in an attempt to raise educational standards and achievement levels, and while children struggle to pass competency tests, it's important that education not lose its heart and soul.

Or, as a child might say, we shouldn't throw out the baby with the garbage.

* * * * *

135

[71]

Neighbors – just a yard away
May 8, 2003

Neighborhood children dig shallow holes in the dirt beneath my backyard deck and construct miniature furniture with sticks and rocks. Their father starts my stubborn lawnmower when my own patience and muscle wane.

Neighbors share brownies, jokes, mulch and advice. We tolerate winter hibernation, then emerge again each spring. But even during coldest times, we shout across icy driveways and shovel snow in a friendly, unconscious rhythm. Weather permitting, we linger at the communal mailbox to gossip, laugh or complain.

So if there's anything more precious than neighbors, I don't know what it is.

Yet something strange is happening in the construction business.

Glancing down the streets of new residential construction, we often see nothing but rows of protruding garages, looking for all the world like gigantic storage facilities. No one sits on front porches, because there are none. Front doors are set back from the street farther than the garages and sometimes crouch invisibly at the side of the house, daring someone to find them. I'm told these structures are called "snout houses."

During the past year, I stopped at building sites on three different occasions to ask construction workers the reason for this popular housing design. None of them claimed to know. (And who, they probably thought, is that crazy old woman, anyway?) A recent scholarly essay suggested that this trend symbolizes the importance of the automobile in our society. But it's hard to believe that the design's original purpose was to showcase our cars.

I've considered other possibilities. Does the layout somehow maximize lot space? Is the shorter driveway intended to cut down on snow shoveling? Was the design purposely developed to increase privacy for residents? If the latter, it's probably working. One could conceivably go for weeks without ever seeing the family next door.

As it is, automatic garage doors gape open in the morning to spit people out for the day, then gape open again to swallow them up for the evening.

Those homes are probably lovely and comfortable, once someone finds her way inside. And perhaps there are welcoming communal patios and playgrounds in the back yard that passersby can't see. I hope so.

What happened to neighborhoods?

First, with sad good reason, we started locking our doors. Then, in our busyness, much of the world adopted a "call before you come" mode. Many of us remember when porches and kitchens maintained open hours for neighbors, friends and sometimes strangers. No reservations necessary; come as you are.

In the surviving old-fashioned neighborhoods, everyone knows where to go to borrow cups of sugar or find a sympathetic shoulder. Every house is a safe target for trick or treating and, if we're lucky, there might even be block parties or parades.

Of course, porches don't guarantee neighborliness, and, conversely, many families break the isolation barrier posed by intruding garages. Determined folk can vault that void to meet the people next door. And it's well worth the trip.

But why does the new architecture insist upon making it more difficult? Interior designers tell us that our furniture arrangement can make visitors feel welcome or otherwise. So can front doors.

Robert Frost writes that good fences make good neighbors but also advises that we make sure we know what it is we're walling out or walling in.

There's certainly more to be said on this subject, but you'll have to excuse me. Because, no kidding, three little girls, dressed up as spies, just came to my front door to invite me to their picnic.

Or, as Mr. Rogers might have observed, it's a beautiful day in the neighborhood.

* * * * *

[72]

You won't hear it from me
June 22, 2003

Readers occasionally suggest I write a column about my pet peeves. But since I hate focusing on the lint of life and don't want to christen my new column location with a litany of complaints, I'm resisting the temptation to wax peevish.

Less charitable folks would probably cave in to an opportunity to gripe.

They'd squawk about stores with ten checkout counters with no more than two of them open for business at any given time. Or, in that same venue, about customers who stand ahead of them in long lines but never dream of locating their checkbook until the cashier announces the total.

They'd go on to criticize unfriendly clerks who seemingly wish people shopped at the competition and didn't bother them.

Malcontents would probably rant about a wide range of other people's noises. They'd complain about car stereos that blast loudly enough to explode pacemakers. They don't even like it when people wash cars in residential driveways, turning the car radio's volume high enough to be heard down the block – figuring everyone else enjoys that radio station, too.

You'd no doubt find a few crotchety people who don't like to hear dogs barking in dissonant concert – neither the big woofers nor the tiny yippers. Even some who claim to be animal lovers squawk about the canine cacophony.

Other grumblers find fault with dogs that sniff crotches while owners look on, amused at their pet's cute habit. And who but a whiner would grumble about pony-size dogs greeting company by putting their paws on visitors' shoulders, nearly knocking them to the sidewalk?

Retired folks, who occasionally get to sleep late, might complain if school bus drivers honk the bus horn on the corner shortly after dawn as one last call to dawdling students. In that same foul mood, they'd scowl at cars parked across sidewalks, forcing walkers to detour through wet grass or into the street.

And can you believe it? There are some seemingly patriotic, upright citizens who don't even care who wins basketball or football games and don't weep when coaches leave or care where they go. So they gripe about being bombarded with all the hoopla.

Those prone to being easily upset can't even enjoy the spring bumper crop of orange barrels and the scenic detours they promote. And they allow themselves to cringe when speeding drivers cut ahead of them to wait (and wait and wait) at the stoplight.

Computer-literate folks raise a malcontented fuss about unsolicited e-mails that promise everything from overnight riches to enlargement of body parts that need enlarged and reduction of body parts that need reduced.

Even some of my own friends complain about smokers, as though someone else's cancer or second-hand smoke was any of their business. Go figure.

Obviously, a column about my own pet peeves would require deviation from my accepting and charitable spirit. So you can understand why I've resisted the temptation.

Sure, I might eventually have a personal complaint or two.

But I'll be keeping them to myself.

* * * * *

[73]

When money's talking, listen up!
July 27, 2003

Barry Bonds, home run record setter, recently agreed to a $90 million, five-year contract with the San Francisco Giants. That contract earns Bonds the status of fourth highest salary in baseball and promises more than some of us earn even during a bumper crop year. Tiger Woods received four million dollars just for participating in a golf tournament – win or lose.

Being neither a sports expert nor economist, I'm hard pressed to think of anything someone could do with a baseball or golf ball to warrant such exorbitant pay.

Since top athletes routinely receive such salaries, I assumed we used the same pay scale in the field of education. But when I checked with a couple master teachers, they insisted their own salaries don't measure up. The claim to fall short of seventeen million dollars a year even if they include what they earn at their second job at McDonalds.

Maybe I exist in some sort of time warp.

The year I was born, the average annual salary in the United States was $1,601. How can someone of that generation even begin to appreciate Venus Williams' eight million dollar a year contract for a tennis endorsement in addition to tournament winnings? (Sure, I've won a couple tennis prizes, too, but the most valuable so far is a pair of athletic socks.)

As though it isn't bad enough that colossal salary discrepancies between teachers and athletes exist, we're told that the discrepancy reflects our national value system. We're told we prize sports above everything else – that we're willing to pay more to be entertained by someone's baseball, football, or tennis prowess than to teach our children and young adults. I do have to admit I haven't seen thousands of cheering fans jam arenas for spelling bees and debates or pay to attend PTO meetings. So perhaps the statisticians are right. If it's true we put our money where our hearts are, the evidence is hard to dispute.

I realize I'm comparing private versus public monies, but there's a finite amount, and it all comes out of the pockets in our own pants. Money does talk – and paying thousands of dollars for reserved stadium seats sends as clear a message about values as voting against a school bond issue.

Of course sports play an important role in our society, and of course children can learn teamwork, persistence, pride, and good sportsmanship from participating – providing they have good role models. But the three R's shouldn't have to compete with sports programs for dollars. Most people aren't averse to athletics as an extracurricular facet of our educational programs. We cringe, however, when athletics assume the primary position in terms of interest, enthusiasm, and allocation of resources, whether we're talking about professional or public arenas.

I haven't any idea how the world got to this point, and don't know how we'd retreat from it even if everyone wanted to.

But as one philosopher said, "If you think education is expensive, try ignorance."

* * * * *

[74]

Read any good CDs lately?
Aug. 31, 2003

With a new school year upon us, students might be relieved to know they won't have to shoulder those backbreaking book bags much longer, because in some quarters, teachers are already sending homework home on CDs. No, not the money kind, but CD as in Compact Disc, as in computers. And I fear we might all be making that transition more quickly than we like to imagine. The term "rare books" could soon take on new meaning. Is it possible that books will someday become as obsolete as stone tablets and slates?

Even though I don't qualify as a bookworm, I have lots of friends who do. But I still appreciate the feel of books, the enticing smells of older books and new ones, the sound of pages flipping, and their inevitable coffee stains.

Besides superior aesthetics, books have other distinct advantages over CDs. We can not only lull cozily on the couch to read, but can also tote books with us into the bathtub or up a tree. We can fall asleep with book on our chest. Sure, agile users could manage the same maneuvers with laptop computers, but those contraptions simply aren't cuddly.

And with books, if no one raps our fingers for doing so, we can write and doodle in the margins or highlight special passages in day-glow yellow.

Even non-readers have lots to lose.

Without books, where would we press flowers, four-leaf clovers, and other mementos? The cautious among us would no longer be able to hide the family jewels in a hollowed out volume of *Tom Sawyer*.

And at Thanksgiving time, toddlers usually sit on two volumes of the *Encyclopedia Britannica* to reach Grandma's dinner table. How many CDs do you suppose that will take?

Baby's first books are colorful, chewable & washable. Will some entrepreneur invent chewable, washable CDs?

I once lived with a wealthy widow whose sunroom included floor to ceiling built-in bookcases. Unfortunately, she didn't enjoy reading, so she solicited contributions from friends and arranged their donated books by color on the shelves. But with the new technology, we have access to the complete works of Shakespeare or an entire set of encyclopedia on a CD or two. What happens to beautifully bound volumes that have lined our shelves, and how will nonreaders decorate their home and impress other people at the same time?

I wonder. Will books soon go the way of carbon paper and end up in some great unused bookstore in the sky? Letters, pens, and stationery are nearly passé already. I won't soon forget the puzzled look on the face of a young clerk when I asked for a bottle of ink.

Children already inquire, "Grandpa, what's a record player?" Will they eventually be asking, "Grandpa, what's a book?" Is it possible that bookworms will gradually metamorphose into CD worms?

Obviously, this book/CD issue raises a lot of questions for which I have no answers.

We might well love those shiny CDs. But only books can love us back.

* * * * *

[75]

What goes down must come up
Sept. 28, 2003

This isn't a column about indigestion or stock market predictions. It's about packrats and their offspring.

Most of us, particularly those of us qualifying as seniors, vow twice a year to downsize. Yes, the diet kind, but also downsizing defined as getting rid of useless treasures we've accumulated over the years.

Often, it's a losing battle. Just when we're determined to reduce our inventory, an irresistible garage sale lures us from our resolution and we add yet another wind chime, filing cabinet, or box of infinite possibilities to our stockpile. We buy a new chair, but can't face getting rid of the old one in case some great grandchild (as yet unborn) needs it for her first apartment.

But, following a recent epiphany, I crowned myself Downsizing Queen.

It happened as I carried items to the basement tomb where I bury my treasures. Suddenly, I realized I'd never use that stuff again, and that either I or my heirs would have to lug it all out of there someday. Hence my new mantra: What Goes Down Must Come Up.

When Newton announced that what goes up must come down, he wasn't discovering gravity. He was referring to attic storage.

If you've ever been party to cleaning out someone's house after thirty or fifty years of collecting, you know what I mean. I don't know what heirs are supposed to do with photos of people they don't even know, the first computer ever made, or curtain rods that fit windows three houses ago. They probably won't even appreciate the bowling trophy we won in 1950. Do we think we keep ourselves alive by keeping our memorabilia alive?

But let's be fair. Perhaps we aren't packrats. Maybe those boxes of miscellany and the green futon belong to our son who already left home and lives in spaces smaller than our storage space. Maybe he's interning in Africa. Or maybe his new wife doesn't want his artifacts in her house. How many years do we give him to carry it up those stairs himself before we donate it to a garage sale?

Since my epiphany, the goal is to dispose of something as soon as I'm through with it. Is there a risk I'll want it sometime in the future? Statistics say not, but it's easy to talk myself into believing the orange chair will match my next living room or that I'll wear my prom dress again.

Some of us regret not having an inheritance for our children. I suggest that even if we have little to leave our heirs, the greatest gift of all might be what we don't leave them – sixty years of useless accumulation.

Don't get me wrong. Even the Downscaling Queen still has plenty of stuff. But, from now on, if you see me carrying boxes, I'll be headed up the basement stairs rather than down.

* * * * *

[76]

Random acts of meanness
October 26, 2003

David Blaine is a London magician who performs magic and illusions on the street for passersby. Although well known for levitating himself from a standing position, that's the least bizarre of his antics. He once spent sixty hours encased in a block of ice and once allowed himself to be buried alive for seven days.

Most recently, he enclosed himself in a plastic box that dangled in the air near the Thames River, aiming to survive midair for forty-four days with nothing to sustain him but water, determination, and lip balm.

Unfortunately, a few mean-spirited onlookers created problems. They shouted insults and pelted him with eggs and golf balls. One man launched paint-filled balloons at him with a catapult. Another deliberately damaged the unit supplying water to his cage.

Never mind for now why Blaine chose to dangle in a plastic box, let alone freezing and burying himself. Wonder instead about the motivation of his detractors.

We've occasionally spotted their ilk in our own neighborhoods. They're anonymous folk who knock down snowmen and smash our Halloween pumpkins in the street. They drive cars over lawns, knock down newly planted trees, and overturn headstones in cemeteries. They set their dogs free to dig up what we nurtured. In New York City, they reportedly gathered on the street to encourage a potential suicide to jump from his perch on a high ledge. Judging by the plethora of such stories in the news, their ilk is all too alive and well.

Although the blatantly mean-spirited destroy property and spew epithets, we hardly have to hurl rocks or shout obscenities to qualify as cruel. Some of the malevolent among us sling arrows with a demeaning glance, a single hurtful word, or deliberate neglect. Some manipulate fellow human beings behind the scenes for their own gain or spread stories that don't meet the triple criteria of true, kind, and necessary. And perhaps deadliest of all, passive tactics require nothing but silence when someone could use a kind word.

Meanwhile, back in the dangling plastic box, Blaine broke his own silence to speak to musicians who stood beneath him singing John Lennon's song, "Imagine." "Imagine all the people living life in peace... " In explaining why he moved into the box in the first place, Blaine told them that "life is poetic," and "love is everywhere." He didn't try to explain the insults, eggs, golf balls, and paint balloons.

Popular bumper stickers promote random acts of kindness. Has anyone has ever discovered what breeds random acts of meanness?

Emma Goldman once explained the phenomenon with a trickle down theory, suggesting that organized violence "on top" results in individual violence "at the bottom." On the other hand, I wonder if individual kindness at the bottom might not result in organized kindness at the top.

It would be an interesting experiment with nothing whatsoever to lose.

Just imagine.

* * * * *

[77]

Famous last words: gobble-gobble
November 23, 2003

In an old television episode of WKRP in Cincinnati, employees at the radio station devised a Thanksgiving promotion. They loaded a couple dozen turkeys into a helicopter and, at the designated altitude, released them to fly over the downtown area. Shortly after shooing them out, however, they discovered that domestic turkeys can't fly. A horrific climax for sure, as staffers scrambled to clean up the carnage and salvage their own reputation.

Determined to commit no turkey faux pas myself, I researched the subject as tribute to forty-five million birds sacrificing their lives for holiday tables this week.

Here are the facts, so let's talk turkey.

* If you hunt your own bird, you'll learn that, unlike the domestically reared variety, wild turkeys fly for short distances at speeds up to 55 miles per hour and travel up to twenty-five miles per hour on the ground. You might track them by their gobbling, which on a still day can be heard a mile away, but they are hard to sneak up on because of their wide field of vision. Only Tom turkeys gobble. Females make a clicking sound.

* If you don't succeed in bagging your own dinner, your turkey might have died of natural causes. Apparently they can drown if they look up when it's raining. And they sometimes have heart attacks. Those living near Air Force test areas over which the sound barrier was broken were known to drop dead from the sonic boom.

* Meanwhile, back in the kitchen, four-month-old turkeys are dubbed fryers. Five- to seven-month-olds are roasters, and one-year-olds

are yearlings. Any turkey fifteen months or older is referred to as mature…
or simply as white meat and dark meat.

* Turkeys showed up long before Columbus or the Pilgrims.
Scientists reportedly found turkey fossils that are ten million years old.
They, the turkeys, were later domesticated in Mexico and taken to Europe
in the sixteenth century. In England, they used to be walked to market,
wearing booties to protect their feet. They were also walked to market in
the United States, but probably barefooted.

* Modern breeding techniques sometimes cause turkey breasts to
grow so large that the turkeys fall over. And as if that weren't bad enough,
they develop a fleshy growth under their throat, called a wattle. Females of
a more advanced species call in plastic surgeons to correct these unhappy
circumstances.

How did the word turkey come to signify a theater production that
flops? Or an inept person? On the brighter side, they did have a country
named after them.

Nearly sixty years ago, the National Turkey Federation began pre-
senting a live turkey to the U.S. President on Thanksgiving… not expressly
as political commentary, but supposedly just a traditional gift. He pardons
the turkey and sends it to live out the rest of its days on a retirement farm.

Not a particularly auspicious ending, but it sure beats a helicopter
ride.

* * * * *

[78/167]

It's been a year of small potatoes
December 28, 2003
January 23, 2012

Like some boorish houseguest, my year overstayed its welcome. It
arrived innocently enough, but lugged valises full of loss, near loss,
disappointments and challenges. Fortunately, it's promised to pack up and
leave for good midweek.

Everyone's had a year like that at one time or another. If 2003
wasn't yours, you still know what I mean.

I recalled the time I organized a church service. Being the cheerful,
optimistic sort, I planned a service of praise and joy. The organist, however,
had already decided to play a requiem and wouldn't budge from his program. His funereal wet blanket didn't fit into my plans.

I mumbled for a while, then accepted the requiem into the program just as we've learned to accept it into our lives.

We'd like the world to be an uninterrupted celebration, but as we float along, feeling genuinely happy or at least neutral, misfortune strikes. We're reminded time after time that life is an unpredictable mixture of joy and sorrow. Every day, the world topples over on someone who had been sitting on top of it.

I read that the Viennese have a word for the ability to carry on the business of life despite a multitude of ups and downs. Translated, their word means getting by for long periods of time on little sausages and small potatoes – the ability to cope and muddle on.

The most painful crises seem to come out of nowhere and are totally beyond our control. Isabel Allende said, "The really important things in life are never planned. They just happen. And when the pain comes, we're soaked in it. We soak up pain like a sponge soaks up water. Just when we think we can't take any more, we do."

We ask, "Can't the requiem be omitted or played later so that it doesn't interfere with our celebration?" As I learned, the answer is "no."

Most of us have watched children learning to float in a swimming pool. Over and over, they flail their arms, kick their legs and sink. Finally, maybe after several tearful sessions, they learn to trust. The water holds them up when they quit kicking and flailing. In times of loss, maybe we don't have to expend our energies searching frantically for a life preserver – for answers to the why and how of tragedies. It's not a grasping time. It's a time to rest and receive.

In troubled times, requiems are often the loudest music we hear. We temporarily forget how much strength is available from family, friends, our sense of humor, common sense, our faith, our creativity.

It's easy to sing while sitting on top of the world, but tragedies don't have to shatter our underlying trust and capacity for joy. Even during times of little sausages and small potatoes, there is reason to rejoice.

Nonetheless, welcome Baby New Year! Welcome!

* * * * *

[79]

A little bit of knowledge
January 25, 2004

Instead of making New Year's resolutions that tend to lack tenacity, I've spent this month taking inventory of what I learned last year. Most of these gems don't deserve elaboration, but while hunkering down for winter, I'm purging myself of miscellaneous tidbits to make cortex room for critical data like birth date, social security number, and my name.

Throughout the year, internet sources and news articles piqued my curiosity and answered questions I'd not dreamed of asking. If life depends upon this information's being correct, however, get a second opinion.

You might need to know for some reason that cockroaches can live nine days without heads before starving to death. That snails can sleep for three years and, sadly, that the average candy bar contains eight insect legs.

Did you know that dueling is legal in Paraguay as long as both parties are registered blood donors? And can you stretch your gullibility far enough to believe that more people are killed by donkeys every year than are killed in plane crashes? At least that's what it says right here.

Other intelligence informs me that women blink nearly twice as much as men and that the electric chair was invented by a dentist. Somehow we knew that.

My favorite revelation came from stand-up comedian, Emo, who deadpanned, "It's really too bad that none of our states ends in the letter A. The only ones that do are Alabama, Iowa, Arizona, North Carolina, South Carolina, North Dakota, South Dakota, Louisiana, Alaska, Montana, California, Nebraska, Oklahoma, Indiana, Pennsylvania, Florida, Georgia, Minnesota, Nevada, Virginia, and West Virginia." Twenty-one out of fifty! Now what are the odds?

And, when you catch your breath, check out the continents. The letter A predominates again both at the beginning and ending of America, Africa, Asia, Australia, Antarctica.

Obviously, there's no excuse for remaining ignorant when information spurts around us continuously, unsolicited, and free.

I've learned this year from personal experience that the amount of fertilizer I put on the lawn has something to do with how frequently I have to mow.

I've relearned that cookie sheets are hot when they come out of the oven and that good intentions still pave roads to Hell.

I reconfirmed that someone can get by on charm for about fifteen minutes, and after that, had better know something. I was reminded we don't have to change friends if we understand that friends change.

One would think with all this learning, there's little new under the sun. But the new year already presents fresh puzzlers.

Perhaps the number one question comes from a California philoso-phizer who asks, "Has all this evolution been worth it?" Do let me know if you find out.

In the meantime, to the accompaniment of resolutions crashing in the background, good wishes to us all for a peaceful, prosperous 2004.

* * * * *

[80]

There's quite a fire on that cake
February 22, 2004

I celebrated my birthday last month. A delicious one ending in zero. Earlier zeroes elicited some groans, but there comes a turning point when we boast about age, particularly if we enjoy the delusion that we look much younger than our years.

Having reached my promised three score years and ten, and having made no New Year's resolutions, I compiled resolutions belatedly for my birthday.

I'd already announced that I plan to be more truthful than ever before – a pronouncement that frightened the less hardy. One always runs the risk of being arrested for committing truth, and the Gospel of Timidity warns that the truth can also make thee lonely. But I've been practicing the truth business for a long time and consider it worth the risk. I will continue my campaign to convince the world that we're each responsible for our own behavior in spite of creative excuses. I don't intend to be unkind to other human beings, but also won't be accepting rudeness or incompetence with an understanding smile.

As a special birthday surprise, God permanently excused me from serving on committees or holding office. I no longer have to accept the nomination as assistant interim vice president in charge of attendance and lemonade. Sure, one person can make a difference, but it doesn't necessarily have to be me. Someone else will have to save the endangered tsetse fly.

Without a special holy edict, I'm also excusing myself from attend-ing parties where hosts sell baskets, jewelry, pans, or underwear. In fact, I'm not going to visit anyone's house if I know in advance it will cost money to leave.

And you know that list of one hundred books one should read before she dies? I'm simply not going to read them.

Sure, I'll still keep busy. I'm not dropping out. Just dropping into a self-carved niche that fits the edges of a salty old woman.

Basking in the light of all those candles on my cake, I'm reminded that much of age is attitude, and it's all relative. I recently read a 106-year-old woman's reflection on her age. She said, "Being in the 106th year of my life is a bit tedious. The old body is just too darn frail. Oh, to be ninety or even a hundred again when I could get around and do things."

We don't often formalize our wish lists except on birthdays and other gift-getting occasions. But sometimes, during those celebrations, we're moved to prioritize our wishes and resolutions.

Just before Christmas, while adventuring outside of the box, I noticed a mall Santa sitting idle in his sleigh. So I asked if he'd sit on my lap to whisper what he wanted for Christmas. He quickly obliged. While his elf took our picture, Santa confided that all he wished for was good health.

As we extinguish birthday candles this year, so say we all.

* * * * *

[81]

We are what we wear? I hope not!
March 28, 2004

Sunday mornings, in preparation for church, I perform a sacrificial, ritual dance. With minor weekly variations, it consists of hopping around the bedroom, occasionally grasping the chest of drawers for balance, and finally wriggling successfully into pantyhose. For the umpteenth time I wonder why I perpetrate this crime upon myself when I'm sure God would be the last to care about pantyhose. Nonetheless, I bow to standards of what is deemed appropriate for the occasion, and then sit with my legs stuck out in the sanctuary aisle until I'm sure God acknowledges the sacrifice.

I've generally met with failure when trying to dress as fashion demands.

As a result, one might think I'd advocate strictly casual dress, but this is not the case – and the issue confounds me. I'm starting to think the rest of the world is confused, too. What do we really think about our garb and its relevance?

I've been taught that some situations call for "dressing up" to show respect for the event itself or for others who will show up there. Church is probably one of these. Theater performances and concerts might be two others. But, instead, the world has turned into a giant come-as-you-are party.

What ever happened to sartorial splendor?

I don't know the answers. I just ask the questions. Do we behave more professionally if we dress the part? Do students learn better if they look like students? Do brains and courtesy deteriorate when we're sloppily dressed? Will we get into Heaven if we spruce up on Sunday mornings?

Another aspect of the dilemma is that I'd like to be able to walk into a school, an office, or retail store and be met by employees who dress well enough that I can distinguish them from their blue-jeaned customers.

I know, I know! Those folks have some dirty jobs during their workday, and they aren't given bonuses for wardrobe. I plead guilty myself to choosing comfort over class anytime I can get away with it.

The sad conclusion might be that I'd like to dress casually but hold everyone else to higher standards.

Some of my friends actually enjoy dressing up, and they look classy any time they appear in public. If, wearing my grungies, I meet them in a grocery store, I tell them I've just returned from helping migrant workers in the field.

Goethe, in *Faust*, minces no words in expressing his point of view. "You are in the end – exactly what you are. Put on a wig with a million curls, put on your feet the boots with the highest heels, yet you remain in the end just what you are."

So while I'm contemplating my wardrobe, I'm also perusing a book called *Encyclopedia of Gods* which lists 2,500 deities worshiped throughout the world.

I'm looking for one that specifically prohibits pantyhose, even on Sundays.

* * * * *

[82]

Pull over to the side of the road
April 25, 2004

Driving bumper to bumper on a super-clogged superhighway south of Boston, I spotted signs at regular intervals that read, "Breakdown lane. No traffic allowed."

And sure enough, the Powers That Be had provided a lane at the right side of the road for breakdowns. What a great concept! Drivers can pull out of the traffic flow and merge into the chaos again whenever they're ready. Sidelined, out of harm's way, drivers can call for help, solve the problem themselves, or simply give their tired chassis a rest.

Surely, in this fast-paced world, we all need breakdown lanes, and they're not always easy to come by. They aren't built into most highway systems, nor often enough into our daily routines.

Where do we go to get out of the world's traffic when we're tired of bumper-to-bumper or are running out of gas? We provide time outs for children when they can no longer cope gracefully with the world, but what do we do for ourselves?

I'd personally choose a beach location for my respite lane, but the legislature repeatedly ignores my petitions to authorize an ocean for Kansas. So until one is made available, sea nymphs (and the rest of us) would be well advised to keep more reasonable breakdown sites handy in case of emergency.

Therapists' offices might do. Bubble baths, yoga mats, and afternoon naps are cheaper. Others find sanctuary in fishing boats, long walks, church pews or hammocks. If there isn't a breakdown lane on the shoulder of the road, a friend's shoulder works just as well and is softer than asphalt.

Of course we could forget about respites and insist upon driving with worn, damaged, and dangerous parts – as many do. We could push on until we've completely run out of gas or something important boils over.

Don't get me wrong. Respite lanes aren't a panacea. Folks in a hurry will try to drive in our breakdown lanes. At least they did on the Boston highway. There are always those for whom rules apparently don't apply – those who speed past on their frantic way, too preoccupied to care who's broken down or why, let alone stopping to help.

Someone's bound to rock our hammock or pull the plug on our bubble bath.

And, even if they didn't, we can't stay in the breakdown lane forever. An old song recommends we build a sweet little nest somewhere in the west and let the rest of the world go by. But reality reminds us that, all too soon, we have to merge back into traffic.

Frankly, if we can't even get an ocean in Kansas, we probably shouldn't count on formal breakdown lanes on all our highways and byways either. So we simply have to devise our own.

"Little man in a hurry, full of an important worry, halt, stop, forget, relax, wait."

Pull over to the side of the road.

* * * * *

[83/138]

A song for the unsung
May 23, 2004
Nov. 23, 2008

School's out, school's out!

It's time for awards, certificates, blue ribbons, graduations and applause. Whether for perfect attendance, perfect touchdowns, perfect personality, or perfect grades, it's time to offer recognition and appreciation for a job well done. Some of the most talented will garner more than an equal share of accolades and already have one foot poised to enjoy whatever opportunities come next. We wish them continued success in all they undertake.

But when the formal applause dies down and all the traditional praises have been sung, I'd like to offer a song for the unsung. We all know children who have lassoed our hearts even though they get little recognition from the world at large. We are often their only cheerleader, advocate, and fan. Perhaps, even, their only friend. In this moment, we have a chance to join together in a virtual chorus to sing their praises.

Let this be a song for the child:

... who has never hit a homerun nor made a touchdown – but shows up for practice without fail and cheers enthusiastically for his teammates

... who has never made the honor roll – but whose work is always completed on time even at the expense of long hours of study at home

... who has never worn a pair of designer jeans – but who walks tall and proud in the "lesser" brands

... who has never known the security of a peaceful, supportive home – but nonetheless has developed a personal serenity that gives her strength

... who has never been accepted by the small "popular" group of peers – but who is cherished by those who have wisely allowed her into their circle

... who has never been able to deal with the world's demands without extra help and a special boost – but who accepts that assistance with continued high regard for himself

... who has never participated in the mainstream of life because of an illness or severe handicap – but who contributes from the sidelines in whatever way he is able, with the loving help of those who care about him

... who has never been considered "pretty" by conventional standards – but whose smile would melt the heart of even the most demanding judge

... who has never been excited about the choices that excite his friends – but who carves out his own pathway even if he has to travel much of it alone.

Just like those who have earned public awards and applause, these others are also our children, and their wellbeing depends on each of us. Our impact is greater than we might imagine – not only by virtue of what we say to them, but what we leave unsaid. The uncheered and unnoticed are listening for our song. The next time there's an opportunity for a hug, let them know how pleased we are with the person they have become.

All together now, a song for the unsung.

* * * * *

[84]

Hardening of the attitudes
June 27, 2004

When I was a child, Aunt Mary was our county's public health nurse. Occasionally, she made me feel important by letting me help with office jobs a child could handle. One day, she handed me a file labeled "Tuberculosis" and asked me to alphabetize its index cards.

Horrified, I discovered cards with the names of many of my relatives and friends. I kept this terrible discovery a secret until learning later these people were not tuberculosis victims, but had simply taken the screening test.

I kept another anxiety to myself when my parents sent me to the post office for a money order. I assumed we were so poor we were ordering money.

Children often harbor such distortions of reality. One little girl I know thought she'd die of cancer – having heard that was the astrological sign under which she was born.

Misconceptions – minor ones as misconceptions go – and not dangerous if we don't allow them to petrify into permanent false attitudes.

If they do, our ingrained misconceptions become adult prejudices and determine how we treat other people. How many of them do we harbor in our repertoire after we're well beyond childhood? What happens when we incorporate misconceptions into our basic belief system?

I read about a hospitalized paranoid patient who insisted he was a ghost. Therapy and medication hadn't helped, so his psychiatrist used logic. He asked the patient, "Do ghosts bleed?" And the patient answered, "Of course not." So the physician pricked the patient's finger and squeezed droplets of blood to the surface. The patient looked at his finger in amazement and exclaimed, "Well, what do you know! Ghosts do bleed!"

Maybe we don't cling quite that tenaciously to misconceptions, but we do tend to plug our ears to logic. We don't like being confused with facts when we've already made up our minds.

Just as we develop arthritic stiffness with age, there's the danger of developing concept rigidity as well. Oldsters often make gross generalizations about those under twenty. And, from personal observation, there's evidence that younger folks are sometimes subject to premature hardening of the attitudes.

Unfortunately, we oldsters run into young people who automatically consider us incompetent (and probably incontinent) on the basis of perceived age. They assume our gray hair is rooted in atrophied brain tissue. But we're not all headed for a nap. We're probably on our way to sky dive, install computer programs, repair our cars, or dance a jig.

I'd like those youngsters to realize that during senior years, our minds work faster than our legs, our sense of humor sparkles brighter than our eyes, our judgment is more reliable than our balance, and our politics less conservative than our shoes. And if they get too feisty, I'd remind them that old age and treachery often outwit youth and skill.

In the meantime, I'll schedule regular attitude checks of my own – just to be sure.

* * * * *

[85]

Those sweet three little words
July 25, 2004

If the sweetest three little words in our language are "I love you," second place surely goes to that unpopular trio, "I was wrong."

Earlier this year, I discovered a discrepancy on some financial documents sent to me in the mail. After puzzling over them for a while, I called the person responsible for compiling the information and asked for an explanation. She looked at my records and said, "It's my mistake. I was just plain wrong."

Quickly reviving myself, I asked, "You're sure it's not a misunderstanding, or a problem in communication, or a computer glitch?"

But she reiterated, "No, I was just wrong."

How refreshing!

We've somehow turned into a defensive society, quick to spew excuses, rationalize, or shift the blame to others. Are we no longer responsible for our own behavior? Are computers always to blame? Can a lawsuit absolve us of all our foibles?

Because of the irresponsible and litigious trend in our society, Stella Awards are given each year on line to those most clearly deserving. The awards are named after Stella L., age 81, who spilled hot coffee on herself and successfully sued McDonalds for her burns.

One of the 2003 awards was presented to a luckless man hit by lightning in the parking lot of an Ohio amusement park. While many of us naïve folk would dub this an act of God, the victim's attorney filed a suit against the amusement park. He claimed the park was remiss for not warning people to stay inside during a thunderstorm.

Kudos went also to a 270-pound New York City man who claimed to suffer from obesity, diabetes and heart disease because, as the complaint alleges, "fast food restaurants forced him to eat their fatty food four to five times a week." He filed suit against four of the major fast food chains for not having warned him that junk food wasn't good for him. This particular case got thrown out of court twice. But if the courts lighten up a bit, I'll have to consider filing suit against my good buddies Baskin, Robbins, Edy, Ben and Jerry.

As farfetched as these examples appear, we shake our heads and believe. Because most of us have witnessed litigation seemingly gone berserk closer to home.

I'm sorry to sound so blatantly old fashioned, but I still believe we're pretty much responsible for our own mistakes. Casting blame has become such a national pastime that competition for the Stella Awards is more intense than for the Oscars.

I'm personally inspired to establish an award to honor those folks with enough integrity to acknowledge errors when they goof and to accept personal responsibility for their own behavior.

I'm going to call it the Ashley Award in honor of her blessed three-little-word explanation: "I was wrong."

* * * * *

[86]

Writing styles and writing styles
August 22, 2004

Years ago, attending my first writers' conference, I accepted an invitation to attend the evening reception for a prominent visiting author. I spent considerable time that afternoon choosing an outfit that would exude competence and at the same time lavish proper respect upon our guest of honor.

I reluctantly submitted to a popular elastic monstrosity, known euphemistically as a panty girdle, and donned my classic black Sunday dress. I chose black heels high enough to impress onlookers but low enough to prevent a disastrous tumble. Other young women put on comparable outfits and we passed our mutual inspection with flying colors. We fairly reeked with equal parts literary confidence and cologne.

That evening, after an appropriate period of hors d'oeuvres and anticipation, we guests applauded The Famous Writer's entrance. But when she sauntered into the room, I teetered on my high heels in amazement! No elasticized sartorial splendor here! Our honoree wore a shapeless purple sweater, wrinkled plaid skirt, and sported white ankle socks beneath brown leather sandals. Her hair fell in terminal disarray around a face left entirely *au naturel*.

Obviously, I was not yet a real writer and had lots to learn about rules of the game.

I've done some thinking since that first encounter with the literary elite. Of course, I've conscientiously practiced writing. But in addition to developing my writing style, I've also worked to develop my writing outfit. Lounging at home and making brief sojourns into the larger world, I'm usually content to look like an ordinary person. But I feel obligated to assemble some stylish literary gear before my own inevitable public reception.

I've long since gotten rid of the panty girdle and little black dress and have decided, instead, to adopt a lean and hungry look accessorized with eccentric accents. For my public debut, I'll wear seriously snug black tights topped with a tee shirt that bears some obscure philosophical message. Two slender cigars will protrude slightly from the breast pocket of my tweed jacket. I'll wear a knitted red tam regardless of the season, and sport dangling beaded earrings. There's no decision to make about shoes, since upon researching the subject, I've learned ankle socks and sandals are mandatory.

I'm practicing something casual with my hair, though it takes hours to accomplish the exact disheveled aura I'm after. I've more successfully achieved the requisite distracted look – a look acknowledging that, although part of me appears to be present, most of me is on a park bench somewhere else – writing, brooding, sipping cappuccino.

Perhaps for practice I'll set up shop every morning at the back table of local coffee shop and jot literary inspirations on napkins. I'll audition my costume while alternately assuming pained and thoughtful expressions.

Since my Famous Writer reception isn't exactly scheduled yet, details are sketchy. All I know for sure is that young literary pretenders from across the nation will be there; and dress will be casual.

* * * * *

[87]

Hail to thee, our alma mommy
September 26, 2004

College students recently left the nest again to settle in for the school year… to settle into coed dorms with laptops, cell phones, and no parents. I promise not to reminisce about trudging to class through six-foot drifts of snow, but college in the 1950s on my small Methodist campus would qualify as prison to today's students.

We certainly didn't have coed dorms. No men were allowed beyond the dormitory lobby except for our resident "house father." An older student, his job was to protect us women from danger, to change light bulbs and kill scary bugs. When he came within shouting distance of our hallway, he hollered, "Man on floor," lest he find one of us in our bathrobe or less.

Our "house mother," a sixty-ish otherwise retired woman, served as our *in locus parentis*. She made and enforced rules, offered shoulders to cry on, and settled minor disputes.

And, yes, she punished for rule infractions.

Curfew tolled at 10 p.m. on weekdays and a bit later weekend evenings. A student monitor at the lobby desk made sure we signed out, telling where we were going, with whom, and when we'd return. If we signed in late, we were "dormed" – the equivalent of being grounded.

The housemother made weekly inspections of our rooms to make sure they were kept clean and the trash can emptied. I never understood why we couldn't have even two inches of trash in a two-foot tall trashcan, but protests got me nowhere.

One night each month we residents had what amounted to a family meeting. We gathered in our pajamas for a 10:30 dorm session at which time the housemother ordinarily brought up subjects like lint in the dryers or noise during quiet hours. But one night, the dean of women called an extra meeting herself and came clear across campus to discuss the horrifying ramifications of a condom being found in our parking lot. At that time, I was naïve beyond legal limits, even for the 50s. I'm hoping I didn't raise my hand to ask what a condom was. So let's pretend I didn't. I mostly remember wondering what those bad girls at the other end of the hall must be up to.

Guys and girls dressed up for dates rather than going out in grungies, and girls routinely stayed home one evening a week to wash their hair. We dressed in Sunday best for dinner in the dormitory dining hall each Wednesday evening and attended mandatory chapel services Wednesday mornings. And okay, I admit it – we had a May Pole dance in the spring.

Does all change qualify as progress? I suspect if colleges enforced that same set of rules today, adolescents would clamor to stay home. Were we somehow better off living the life of Beaver Cleaver? In retrospect, the rules were pretty formidable and I followed most of them. But you know what? I'm starting to think those bad girls down the hall had more fun.

* * * * *

[88/162]

The sick have their day
October 24, 2004
April 4, 2011

After decades of study, mathematicians finally came up with the definition of a split second. Previously, it was defined as the time it takes for impatient drivers behind us to honk their horns when traffic lights turn green. But no more.

A split second is now defined as the length of time it takes folks to begin talking about their own, or someone else's, ailment after we've mentioned ours.

A book of etiquette has been developed to prescribe acceptable behavior during this split second interval. Here's the gist of what it recommends.

The primary rule is that the first person to mention his ailment gets to be Impaired Person for that day. The rest of us bite our tongues even if it makes them bleed.

For example, if a friend tells us he's been kicked by a butterfly, we can speak nothing but words of sympathy even if during our morning shower we discovered we're growing a tail.

We avoid comments like, "You look awful," and refrain from mentioning that our uncle Joe had the same ailment, only worse, and he died from it.

If the designated victim of the day is lying in a hospital bed with both legs in casts and her head wrapped in bandages, we don't say, "Boy, you sure were lucky." She probably doesn't feel particularly lucky and may well come after us when she's back in fighting form.

It's tempting to tell her it could be much worse and advise her to count her blessings. But she doesn't care right now that other people are in worse shape than she, because she isn't vying for worst.

If our ailing friend is a concert violinist and laments that since he just lost three fingers he will no longer be able to play the violin, we don't tell him that as a child we took some violin lessons and still can't play Yankee Doodle. Although relatively subtle, the problem here is obvious, isn't it?

We don't give advice unless asked. Free advice, they say, is usually worth what one pays for it, and unless friends request it, they probably aren't listening anyway. It might not be the best time to share our family's remedy or offer samples of our prescription medications.

We don't whisper that their physician isn't the one we'd personally recommend since we've heard gossip about his marital problems.

And unless we're certified as All-Knowing, we don't tell them God doesn't give people burdens they can't handle. Because, apparently, sometimes He does. And, finally, we don't tell them their ailment happened for some cosmic reason. Because perhaps it didn't.

Obviously, this new definition of a split second is not only a mathematical breakthrough but also a test of character. If we can't say something helpful during that crucial split second interval, maybe we should, literally, bite our tongue. Hard. Then, when it's our day to be Impaired Person, we can talk about how much it hurt.

* * * * *

[89]

Remember your power
Nov. 28, 2004

While attending my first year of graduate school, I rented a room in the home of an elderly widow. Technically, my monthly payment covered just a bedroom, but Mrs. G. allowed me kitchen privileges and invited me to watch television with her in the living room.

One particular evening, we chose to watch the biography of Joan of Arc. We sat together through Joan's childhood, her visions, the country's political/religious struggles and, finally, reached the story's climactic scene. But just as some French official leaned in to light the pyre beneath Joan's feet, Mrs. G. got up and shut the television set off. Startled, I asked why she had done that. And I've remembered her simple answer all these years.

"Too intense," she said. "Too intense."

Luckily, I already knew the story's ending because I was in no position to bargain.

But I think now, in retrospect, Mrs. G. was on to something.

Few folks dispute the idea that foods we allow into our bodies leave their indelible mark. I'm equally convinced that music and other stimuli we allow into our brains affect our level of tranquility and our behavior. To paraphrase another's observation, we each have within us both a serene and a frantic animal. The one that thrives is the one we feed.

All of which brings us back to Joan and her aborted television appearance.

Regardless of what researchers might discover, television has to affect children and adults as well – our moods, our range of interest, and our behavior. Parents often lament their children watch too many hours of television. I'm no electrical engineer, but all on my own discovered that the little button that turns the set on will also turn it off.

We need to keep one finger on that button for the children's sake, if not our own.

I think the reason I've remembered Mrs. G's comment so long is because of the infinite, imaginative possibilities. How amazing it would be to be able to neutralize difficult times in our lives by declaring, "Too intense." At which point we simply shut them off. We could zap the angry person shouting at us, switch off threats of illness, and do away with worries about situations over which we have no control. And, certainly, we'd not have to watch anyone being burned at the stake.

Even the most casual observer can sense just by standing on a street corner that the world's dial is set on "frantic." So why do we add to our internal chaos with television and movie fare of cop chases, burning buildings, hospital emergencies and mass murders?

Before someone shakes a knowing finger, I confess to watching far more than a healthy portion of shoot-'em-up television. I'm even traumatized by the evening news.

But sometimes I look over my shoulder for Mrs. G. Although probably wielding a remote control by now, she'd click that little black "off" button and rescue me from mayhem again.

* * * * *

[90]

Who's who and who isn't
Dec. 26, 2004

I can't help it. I keep thinking about the Sneetches. You might remember those Dr. Seuss creatures who established a hierarchy defining which Sneetches were more worthy than the rest of the Sneetches.

According to their guidelines, those who had bellies with stars outclassed the Sneetches "with none upon thars."

You'll have to re-read the story if you don't remember all the complications and confusions that resulted from trying to keep their discriminations straight. But if you don't have the book handy, just grab a history book instead. Not the Sneetch history book, but our own.

As a nation, we've gone through a changing list of Who's Inferior and are still revising it. If we're as confident and comfortable in our own skins as we profess, why do we always have to elect some group as second-class citizens? Or worse, to decide that the planet isn't big enough for both of us?

Back in the 1850s there were supposedly "scientific and biblical" justifications for slavery. In the early 1900s, opponents of women's rights spouted "scientific and biblical" reasons why women should stay home and be denied the vote. As recently as the 1950s we heard speeches about the "scientific and biblical" reasons to preserve racial segregation.

Now, years later, we've wised up to the inequity and inhumanity of slavery, have encouraged women to participate in the workplace and have accorded them equal voting rights. Segregation is outlawed. We not only pride ourselves on our own inclusiveness and freedom, but spend a fortune in lives and dollars to spread these values abroad. For better or for worse, we've become internationally known as fighters for the underdog.

But here at home, it's business as usual. We're still bombarded with the "scientific and biblical" reasons that gays are inferior and their lifestyle damaging to the moral fiber of our country. How long do we have to wait for this prejudice and discrimination to go the way of all the others? Just four more years?

Of course, acceptance and equality don't happen all at once – either here or elsewhere. Some in the majority group are true believers and work for genuine equality while others mouth the right words in public and know when to keep quiet. As a nation, we still struggle with what to do about the elderly, the handicapped, the poor, ethnic minorities, and the mentally ill. Where do we put them in the hierarchy of human value?

Strange. One would think that believing in God would relieve us of playing God ourselves. Go figure.

Only the most arrogant of Sneetches would claim to know why, in all our diversity, we are put on earth in the first place. But since we're here together, it might be best to forget about stars on the belly and help each other through life with all the kindness we can muster.

Then we'd have not only a happy new year but a happy new era.

* * * * *

[91]

You can quote me on that
January 30, 2005

"Never sleep with anyone crazier than you are, and never eat anything bigger than your head." No doubt about it, that's good advice.

I wouldn't have risked spouting quotations right now, but 2005 is steaming ahead, and it's already late to be sharing wisdom for the new year. Fortunately, I've collected life-altering quotations since high school and have five hand-written notebooks full. The quotes were gleaned from bumper stickers, television shows, books, friends, and legitimate gurus. Thus, with some trepidation, I undertake the task of illuminating the unilluminated.

Sadly, some purists turn up their noses at quotations. I believe it was the venerable Mark Twain who dubbed quotations "the literature of the illiterate." But, ironically, I bet he'd be pleased to know I'm quoting him.

On bad days, when I can't readily remember my phone number or birth date, I can still recite hundreds of quotations. Mercifully, I don't recite out loud every time one comes to mind.

So, scoffers notwithstanding, pithy aphorisms frequently stick in our minds and remind us of underlying truths. Although I can't usually cite the authors, their wisdom is scrawled like graffiti on my brain.

For example, guess who saw me through diet and exercise when motivation lagged. It was some anonymous guru who asked, "If you don't take care of your body, where are you going to live?"

In tough times, flashing red graffiti reminds me "This too shall pass."

And the antidote for regret? "The past is past and cannot be changed."

If I'm about to make the same mistake I made last week, a knowing voice scolds, "If you do what you've always done, you'll get what you've always gotten."

If someone makes a habit of treating me badly, I eventually recall another bit of terse advice. "When someone shows you the truth about themselves, believe them the first time." And how can we sort good guys from bad? "The best measure of the greatness of a man is his willingness to be kind."

Theology needn't be long-winded either. Gandhi is credited with telling us "If you don't see God in the next person you meet, it's a waste of time to look for Him further."

Maybe, as cynics claim, "if we can put our philosophy of life in a nutshell, that's where it belongs." And, obviously, simple quotations don't cover any subject in depth. Their job is to provide mental shortcuts to ageless truths.

My notebooks, reviewed chronologically, also serve as a diary. The progression of quotations reveals changes in my sense of humor, spiritual growth and values... a trek from stodgy adolescent to salty old woman.

The most recent notebook addition comes from a recurring internet missive and is my final illumination for 2005. "Life is not a journey to the grave with the intention of arriving safely in a pretty and well-preserved body, but rather to skid in broadside, thoroughly used up, totally worn out, and loudly proclaiming, 'WOW what a ride!'"

Happy New Year.

* * * * *

[92]

Sleep: don't let it keep you up
February 27, 2005

Pulling the bed covers over my head to extend nighttime just a little longer, I think of those icons of industry who make the rest of us look lazy.

Thomas Jefferson didn't require eight regular hours of sleep. He worked several days in a row and caught up on sleep later – sometimes sleeping as long as thirty-six hours straight.

Boris Yeltsin slept just four hours a night, got up at 5:00 a.m., read contemporary literature for two hours, then did his morning exercises.

The *Book of Lists* cites others who shorted themselves on sleep. Comedian David Brenner did the math, figuring if he slept only four hours a night, he could bank 1, 456 hours a year.

In view of the blessing of sleep, insomnia must be one of those hells on earth. The list of well known insomniacs includes Marlene Dietrich, Judy Garland, W.C. Fields, Groucho Marx, Mark Twain, and Teddy Roosevelt. Mr. Roosevelt is said to have alleviated his affliction with a shot of cognac in milk.

Most amazing of all, Tomas Izquierdo, a Cuban born in the 1930s, reportedly hasn't slept since World War II. A surgical trauma left him with nightmares so severe he prefers staying awake. He is known in his hometown as "Tomas who doesn't sleep."

Meanwhile, back on the Beauty Rest, most of us sleep away an average of twenty-five years during a lifetime. As we grow old, we're said to need less sleep and we sleep less soundly. To make up for this, our biological clocks allow more naps.

I don't particularly subscribe to the nap theory, but do notice that my recliner, in its old age, occasionally insists upon an afternoon snooze with me in it. With winter upon us, the urge to hibernate rears its sleepy head regardless of the chair.

It used to be, for example, when we pulled out a fluffy pillow after lunch to rest at our workplace, someone wrote us up in the personnel file for goofing off. But now, empathetic executives sometimes promote those brief respites to the status of power naps and they're actually being encouraged at a few nurturing job sites.

As for insomnia, someone rightly suggested it isn't a problem unless we care. So if we don't have to set a morning alarm and are content to read, iron clothes, or practice our trumpet at 2:00 a.m., we can snore to the tick of our erratic internal clock without suffering any dire consequences.

Scientists have long studied the nature of sleep. I don't dwell too long on the scientific explanation and would rather consider sleep a mysterious blessing.

Sir Philip Sidney gets as scientific as I like when he writes, "Sleep, the certain knot of peace, the baiting-place of wit, the balm of woe, the poor man's wealth, the prisoner's release, the indifferent judge between the high and low… "

Lured once again into the recliner, my last waking thought extends heart-felt sympathy to that icon of insomnia, "Tomas who doesn't sleep."

* * * * *

[93]

We all play the waiting game
March 27, 2005

"So," they sometimes ask impatiently, "what are you waiting for?"

If we dare begin a list, it soon becomes obvious we spend a generous portion of our lives just waiting. We wait for spring, mail, test results, weekends, promotions, payday, visitors, tax returns, rain, holidays, bedtime and phone calls. We wait for our ship to come in, the other shoe to drop, the pot to boil, the dough to rise, or the apocalypse. A few diehard intellectuals are still waiting for Godot.

Our moods vary, of course, depending on what we're waiting for. Are we bored? Excited? Eager? Afraid?

And we wait absolutely everywhere. Airports are constructed with the sole purpose of catering to waiters, as have the multitude of aptly named waiting rooms in office buildings and medical facilities. We bide our time in line at movie theaters and concert halls, in school gymnasiums, in traffic, and at checkout counters.

You'd think with all this practice, we'd get good at it, but, somehow, the experience hasn't made us much more patient. We're willing to wait a maximum of two minutes for a hamburger, two for a traffic light, and ten seconds for a computer download.

A couple truths become obvious.

First of all, it's increasingly clear that time is fickle. Rather than proceeding at a predictable ticking pace, it slows down or speeds ahead depending on what we're waiting for. Even with no knowledge of physics, we come to believe in the relativity of time. If we're awaiting execution, hands on the clock virtually spin. Or so they tell me. Those same hands drag slowly around the clock face when we anticipate Saturday respites after long frustrating work weeks. And is there any longer wait than waiting for a loved one to return home?

Henry Van Dyke wrote, "Time is too slow for those who wait, too swift for those who fear, too long for those who grieve, too short for those who rejoice... "

And secondly, if we're always busy waiting for something, what becomes of now? Anticipation is harmless, even invigorating, unless we somehow miss out on life in the process. Regardless of what we wait for and how unfulfilled we feel until that event comes to pass, the single moment at hand is absolutely the only one we have at our disposal.

A wise man once compared the present to the thinness of a knife blade – the past already gone and the future forever elusive. Now is the only time available to us.

So while we're busy waiting, what do we do with those moments, hours, days?

In our impatience and eagerness, we sometimes feel as though we're spending life in a gigantic waiting room. And perhaps we are, in more ways than one. But while we're waiting for whatever comes next, maybe we should relax, count our blessings, and enjoy the piped in music. Or, when all else fails, find a way to compose our own.

* * * * *

[94]

Are there any volunteers?
May 1, 2005

I've delayed writing this column for a long time because of the possible response. So if you read it, vow not to contact me with offers.

The subject is volunteerism, and heaven knows, I've tried.

I'd checked my deodorant, practiced smiling in front of the mirror, brushed up my resume and honed my interview skills, but nothing helped. Let me share some of my attempts to volunteer over the years, right here in Topeka town. Names have been omitted to protect us both.

I wrote a letter to one local organization offering to teach parent workshops to their clients for free and outlined my credentials, having taught such workshops for over twenty years. They did not respond.

I offered to read to young students after a teacher made the request, but subsequently was not invited. I offered to make a presentation to a class of high school students on a timely subject, and the teacher apparently forgot we had discussed it.

I responded to one social service agency's request to help organize an office, but when I got there learned the employee didn't want her office organized. Only her supervisor did. So they decided to put me on call for future projects. They haven't called.

Another organization advertised for someone to write a monthly article for its newsletter. When I applied, they said the job had been taken, but they had another writing position and would call me back. They didn't.

I volunteered to teach a community writing workshop for children at no charge to anyone. No one enrolled.

I signed up at another prominent agency and, after they interviewed me and read my credentials the interviewer said, "You have so many skills we'll save you for something special." That was about four years ago and I haven't yet heard. Something special might be turning up any day now.

Saddest of all, the blood bank won't even take my blood anymore.

Someone of a more humble nature might take these rejections personally. But I've shored up my self-esteem and have since succeeded in finding a couple niches where my talents can meet someone else's need. Of course, I speak my rejection truths with tongue in cheek because I know there are multiple openings for agency volunteers in the community – many of which would probably accept even me. But the rejection situation got to be so amusing I started keeping my list.

I thought about the Boy Scout so eager to do good deeds that he insisted on helping elderly women across the street when they didn't want to go. I hated, however, to force myself on anyone.

As I advised at the outset, don't contact me. I'm already busy. Certainly I'm bold enough to have pursued all of those lost opportunities further. But I'd remind agencies to stay acutely alert to those who raise their hands to volunteer. Some of them may be too short to be seen over the crowd or too timid to ask twice.

* * * * *

[95]

We learn to bend in the wind
June 7, 2005

Just as others remember exactly where they were when they heard of Kennedy's assassination, I have total recall for the moments I first heard about microwave ovens and VCRs. I scoffed, warning the teller of microwave tales that those ovens would poison us, and told the VCR messenger there weren't any TV shows worth seeing twice. So why record them?

It's all about change. Although we're used to changing clothes, lanes, jobs and flat tires, we're slower to change our habits and our minds to acknowledge shifts in life. It may actually be true that the only person who genuinely welcomes change is a wet baby. We hunker down into inertia and chant, "If it ain't broke, don't fix it," but we usually discover the world won't wait for our approval to move on.

Many years ago I vowed to relocate to the moon if ever required to learn the computer or metric system. Metrics still elude me, but I'm on good terms with computers now and mastered those VCRs and microwave ovens as well as ATM machines, online banking, answering machines, debit cards, self-checkout at the grocery store and Ebay.

Alphonse Karr is credited with saying that nothing is permanent except change. He might be right.

Sometimes we get to choose whether to accept innovations and sometimes they are forced on us. To make matters worse, while we're busy adapting (or not) to changes in our personal universe, the world offers up changes in the ozone layer, wars and rumors of wars, terrorism alerts, floods, famines, political intrigue and morality issues.

We often feel powerless in the face of these developments and rightly refuse to view all change as progress. Often, we quietly acquiesce. Sometimes we decide to fight the good fight, tilting at Don Quixote's windmills.

But even when change is indicative of genuine progress, it's hard work. How do we manage the shift comfortably?

Kansas offers the perfect analogy on windy days.

When I first moved here, forty- and fifty-mile wind gusts proved a bit intimidating. Watching and listening from the shelter of home was scary enough, but caught outside in traffic was worse. I remember pulling up to an intersection in my car, momentarily held captive by the red traffic light, watching it swing back and forth above me on poles that swayed rhythmically in the wind. When the light finally turned green, I was relieved to get out of that intersection, having expected the poles to crack and the lights to crash down on the car with me in it.

Of course there was no crash. As I learned later, the poles are designed to sway with the wind and would, indeed, have cracked and crashed had they been rigid rather than flexible.

In our personal lives and in the larger world, crises often impose changes that appear insurmountable. But as someone recently reminded me, change doesn't mean life's over. It means it's altered.

Poles and people. Bend or break.

* * * * *

[96]

Men can let it all hang out
June 28, 2005

Inequality of the sexes rears its shameless head in the strangest places. And though I'm not a strident feminist, a recent realization inspired me to take action.

Wanting to remain objective, I painstakingly researched this question: What do people do when they develop a stomach, gut, paunch, or just plain belly that has to be toted around with them? Without any preconceived notions, I systematically observed subjects in malls, restaurants, and concert halls. When I computed the data, sexual differences in adopting a solution became all too obvious.

My statistics reveal that healthily bellied women resort to elastic bands in their slacks, leave shirttails hanging out and occasionally succumb to temptation by purchasing maternity pants with those expanding belly pouches. As a matter of fact, there's never been a socially acceptable excuse for female abdominal bulges except pregnancy. A group of us recently lobbied for the return of muumuus but, alas, the fashion industry remained unimpressed.

Men, on the other hand, obviously (very obviously) have adopted a universal solution. Pretending nothing has changed since high school, men wear the same pant size all their adult lives simply by shifting their belt further south if a paunch appears. The belt fastens below the belly and, above the buckle is a tightly stretched tucked in shirt, hiding what looks like some great surprise. It's become the norm – a practice so widespread it rarely receives comment. Society nods approval by its silence. If women adopted that solution, we'd quickly be apprehended by the decency police or fashion patrol.

It's entirely possible there are physiological reasons for men's lowering their belts. Perhaps pulling their pants up to the waist would result in wedgies or worse. If so, I really don't want to hear about it, but trouser designers should take the idea and fly with it.

Don't get me wrong. This diatribe isn't criticism. It's sheer jealousy. I confess to having experimented, lowering my belt in the privacy of my own boudoir, letting the pant waistband nestle beneath the belly and rest on the hips. That moment of emancipation far surpassed the thrill when, years earlier, I abandoned high heels, panty hose and girdles.

Fashionable young women have recently begun wearing low-cut slacks that expose their navels. Is this the modest start of a downward trend? Are they on to something? Kathryn Hepburn defied tradition by making slacks her trademark outfit long before it was considered fashionably correct. It caught on and is here to stay.

Who, I wonder, was the male pioneer who first lowered the bar? Surely there's a memorial to him somewhere. I'm convinced that's precisely what we women need – a leader, a hero. Some courageous female who dares drop her belt beneath her belly and go public.

Maybe we'll schedule a specific day for Everywoman to let it all hang out – a national awareness, fairness day. I'm much too cowardly to lead the parade, but I'll definitely be there.

* * * * *

[97]

Silliness needs no reason
July 26, 2005

One evening this May, I answered the doorbell to find six smiling teenage girls on my porch. I knew none of them. With no motivation except silliness, they sang a Christmas carol, then left as anonymously as they arrived.

I hope they don't lose that spirit.

How often as children did we hear adults admonish, "Don't be silly?"

Some of us obeyed but, fortunately, some of us didn't.

Recently at a backyard party attended mostly by over-sixties, I asked folks to share their silliness escapades. Without further prompting, one spirited lady performed her rendition of "Shuffle Off to Buffalo." Another guest demonstrated a silly walk he enjoys performing on public sidewalks. A 72-year-old grandmother confessed she'd recently turned somersaults for her grandchildren. The king of silliness himself performed R-rated tricks with a table napkin.

I personally know of otherwise respectable old people, in otherwise respectable restaurants, who entertain themselves at the table by hanging spoons from their faces.

A younger friend pretended to be Swedish, complete with the accent, while shopping at the mall. Another, a professor, wore an ape costume into his classroom and tossed bananas to the students.

A Colorado peer tells me she once took her daughters on a spontaneous chocolate tasting spree. They bought boxes of chocolate of every variety and ate all of it.

A decidedly free spirit in Virginia engaged in unauthorized preaching from a stump at the entrance of Jerry Falwell's Liberty University. His twenty-minute raving about the next-to-last days drew little attention, in spite of the fact he was wearing a Christmas toboggan hat.

Happily, I'm not immune to the silliness bug.

A fortyish friend who is my frequent partner in spontaneous silly pursuits, sat with me on Santa's vacated couch at the mall, hoping to entice shoppers to sit on our laps. On another outing I found myself pushing her around the aisles of a department store in a shopping cart.

But there's more to be done. I smile when I think of the fellow who periodically walks up to a stranger and somberly announces, "My uncle used to work for the telephone company." I've got that escapade on my to-do list.

Silliness has no purpose except to be. And yet, it's among the most precious of attributes and is important to emotional survival. It hurts no one and brings perspective and humor to the world. Besides, it's cheaper than therapy. I worry about those who never do anything silly. It makes me want to muss up their hair and holler, "Tag! You're it!"

Someone said a good friend is one who will bail you out of jail, but that a super good friend will be sitting beside you in the cell, exclaiming, "Dang, that was fun!"

Although authentic silliness doesn't usually land us in jail, I wish us all a streak of silliness and a flock of certified silly friends.

* * * * *

[98]

Home is gateway to the world
August 23, 2005

As summer draws to a close, I'm expected to report on my vacation travels. Is this a joke?

If you want to hear about the Taj Mahal, Grand Canyon, or Great Wall of China, you'll have to ask someone else.

You might consider asking someone who's periodically traveled out of the country – or the state, or the county; someone who leaves her street more frequently than I; someone who takes photographs, fills shelves with souvenirs, and enjoys a personal relationship with AAA. I've never complained about my passport photo, because it's never left its case.

You might think I'd be miserable under such self-imposed confinement. But unlike involuntary stay-at-homes, I'm not the least bit jealous of travelers. Gadabouts will never understand my contentment nor even imagine all the interesting places I've been without benefit of visa, plane tickets, Dramamine or luggage. I'm simply not as geographically limited as folks may think.

Where have I been, you ask with feigned interest? Well, lots of places.

Without ever leaving my doorstep and with tongue firmly in cheek, I have been out on a limb, behind the eight ball, on top of the world, at the end of my rope, up a creek, down in the dumps, and sometimes out of my mind. I have crawled beneath contempt and at times soared above reproach. I have gotten lost in thought and ventured out of my element. I've been known to spend time under the weather or, on a particularly busy day, have been beside myself or got ahead of myself.

Sometimes I loiter a few days between a rock and a hard place or visit the point of no return. Occasionally I lag behind the times or dash beyond the call of duty.

I've spent months in the State of Tranquility, weeks in the State of Confusion, and enviable days in the State of Arousal. I take short trips right up my alley, but have also endured longer treks to Hell and back.

It's challenging, if not impossible, to take pictures of those exotic places. Travel agencies provide no brochures and no one has yet captured the settings on post cards. Such trips don't make good fodder for holiday letters to relatives so, instead, I resort to boasting about my dog's new tricks, exaggerating the extremes of Kansas weather and bemoaning election results.

Many agree with Thomas Fuller who proclaimed, "He that travels far knows much."

But my ancient friend Lao Tse said, "A man may know the world without leaving his own home. From his window he can see the supreme Heaven... "

So when I meet folks who have also limited their travels to my kind of unadvertised touristy spots, we nod in quiet understanding and settle in to watch our friends' vacation videos. You know, videos taken in Colorado, Africa, Egypt, and France.

Places like that.

$$* * * * *$$

[99]

More than sheepskin required
September 27, 2005

Last month, ABC news anchor Peter Jennings died of lung cancer.

Accolades appeared in television, radio and newspaper reports, with surely more to emerge as broadcasting history writes itself.

He will be remembered for coverage of the Vietnam War, the fall of the Berlin Wall and terrorist attacks of September 11, as well as for his daily reports of less spectacular national and international news.

In reading details of Jennings' biography, I was struck by the number of his awards and achievements, but even more so by what wasn't listed there.

As it turns out, Jennings hadn't attended college. But wait – there's more. He hadn't graduated from high school. Without much imagination, one can picture this bright, articulate, handsome, sophisticated man dressed in academic robes, standing on the steps of an Ivy League library or teaching classes there.

But instead of pursuing a formal education, Jennings had pursued his passion, surely having no idea himself of the success he would achieve against all odds.

I certainly don't dismiss the value of formal education. I like the idea of my surgeon having studied the Scalpel Manual and my French instructor being taught the language before teaching it. I even went to school several years myself.

But I'm wondering what would happen to a young Jennings in today's work world.

We regularly hear about the high school dropout rate, and stay-in-school promotions warn dropouts that they'll earn forty-two percent less during their lifetime than will graduates. Government agencies and large companies often require applicants to have a college diploma to be considered for a position. Aware of that requirement, many students seek "that piece of paper" with little passion or direction.

But what happens to the adolescent who doesn't finish high school or the older adult who didn't attend college? Perhaps they didn't fit the formal education mold or lacked resources and support to attend. But many have the intelligence, heart, creativity, and passion to make a meaningful mark in the world. And perhaps their mark could be made without college algebra or knowing the capital of Afghanistan.

In Jennings' case, it's said that his career took off when he "was noticed by" some executive of a fledgling television network.

Are there employers today who glance up from the formal resume to look for sparkle in an applicant's eye? Do they appreciate the contributions someone who lives "outside the box" could make to their organization? Can they find ways to give extra credit points for life experiences and solid character?

Like Jennings, in order to thrive, we all need someone who notices. To potential employers I'd say, "Sure, it helps if an applicant sports an academic gown and carries a pouch full of sheep skins. But look first for the passion."

* * * * *

[100]

The view from my mountaintop
Oct. 25, 2005

This is my 100th column. A conversation with friends inspired me to mark the occasion by listing some of the guidelines I try to live by. I offer my list from this virtual mountaintop, sparing truth-seekers the steep climb. I also offer it as a challenge for readers to consider compiling their own lists. A skeptic once said, "If you can put your philosophy of life in a nutshell, that's where it belongs." Here's mine anyway, its tenets in no special order.

- Adopt as the central fact of life that you won't be here on earth forever. This awareness will influence your choices and your attitude.
- Develop honesty with yourself and others, about how you feel, what you need, and how you live your life. Never be afraid of what you discover about yourself. Embrace it. Then you'll be free to change whatever you aren't pleased with.
- Be kind.
- We're all more alike than different. Where differences do arise, respect and protect them. Honor diverse gifts. There is no one to envy or idolize and no one to whom you should feel superior.
- Recognize what money can and can't buy – the good and harm it can do.
- Keep learning. Don't be afraid to try something new. Enjoy doing it badly.
- The past is past and cannot be changed. Not with tears, argument, anger, or prayer. Acceptance of this fact is the beginning of forgiveness and foundation for moving on. Learn from the past, then let it go.
- Cherish friends and family and don't give up on them.
- Remember that you remain in control of your attitude even when you lose control of other aspects of your life... things like your driver's license, your home, your loved ones, your health, your wealth.
- Laughter and tears are the best medicines. Laugh especially at yourself because there's probably no one funnier. Take your work seriously without taking yourself too seriously.
- Love.
- In times of difficulty, remember that this, too, shall pass.

- Take care of your body or you'll have no comfortable place to live.
- Leave everything a little better than you find it.
- Be thankful.
- Don't worry much about what other people think about you. It doesn't often matter, and they usually aren't spending much time thinking about you anyway.
- Allow yourself to believe in a higher power. Name it if you like, whatever you choose. Then pursue it through life's twists and turns until it catches you.

Now, all that being said, hustle back down the mountain and write your own list.

* * * * *

[101]

Beyond the turkey and gravy
November 27, 2005

Browsers and buyers passed through the narrow aisles of the July craft show. The huge gymnasium was hot and, since tiny fans high in the vaulted ceiling offered no relief, most shoppers hurried about their business, eager to get outside again. One person began blending into the next and there was little sense of joy.

The sterile mood was broken by the voice of a child saying, "Look, mama, look!" I turned to see a slender, blond boy about four years old. He had paused in the aisle and, with wonder in his eyes, pointed to the ceiling. Those around him stopped to see what he had discovered.

High in the rafters, at the opposite end of the gymnasium, was a green balloon. It had been stuck there all morning. As we focused on the balloon and shared for a moment in the boy's pleasure, the balloon mysteriously started traveling slowly across the giant room. It stayed at ceiling height until it reached our end of the gymnasium, then drifted downward across the bleacher section, then across three rows of craft booths, and floated directly to the little boy.

It hung in front of him, its string dangling below, while bystanders looked on in amazement. Too stunned to respond, the child neither spoke nor moved. Someone shouted, "Grab it!" and I heard myself urging more quietly, "You can have it. It's yours."

He reached out to claim his prize, grasped the string, and resumed his walk down the aisle. Boy and balloon were rescued from the heat and tedium of the day. And for a moment, so were we all.

Yes, the story is true.

Beyond the turkey and in spite of the world's bad news, Thanksgiving week seems an appropriate time to express gratitude for myriad miracles surrounding us.

Of course, if we refuse to declare a miracle until our tap water turns into wine or our parakeet rises from the dead, we could have long wait. But if we pause long enough and quietly enough, we recognize the smaller miracles on our path. Sometimes we write them off as coincidences, but even those have been defined as God's way of staying anonymous.

Among those unheralded miracles? The way a spider's delicate web remains undisturbed during winds so strong that chairs are blown off the porch. The intricate design we discover when we slice through a carrot. The way broken bones mend and the way our bodies go to sleep when we need rest. The way we sometimes make eye contact with a total stranger but experience a brief connection that is ages deep.

Cynics won't be impressed and could even write off the balloon episode as a function of room temperature and airflow. But then, they didn't see the little boy's face.

Maybe in our hectic lives and in the face of so much tragic news, just noticing is a miracle.

* * * * *

[102]

The man in the truck
December 27, 2005

I grew up in a tiny Ohio county seat that sported a classic village square. Its grassy park area hosted a cannon, gazebo bandstand and iron hitching posts. The cannon wasn't functional, the bandstand stood empty, and cars had eventually replaced horses.

We citizens were a homogeneous lot and most of us knew each other. There were a few we dubbed rich, but it was largely a town of middle- and lower-class neighbors. Our WASP-ish population included a few Catholics, one black family, a retarded child, and a woman who dressed like a man. It was otherwise a sheltered, simplistic corner of the world. It was easy for us to assume nothing existed beyond the city limits and, if it did, it would be another town filled with people just like us.

One day when I was ten years old, I had been sent on an errand to the post office. Heading home with my mission accomplished, I stopped at the square, waiting to cross the street.

176

I casually glanced up as a truck passed in front of me. I looked at the unfamiliar driver who neither noticed me nor looked in my direction. But I quickly caught my breath with an insight so profound that the moment lodged in memory.

"That man has a life of his own," I realized. "He is going somewhere I don't know about, has a family I haven't met, and has ideas and wishes that may be different than mine. He is just as important to him as I am to me."

There was no formal ceremony, but that startling incident served as my initiation into the human race. I didn't tell anyone about what happened on that corner. I tucked the memory away with other revelations about wars and flowers and evil – revelations grownups might not have understood.

Membership dues in the new club were surprisingly high. I couldn't be an enthusiastic booster of our school sports teams. I understood why our team would like to win its game, but I knew how badly the other team would like to win, too. I was a Protestant but sensed how deeply the Catholics must have felt about their own faith, since I cherished mine. Membership stood in the way of being a zealot. It made me cry for the enemy who had been wiped out by "our side" and made it difficult to hate those who were supposed to be hated. How could I take an assertive stand of "Us against Them" when all of Us were One?

Looking back to that peaceful town square, the revelation of humankind's oneness seems a trifle heavy for a little girl. It's a trifle heavy for a big girl, too. My childhood village and its simplicity are distant now. But I have since tried to glance up at corners in order to stay in touch with that man in the truck.

Trying even harder is my New Year's resolution.

* * * * *

[103/169]

Taking it with me
January 24, 2006
April 30, 2012

Archaeologists recently uncovered mummies in the deserts of Peru. They discovered that along with each body, mourners had buried items their dear departed would need in the afterlife. Among these were food, bowls, and skulls of sacrificial llamas.

It's always something. I'd already written my will and signed powers of attorney. But none of these documents asked what I wanted buried with me. The idea of packing for the trip is intriguing since I'd previously been led to believe I couldn't take it with me. Since we can't know for sure whether the afterlife provides every necessity, it can't hurt to be circumspect.

Consequently, I've been compiling a supply list to file with other important documents. Reserving the right to modify my packing list at any time, here's how it stands right now.

I want my eyeglasses. After waiting and wondering for decades, I want to see the afterlife in focus. And pack my digital camera. Given an imaginative bent and tendency to exaggerate, no one would believe what I'd seen if I didn't have pictures to prove it.

Include lots of pencils, pens, and paper. These are survival tools and I might be asked to write a column for the Celestial Times. I'll also need a thesaurus and dictionary. Can you imagine the torture of spending an eternity wondering what syzygy means or trying to think of a synonym for ethereal?

I am concerned when I recall the suicide of a group of Heaven Gates cult members who each was prepared with a bag full of quarters. I've always wondered if they were expecting to find slot machine and pay phones in the afterlife.

There are also some intentional omissions from my list. I plan to pack light since, if the next life is anything like this one, the more one accumulates the more one has to take care of. First of all, I'm hoping there's no need for sacrificial llama skulls, so don't bother arranging for those.

Secondly, I'm omitting food items. They're perishable. Besides, if there's anything I know for sure, it's that there will be unlimited milk, honey and manna. I'm planning to order ahead for ice cream.

For sure, I'm taking no clocks or mobile phones. I've seen enough of both for this lifetime and the next.

It might be politically correct to request that a Bible be packed with my stuff, but whatever reference turns out to be the Holy Book of Choice, there will be one in each nightstand. Besides, if I have questions, I can ask the authors in person.

And, mourners, just for fun, please devise some hoax to put in my casket – maybe a message written in gibberish for future archaeologists to puzzle over when they carbon-date my remains. Sure. Cynical friends will sneak a fan and cold drinks into the casket in case it's exceedingly warm where I'm going. But that's what friends are for.

* * * * *

[104]

When it walks like a duck
February 28, 2006

On a recent chilly evening, I was walking my usual route when the usual dog barked at me from behind the usual wooden fence. Since he was one of those hyperactive yippy breeds his noise could scarcely be called barking, but it never failed to startle me.

He had enjoyed this game with passersby often enough that he had pawed a hole beneath the fence and was able to poke his furry white head out and watch his victims jump. It obviously wouldn't take many more nights for his whole body to make the grand escape – possibly to nip some heels.

More for my own protection than his, I walked around the corner into the homeowner's front yard, hoping to find something to block the hole. Sure enough, there was a pile of decorative rocks around the base of a newly planted tree. I chose a large rectangular one that might best fit and headed out of the yard toward the sidewalk.

At that exact moment, headlights beamed on me and my path. The homeowner had pulled into his driveway and caught me red handed. I was wearing a dark hooded jacket popular with perpetrators on cop shows and knew immediately the jury would consider my rock to be smoking gun evidence.

But first I had to deal with the man driving the truck. I could already see through the windshield that he was a big guy and that he wore military fatigues. A young boy accompanied him and probably would be called to the stand as witness for the prosecution.

But when the driver-homeowner got out, he faced me on the sidewalk and posed a question I will not forget.

He simply asked, "Did I miss something?"

Amazing! Instead of adding up the apparent evidence and making a judgment, he first considered the possibility that he didn't yet have all the information; and he was asking me to fill in the blanks. In spite of my dark hooded jacket, this stranger gave me the benefit of the doubt rather than assuming I was stealing rocks to finish my patio.

Since his approach made me feel like neither a criminal nor crazy person, my explanation came easily. He thanked me and took the rock around the corner to block the hole.

Since then I've wondered where he learned that question and the attitude it conveys. Did he first hear it when his mother found him spray-painting the cat or wearing muddy cowboy boots to bed? And has he already passed the question on to his lucky young son?

I smile each time I think of the incident. We're often so quick to judge, thinking the worst of others and jumping to conclusions. In both personal encounters and those in the wider world, we don't routinely stop to gather facts.

If it looks like a duck, walks like a duck and quacks like a duck, does it absolutely have to be a duck?

Or could we have missed something?

* * * * *

[105]

People who live in class houses
March 28, 2006

A friend and I have a running argument. Although we try to avoid the subject, it pops up periodically when I say something like, "What an outrageously pretentious house!" or "Who would ever pay $100 for dinner?" Her predictable retort is some variation of, "People deserve to live in beautiful homes and eat delicious food." Three comments later, which we have pretty thoroughly rehearsed by now, she calls me a Reverse Snob and watches my hackles rise. So far, that's where we end the discussion, since neither of us welcomes any further arousal of my hackles.

I've at least figured out what she means by Reverse Snob. She accuses me not of looking down on the poor (as a genuine snob would do) but of looking down on the rich.

This argument doesn't stem from economic differences between us, because we both grew up poor and have by now fitted ourselves into about the same size IRAs. So, rejecting the title she gives me, I am left to explain the conflict to myself with the ultimate goal of explaining it to her.

I've decided it's not a matter of reverse snobbery, but something that has to do with social conscience. People do deserve to have beautiful homes and good meals. But which people? The better part of me answers, "Every people."

So I've concluded I don't like pretentious houses because they make me look at myself. And that disrupts my internal poise. My conscience insists no one should live like that when there are hungry people across the ocean or across town. But where to draw the line? Perhaps I shouldn't live the way I do either. Shakespeare speaks of awareness that creeps too near our conscience.

Although television shrinks the world daily, the desperately poor often live so far away, so anonymously, they are in danger of becoming invisible. I'm wondering what would happen if a destitute family moved into their dirt hut right next door to us. What if we learn their names, see their faces, and witness their struggle up close and personal?

Wealthy families in class houses have hearts the same size as the rest of our hearts and often make that clear with charitable contributions larger than most of us could even imagine. Judging from the pictures of Bill Gates' mega-home, it could house the population of an entire third-world country. But not long ago he donated one hundred million dollars to inoculate the world's children against disease. If I have fifty dollars and don't sacrifice a dime, if I had his millions, would I share a hundred?

It's not a question of wealth or snobbery, reverse or otherwise. It's a question of social responsibility and caring. When some have nothing, how much is too much? And although I've wrestled with the issue for a long time, I still don't know the answer. I just don't want to forget the question.

* * * * *

[106]

Are there rocks in my head?
April 25, 2006

Lately, I've had rocks on my mind and it's resulted in some weighty thoughts.

The story begins back in college, where I somehow ended up in a geology class. The professor, Dr. Rice, (nicknamed Rocky, of course), renovated a hearse and drove us students around the county, explaining geological formations and their origins. I fell in love with his red hair and nasal drawl but forget most of what he said.

One major exception is the geological concept called *angle of repose*. Dr. Rice explained that when rocks tumble chaotically down a hillside, they eventually sort themselves out and come to rest at the bottom in a configuration referred to as their angle of repose.

My weighty analogy? Time and again, we humans struggle through a similar process. We experience virtual landslides when all at once our foundation breaks loose and tumbles out of control. We're bumped and bruised in the process and the slide seems endless.

But somehow, the turmoil eventually ends and we find ourselves settled and safe in a new place. It's just hard to remember that promise on the way down.

Recently, a friend introduced the second heavy rock contemplation by expanding my vocabulary. My new word is *riprap*.

I'm told that riprap is a protective foundation made of loose chunks of stones placed together. It made me wonder what and who make up the riprap of our lives.

I particularly think of good friends and select family members who provide support for our foundation. They may not even know each other, but together create a protective base for our lives.

But I also think of others less caring whose impact plays an equally important role in creating our foundation. Someone once said, "Our lives are shaped by those who love us and those who refuse to love us." That's the other kind of riprap.

After contemplating the idea of riprap, I heard about a third rocky concept with an equally juicy name. That word is *haha* – and it refers to a walled ditch in the ground that serves as a fence without impairing the view. It's said to get its name from the expression of surprise when one encounters it.

I can't help but wonder about sunken fences in our lives that provide structure and limits without impairing our view. Who built them for us – and are there any that should be dug up and filled in?

Enough about rocks, you say? Could the rocks be in my head as well as on my mind? Of course not! I'm obviously just a stone's throw away from discovering something profound and would be stuck here between a rock and a hard place if I didn't share my revelations. I have to be a little boulder than most so that you don't take me for granite.

In spite of the groaning, let me wish us all a comfortable angle of repose, good friends as riprap, and delight upon discovering the hahas.

* * * * *

[107]

Mother's Day postlude
May 23, 2006

Well, it happened again. Or, rather, it didn't happen again. Another Mother's Day came and went without my being crowned mother of the year. And although I waited on the porch for several days and wore my best June Cleaver outfit, no one came to present the tiara.

In the midst of brooding, however, I decided that my own children are the only constituents qualified to vote on this issue anyway. And since they still think they are mentioned in the will, they would probably cast their ballots in my direction.

Waxing more serious, I thought about the complex relationships we all have with our mothers. My son wrote me a letter when he was five years old and it captured his mixed feelings concisely. It read, in its entirety, "Dear Mom, I hate you. Love, David."

Somehow, his sentiments were never adopted by greeting card companies for their Mother's Day line. Neither are there cards that read, "I know you tried, but it just wasn't enough." Or, "Where were you when I needed you?" Or, "You suffered too much to nurture me."

The lucky ones among us have mothers who deserve those flowery cards with loving sentiments. But, in spite of the nature of our relationship, the ties that bind mother and child are sturdy double knots. And when mothers leave us, they often leave unanswered questions or unresolved issues and always a vacancy that can't be filled. Mother's Day, with all the commercial advertising, makes us think about our mothers regardless of how we related to one another and whether we remember them lovingly or otherwise.

I once developed a formula in response to an impossible question asked by a friend who was mourning the recent death of her mother. It might be interesting to plug our own figures into the equation during this holiday aftermath.

She asked casually, as though requesting the time of day, or asking that I pass the salt, "How long before I stop missing my mom?" She asked simply, as though I'd glance at the calendar and assure her the pain would subside by next Thursday. So I offered this equation:

Compute the number of consecutive days you enjoyed being together and subtract the times you drove each other crazy or made each other feel like bad mother, bad child. Then multiply by the hours your mother listened, divided by the years she didn't hear. Next, factor in the warmth she wrapped around you and deduct the times she wrapped in it herself, unaware of your chill. Figure in her laughter and the sound of her voice, the tears you've shed together or alone.

But even if we don't work it out mathematically, consider this. Perhaps we mourn while mothers live, dreading the coming loss, wishing for what can't be. Perhaps we'll mourn forever, for all they gave, for all they couldn't give.

* * * * *

[108]

No secret is safe anymore
June 27, 2006

The bank teller counted out my money – loudly. I was making a large withdrawal and she announced every bill from twenty to three hundred as she flicked them down in front of me. I wouldn't have worried so much except that the man behind me was wearing a ski mask and was prematurely exercising his concealed carry rights. Well, perhaps I exaggerate, but realistically I had no assurance he and his evil intent wouldn't rob me later in the parking lot.

I had considered using the drive-up window for a quicker getaway with the cash, but in that case the microphone would broadcast my transaction both inside and outside the bank.

What ever happened to privacy? Some local pharmacies attempt to arrange privacy for their customers, but the public doesn't always cooperate. Strangers peer over our shoulders as the pharmacist gives instructions for using suppositories, and those same customers stay to watch us write the check.

Medical receptionists verify patient information in a loud clear voice for the benefit of patients who are hard of hearing and for the edification of others in the waiting room. In case onlookers miss the name of a patient during that exchange, the nurse will soon arrive across the room and shout it out for them.

Retailers routinely ask for customer phone numbers or zip codes. At one local store I paid cash for my purchase, but the clerk insisted she couldn't open the cash drawer to get my change until I gave her my address and phone number. When I refused, she somehow discovered another solution.

And who knows whether our phones and e-mail are under surveillance in the government's search for bad guys? Let's don't even go there right now.

A medical insurance form advised me that reporting my Social Security number was optional. It was mandatory, however, that I include my Medicare identification number. Did they not know those are identical, or were they hoping I didn't know?

Privacy, in the abstract, has become a dominant issue. Except for blood relatives, every one of my correspondents has sent me a privacy statement. Those brochures and their counterparts hanging on office walls are routinely printed in God's tiniest font. Having never read one, I can't say whose privacy they protect and I'm hoping it doesn't matter in the real world.

I am equally concerned, however, about the fact that many of us give up privacy on a voluntary basis. Television shows feature families willing to wash their dirty laundry while the world listens in. Others use cell phones in public, broadcasting their business to everyone within a mile. Bloggers keep diaries online, not fearing, but hoping, they will be read by friends and strangers alike. Many wear t-shirts with messages proclaiming the wearers' politics, religion, pet peeves or worse.

But even I succumbed and probably committed the ultimate surrender. I just sent a sample of my DNA for National Geographic Society research.

Big Brother will be pleased.

* * * * *

[109]

The sound bites of our lives
July 25, 2006

From a lifetime of myriad conversations, which words remain with you?

As teenagers, my friend and I often took late-night walks. It was the 50s when walks were safer and doors were left unlocked. One night, we detoured into the Catholic Church and stood in the darkened sanctuary listening to the old building's creaks and groans. Perhaps sensing some timidity on my part, my friend explained, "Nothing is ever still."

I can't count how many times since then I have relaxed by remembering her consoling words when things go bump in the night.

My mother bequeathed a practical sound bite. "You have to eat a peck of dirt before you die." True or not, her folk wisdom encouraged me to let children play in the mud and in general kept me from being finicky about the lint of life.

Over the years, yoga instructors, massage therapists and fitness gurus have reminded me to "Breathe." That bite stands me in good stead thus far.

"Naomi, you've done a damn fool thing. But that doesn't mean you're a damn fool." That's the bite left for me by a college professor assessing one of my less commendable adventures. It's since reminded me to consider the deed apart from the doer and not to generalize from a single instance. His admonition also appears to have something to do with forgiveness.

During an early job after graduation, I complained at length to a well-seasoned social worker about the overtime I put in. He listened to my

185

discourse quietly and patiently, then asked, "Why are you doing that to yourself?" Why indeed? He taught in that one sound bite that I make the choices about how I spend my time, minute after minute.

I think of a younger friend every time I twist a bottle cap or turn on a spigot. Of all the words that passed between us, I remember one simple phrase. "Righty tighty, lefty loosey." Thanks, Dan.

As a college freshman preparing a paper for philosophy class, I wrote that my topic was "of wrist-slashing importance." The professor, feigning horror, wrote in the margin, "Shudder." I remain grateful for his shudder and have never since let an issue rise to wrist-slashing status.

Hopefully, each of us has heard the reassuring bite that tells us, "Everything will be all right." I am eternally grateful for that voice in my own life.

Recently, a wise man reminded me, "You give life to what you fear." That's an enormous bite I'm still chewing on.

Most of us have remnants of hurtful comments in our memories as well. I work to erase those from the tape and try not to foist poisonous ones off on the world.

What sound bites do we ourselves leave behind? Once they escape our mouths, we can be sure someone will carry them around forever. Do our comments reflect the legacy we'd like to survive us, or should we sometimes just bite our tongues?

* * * * *

[110]

A matter of life and death
August 22, 2006

Many moons ago, while awaiting the birth of my first child, I experienced the usual anxieties. I wanted to be as well prepared as possible so began reading how-to-do-it books, including unattended delivery at home. Of course learning so much increased the anxiety rather than reducing it. I eventually comforted myself by realizing every living being had been born and that many women give birth without reading the manual. Granted, some with more grace than others.

The ultimate stress reducer finally arose from the realization that I simply didn't have to know all of those things. Happily, the obstetrician was charged with that obligation.

Forever being eager to achieve well, I recalled what sort of embryo I, myself, had been. I distinctly remember keeping one ear to the uterine wall, listening carefully to conversations between my parents and the doctor to make certain I'd know how to be born correctly. I remember they had to coax me out with logic, tantalizing me with visions of ice cream, oceans and sunsets. Being comfortable where I was, their promises sounded empty, but I eventually trusted them and cautiously emerged to see for myself. I almost missed out on being born by insisting on knowing all the answers and being in control.

You'd think I learned my lesson by now. But since I've more than used up my allotted three score years and ten I'm thinking about end-of-life issues. No, I'm not leaving the planet anytime soon that I know of, but it's not too early to begin thinking. Do you remember that student in your class who always had assignments and term papers finished days or weeks ahead of time? That would be me. And it's déjà vu.

Reminiscent of my worries about pregnancy, I've spent some time thinking about how to die. I, of course, want to do it right so (surprise!) read some how-to-do-it books. But there simply doesn't seem to be much consensus on the issue. As before, some try to entice me—this time with golden streets and starry crowns, but I'm reluctant to forfeit the ice cream, oceans and sunsets since it's hard to imagine anything better.

As before, and all these many moons later, I comfort myself in the knowledge that in spite of the uncertainties everyone seems to know how to die when it comes time. Granted, some with more grace than others.

But I am mostly comforted by the realization that I've been putting my ear to that uterine wall again, trying to learn things I don't need to know and forgetting that someone else is in charge.

Rumi, thirteenth-century poet/philosopher, asked the timeless questions of how he got here and how he would die. Never able to solve the mystery, he concluded with enlightened resignation, "Whoever brought me here will have to take me home."

That's certainly good enough for me. Call it letting go, call it surrender. There are some things I simply don't need to know.

* * * * *

(Achieving well, Mount Union College, 1953)

187

[111]

A rose by any other name
September 24, 2006

If you're searching for projects to celebrate the demise of summer and television reruns, accept this assignment just for fun. Pause in the shade and review your life history by listing all the names you've been called – at least the ones you know about. Completing this assignment guarantees a trip down memory lane and could stimulate interesting dinner table conversation.

My mother named me after her best friend. She wanted me to have a name that wouldn't be shared by six others in my classroom. She certainly succeeded. Her friend's name and mine are correctly pronounced as though ending in the letter "a." Naomi thus rhymes with Tacoma. A couple long-time friends still insist on calling me Naomeeeee, and I have accepted that by now as an affectionate fluke. One friend simply gave up on the last vowel and calls me Naom.

For many years, I was affectionately called Sally by an older neighbor gentleman who became a close friend and benefactor.

I was called Noni by a high school friend who thought everyone needed a nickname and was routinely referred to as Diva by one of my son's adult friends and as Toots by another.

A high school boyfriend called me Darling as he drove his car into the ditch. That was the first in a line of life's sweet nothings, ordinarily minus the ditch.

Through the years I was variously referred to as Mommy, Mom, Mutero, and sometimes in exasperation, Mutherrr! How many more years will it take me to quit responding when a child calls for its mother by any of her various monikers?

I always appreciate it when children call me Mrs. Patterson, but the world conspires against me and few children offer that respect.

At the office, younger patients frequently referred to me as Dr. P. and many of the employees called me GD, which they insist stands for "good doctor." I choose to believe that over some other alternatives.

One man, just once, called me Babe. I presume he's recovered from his injuries by now. Testing the limits, another deliberately distorts my name to Norma.

Three young ladies with whom I used to kid-sit still know me as Mrs. Poppins and I accept the title as a badge of honor.

Even though we sometimes consider nicknames a childhood phenomenon, they seem to keep piling up. I have recently been dubbed

Omi, Nome, and Kiddo, with a brief stint as Rosemary. And since a road trip with a friend, I've become Louise to her Thelma.

I've been called a few names that don't deserve repeating and probably a few that were whispered behind my back. But considered all together the names paint a pleasant and interesting biographical sketch. What does your own list say about your life?

Personally, I can't imagine what it would be like to have just one name. I delight in the variety of mine and in the friends who christen me... over and over again.

* * * * *

[112]

Just a four-letter word
October 22, 2006

One doesn't have to make long speeches in order to make a point. Sometimes single words pack a powerful punch. And since that single word often strikes below the belt, we might not be sure what hit us.

Recently, I've been pondering the word "just." Among its multiple meanings, the word refers to honorable, fair and lawful. It can also mean "precisely" as in the sentence, "That's *just* what I was going to say." There are several other nuances of meaning, all but one of which escape my scrutiny for now.

Think for a moment about the fact that "just" also means "merely."

In that context it minimizes events and diminishes other people or ourselves. Consider, for example, what it means to be referred to as *just* a housewife or *just* a kid.

Sadly, I heard a stay-at-home parent introduce herself as "*just* a mom."

A good friend sometimes leaves messages on my answering machine and introduces her message by saying, "It's *just* me." Apparently, the implication is that she's no one important when, in reality, there is no merely about her.

How many of us have heard the brush off of, "Let's be *just* friends." How demeaning to diminish the meaning of friendship by putting the word "*just*" in front of it.

Spouses sometimes do open battle when one of the partners declares that the infidelity was "*just* a one night stand." Or perhaps they have told "*just*" a little white lie.

Careless others hurt our feelings with unkind words and, upon seeing our reaction, say they were "*just* kidding." They hope in that way to minimize what they have said, albeit a bit too late.

Fitness instructors tell us to "*just* roll over on your back," dismissing the actual physical complexities that maneuver requires. They might as well suggest to those of us with aging or maverick muscles that we stick our elbows in our ears. We, too, take our miraculous bodies for granted until they let us know how vulnerable they are.

Medical professionals often try to console us by insisting their probing will hurt *just* a little bit or they recommend a procedure that is *just* minor surgery. I long ago determined that no surgery is minor unless it is being performed on someone else.

Children learn early in life how much time is really involved when one of their parents promises, "*Just* a minute." And there is no greater minimization than to be told that one's devoted invisible friend is a function of "*just* your imagination."

Children also learn how much that four-letter word minimizes tough situations when they face a plate of Brussels sprouts and are ordered to take *just* one bite.

And speaking of Brussels sprouts, there's a point to all this. Namely, it's wise to taste our words, even the tiny ones, before spitting them out. In the process, we might avoid demeaning other people, their values or their concerns

But then, of course, that's *just* my opinion.

* * * * *

[113]

Learning to say when
November 26, 2006

Although she didn't give the incident a second thought, I jotted details in my mental notebook.

My daughter was a teenager at the time and, as another school year approached, I invited her to go with me to buy some new clothes for the occasion. But she told me we didn't have to do that because she already had enough. Imagine! Enough! Perhaps she simply didn't want to be seen with me at the mall, but I prefer thinking she had grasped the difference between need and want.

Contrasting stories come to mind. First, the hungry Oliver Twist standing with his empty gruel bowl in the orphans' home dining room asking, "Please, sir, can I have some more?" That's genuine need.

Fast-forward to 2006 and the quiz show Deal or No Deal. A recent contestant had just won a guaranteed $800,000 but risked that amount to try for more. The bird in the hand was simply not enough.

What makes us clamor for more and more? Is it greed, entitlement, fear, hedonism or maybe keeping up with those annoying Joneses?

I'd never suggest we give up luxuries or all excess, but we do need to identify excess for what it is and be secure in knowing we would be all right with much less. Garage sales and downsizing are eye-openers. But even when those events confront us with evidence we've accumulated too much, it's hard to part with any of our thirty pairs of shoes. Health campaigns try to make us aware of when we've had enough to drink and enough to eat, but I still don't like to use that modifier when referring to ice cream.

An old proverb says, "Enough is as good as a feast." That's an interesting idea to contemplate while our bellies are still rumbling with Thanksgiving leftovers. Even if our cup is already overflowing, it may be hard to say "when."

But too much of a good thing isn't the only excess. We've all had too much of more disturbing excesses as well. We've had enough war, enough crime, enough scandal, abuse, incompetence, discrimination, indifference and deception. We've hollered, "When!" but since no one comes to our rescue, this cup also runneth over.

In the 1976 movie, Network, an agonizing newscaster leaned from his high-rise office building window and urged listeners to go to their own windows and shout, "I'm mad as hell, and I'm not going to take it anymore!" Apparently, some messages are timeless.

As for my own method of protest, I'm considering organizing a march on Washington. Participants will form picket lines and each of us will hold a sign. The print will be large enough for even the blindest politician to see without his glasses and the message will be a single word. That doesn't sound like much, but we'll take pains to choose exactly the right one.

And that will be enough.

* * * * *

[114]

End-of-the-year exam
December 24, 2006

Before dulling our senses with holiday goodies, let's lay visions of sugarplums aside and challenge ourselves with this two-part internet quiz.

First, let's name five recent winners of the Heisman Trophy, five winners each of best actor Academy Awards, Nobel peace prizes, World Series championships and Miss America contests. And, for extra credit, who are the five wealthiest people in the world?

If you didn't exactly cover yourself with glory in responding to Part One, join the club. I flunked the test royally myself.

It's clear that few of us remember yesterday's headlines. As the anonymous author of the quiz reminds us, those folks were not second-rate achievers but the best in their fields. After they step down (or tumble down) from the podium, they display medals and plaques in their dens while the rest of us move on to whomever is next.

And now a chance to raise our test scores with Part Two of the exam.

Name five teachers who helped guide you through school, five friends who supported you through a difficult time, five who made you feel special and appreciated, five who taught you something worthwhile, and five people with whom you always enjoy spending time.

Did you find those answers easier? Most of us do. And that's because as we struggle to survive or win our fifteen minutes of fame, we realize at some level that the people who make a difference in our lives don't have to have a mantel full of trophies or pockets full of cash.

One successful executive displays an eye-catching photo on his office wall. It depicts a turtle sitting atop a wooden fence post. He explains its meaning by telling visitors it serves as a reminder that when we see someone in high places, we know they didn't get there by themselves. Somebody had to help.

In my psychology practice I frequently worked with adults who had made decent, comfortable, well-grounded lives for themselves in spite of deprived or traumatic childhoods. I often asked them, "Who saved you?"

In response, they shared stories of teachers, grandparents, friends, counselors or even total strangers who entered their world in ways so significant their lives were influenced forever. These benefactors weren't folks with the most money, most trophies or most name recognition. They were people who genuinely cared. My own list includes a high school teacher, a grandmother, a church youth leader, a minister, a college professor, and two special neighbors.

Just as we cannot always know the impact we've had on others' lives, our own heroes may not realize how much their association meant to us.

During this season of giving, it might be fitting to remember those who shared their hands and hearts with us. It's never too late to honor them for boosting us safely to the tops of our fence posts.

What greater gift?

* * * * *

[115]

Can you hear me now?
January 28, 2007

Does no one read my memos?

In early December, as a public service, I suggested New Year's resolutions for other people to make. I'd already adopted a resolution for myself but hoped to save busy or forgetful people the trouble of thinking up their own. I mailed them to the appropriate transgressors and waited eagerly to feel the world spin more smoothly as my proposed resolutions were adopted.

I didn't expect thank you notes, so that wasn't a disappointment. But here it is nearing the end of January and there's no evidence my suggestions made any impact.

It's obvious the ills of the world haven't been remedied. For example:

* UPS delivery persons still drop packages on my porch without so much as ringing the bell. Sometimes I discover them that same day and sometimes not.

* Otherwise friendly people still allow their dogs to pee or worse in my yard. I had asked them to teach pets what our own mothers taught us. If you're going somewhere, go to the bathroom before you leave home.

* Drivers apparently tossed my suggested resolutions out their car windows along with the candy wrappers and beer bottles. They haven't yet reduced the volume of their stereos nor pulled over before using cell phones. I had specifically recommended they not blast their horn with the remote key pad when I am standing within heart attack range. And I obviously didn't get through to the lazy, arrogant jerks who park in handicap spaces without benefit of a disability.

*Television newscasters totally ignored my urgings to quit referring to each other as "you guys."

*Self-destructive slow learners continue puffing cigarettes inside my personal smoke-free zone.

* It was also fruitless to recommend that sales persons quit hiding from customers. Allee-allee in free! I give up. Where are you?

*I urged cashiers to count out change to customers rather than handing us a fistful of money, expecting us just to trust their accuracy. And, could they please work with management to see if more than two of the dozen checkout lanes can be open when there are lines of people waiting?

* In the interest of fairness, I asked customers to have checkbook and pen ready and the check half written by the time the cashier announces their purchase total.

And, please, further resolve not to sneak into the grocery express line with forty items.

In the meantime, I'm making excellent progress sticking to my own resolution. I resolved to be more tolerant of human foibles to make sure I don't get upset by little things. I simply don't like to spew more negative energy into the universe than is already there.

It would, of course, be lots easier for me to succeed in keeping my own resolution if everyone else worked on theirs.

* * * * *

[116]

An artist's lesson in bronze
February 25, 2007

Details of the chicken story remain sketchy. But as early as I can remember, my parents weren't on speaking terms with my aunt and uncle. All I knew was that the rift had something to do with a longstanding disagreement over chickens. The feuding relatives are all dead now and didn't ever bother to reconcile with one another or clarify details of the argument. With that background, it's no wonder I've had trouble grasping the concept of forgiveness.

It sounds simple enough when we're told to forgive and forget, and I've read that the beginning of forgiveness is realizing we can't change the past. But how can we forgive seventy times seven as has been prescribed, when once is difficult enough?

Sometimes we manage to stifle the outrage, but quietly nurse our grudges, leaving them poised to emerge at a moment's notice. And regardless of our otherwise failing memory, we often remember slights and hurts, licking our lips and secretly relishing the deliciously bitter taste of revenge.

Chicken wars are challenging enough. So how do mere humans forgive heinous trespasses like murder of family members or innocent school children? As a psychologist I can't help thinking about repression and denial when the seeming saints among us claim that all is forgiven. I've never believed the adage that to understand all is to forgive all.

Just as offenders often mouth the words "I'm sorry" without genuine regret, so might we flippantly mouth the words, "I forgive you." I've concluded that at least for now in my imperfect state, I have to ask someone more benevolent and spiritually advanced than I to consider forgiving the big ones.

Recently, however, the world had an object lesson to teach – a metaphor for forgiveness of at least life's smaller transgressions. Perhaps that's a reasonable place for us neophytes to start.

The lesson presented itself when a local artist, working in bronze, invited friends to his studio to observe a pouring and, after pieces were fired, to help break finished bronze figurines from their molds. Mostly we watched the master at work.

We noticed that in spite of the artist's experience and expertise, there occasionally were tiny flaws among the largely perfect bronze pieces. Some had cracked while being fired; others sported anomalies that couldn't be filed away. Neither met his standard of excellence.

But the artist took it all in stride. We watched as he examined the pieces carefully, then tossed each imperfect figurine back into the fiery melting pit. We watched as the imperfect bronze pieces reached their melting point and were transformed again into fluid, glowing possibility, ready to be poured into another mold tomorrow.

So that's the lesson! More than half a century after the chicken wars I'm learning a simple definition of forgiveness from the artist's work in bronze. There were no excuses. No demands. No promise for tomorrow.

Just another chance.

* * * * *

[117]

Life in slow motion
March 25, 2007

Four years ago I was diagnosed with Parkinson's disease. When the neurologist made his pronouncement, I'm afraid I shared my favorite expletive.

Since then I've shifted from zoom to plod. Scheduling an hour to get dressed sometimes puts a crimp in my social life and I simply don't sign up for foot races. I've exchanged typing eighty accurate words a minute for a sloppy hunt and peck with one hand. I've surrendered unconditionally to buttons, zippers and shoelaces.

In pursuing answers, I've studied gurus who claim we create our own realities by our intent. The idea of my having selected Parkinson's is alternately enticing and annoying. I'd like to think if given a clear choice, I'd have chosen indigestion or a head cold.

But I'm convinced attitude is a powerful aspect of management and treatment of any malady. If there are other psychological aspects involved, attitude is way ahead of whatever comes in second. It's the one thing we can keep nailed down when everything else comes loose.

Make no mistake; I'm not thrilled with this condition. And I'm fully aware of the usual progress and outcome. I've been frustrated, sad, frightened and sometimes worried about those who worry about me. I haven't been angry since I don't know whom or what to target.

I can't believe (yet) that this illness imposed itself in order to teach me some life lesson, but I've learned several things anyway.

My primary task has been learning to accept and even ask for help – not easy for a stubborn old woman. But, usually, I no longer cry when someone helps me into a car or cuts my meat. I keep a honey-do list at home and visitors find themselves changing light bulbs or addressing envelopes. I can't count how many friends and total strangers have lifted, reached, stooped or bent in my behalf –and I am grateful.

I've reconfirmed that people are kind. They are as ready to help as I would be if the situation were reversed. I'm fortunate to be able to hire some assistance as well, but the generosity and caring shown by these people is beyond what money alone could buy.

I've learned to be choosy about the company I keep, and there appears to be a special magnetism that draws like-minded people into my circle.

Most interesting to me is a renewed awareness of the still, calm, unchanging core – call it what you will – that endures through whatever adventures our bodies undertake. There are some benefits to this slower, more reflective pace and that's where I hope to keep my focus.

At the end of that first neurological session, I asked the neurologist, "What is the best possible outcome with this disease?" He said, "Some people get well and we don't know why." I choose that one. In the meanwhile I'll try to keep a good attitude. And if that doesn't alleviate Parkinson symptoms, I guess I'll just be stuck with a good attitude.

* * * * *

[118]

Fly away or disappear?
April 22, 2007

In 2001, an NPR episode of "This American Life" explored the subject of superpowers. Not the international kind. Think Spiderman and Wonder Woman.

The program moderator asked listeners to consider a supposedly "age old question" that was new to me. Here it is. If you could choose between having the power of flight or of becoming invisible at will, which power would you choose? And why?

Rules stipulate that if you choose flight, you can fly up to one thousand miles per hour – wings optional. If you choose invisibility, your clothes will also become invisible as you disappear. In either event, you will be the only person in the universe to have whichever power you choose.

Invisibility gives me trouble. It sounds as though it would be primarily useful to those with criminal intent. One could sneak into movies or into gym locker rooms or listen in on conversations as others gossip about us.

Perhaps invisibility would be an asset in fighting crime if one were so inclined and that same power would come in handy if a mugger approached us on the street. Shy people could disappear into their shells and fugitives could stay unfound forever.

Superman chose the flying option over invisibility and proved how handy it could be in fighting evil. We could use that power when we have to travel faster than a speeding bullet. It would be gratifying to pass up traffic jams and in the process avoid tollbooth fees. We could earn our living as trapeze artist or play Peter Pan on stage without benefit of wire harness.

Of course flying could be used for evildoing as well. An airborne criminal could elude law enforcement and maybe even carry an accomplice on his back. He would probably have to file flight plans and would run the risk of colliding with larger aircraft. He'd get bugs and birds in his teeth. And of course there's the problem of what to wear.

But in spite of any downside, I definitely choose flight. Older folks often feel invisible already and flight offers freedom from human physical restraints.

I used to dream occasionally that I could walk several inches above the ground. I didn't think to flap my arms at the time, but the idea of flying without benefit of airports or planes is enticing. In fact it's an easy choice compared to invisibility.

When this superpower is bestowed I might eventually use it to help save the world. But first I'll don scarf and goggles and make a nostalgic flight to the Atlantic coast. There I'll visit my special beach to thank guardian seagulls who always hovered during my solitary ocean swims.

Then I'll come home to spend at least one summer circling tree-tops and playing follow-the-leader with neighborhood birds I've previously known only from a distance.

I'll keep loving watch over friends and smile to see them looking up, wondering aloud:

"It's a bird! It's a plane! No! It's... "

* * * * *

[119]

Cook of the month?
May 27, 2007

Although I'd won no culinary awards, my long-suffering husband didn't complain about meals. They were reasonably attractive, regularly served, and non-toxic. Perhaps as a reward for his years of tolerance, I decided one weekend to prepare a gourmet dinner.

It took some time to sort through the stack of recipes that, with all good intentions, I'd clipped from magazines over a period of twenty years. But after the initial selections and process of elimination, a spicy leg of lamb was declared the winner. I prepared a grocery list, shopped for necessary ingredients, taped the recipe to a kitchen cupboard door for quick reference, and spent much of the afternoon following intricate instructions.

Then *voila*! In spite of my amateur status and lack of faith, I created a masterpiece. It even looked like the picture in the magazine.

That evening at dinner, I served the lamb without fanfare, awaiting my husband's spontaneous accolades. As I watched from the corner of my eye, he put the first bite into his mouth, chewed cautiously, and asked in a polite, but puzzled, tone of voice. "What is this? It tastes like rotten sock."

Perhaps it was the initial shock that allowed me to answer simply and quietly, "It's leg of lamb." He wasn't in the habit of criticizing meals, and I wasn't in the habit of answering criticism simply and quietly. I can't remember how many bites he took beyond that first one nor what I did with leftovers. In my haste to gain composure, I even failed to ask how he knew what rotten socks taste like. But turning the other cheek, I cooked another special dinner the next evening.

Creating my own recipe this time, I poured a can of stewed tomatoes into a small casserole dish. To this I added one of our son's frayed, graying, athletic socks. I covered the sock completely with the liquid mixture, garnished with chopped onions and chopped green pepper, and simmered... in more ways than one.

At dinnertime, I set the colorful, bubbling casserole in front of my husband. Again I quietly awaited his reaction. He dipped his spoon into the dish, but encountering something solid, abandoned the spoon in favor of his fork. After two or three unsuccessful attempts, he finally lifted the sock part way out of the dish and asked, incredulously, "What's THIS?"

"Now THAT," I explained quietly, "is rotten sock."

As I recall, he was silent.

Lest someone consider me more vengeful than I really am, rest assured there was another dinner already prepared for him. And lest someone consider it folly to waste good food, it wasn't wasted. He must have learned something from the experience because he didn't complain about meals again. And since that evening, women all over town have asked for copies of the Rotten Sock recipe. It's become my tribute to gourmet cooks everywhere.

* * * * *

[120]

The jailers and the jailed
June 24, 2007

One of my good friends resides several miles to my left in matters political. When such discussions arise, I frequently just listen quietly from my own position of comfortable apathy. But I'm jealous of his determination to put beliefs into action – to stick to his guns and try to make a difference.

Recently, he used a powerful analogy with an intriguing image. So I'm taking two giant steps to the left long enough to hear him out.

He spoke about what he saw as government intrusion into our lives in ways he considers unconstitutional. In that context, he said, we are all prisoners – trapped inside a circumference of iron bars. Those on the fringe of the group see and feel the bars while those positioned toward the center of the masses do not. They are unaware of being imprisoned and even find it hard to believe the bars exist.

In college I experienced a vivid Technicolor dream with a similar analogy. In the dream I was looking out a tower window. It was snowing, but instead of white, the flakes were pink and light blue. I ran to tell the others, but they didn't believe me and wouldn't even come to the window to look.

We might argue that the oppressed should fight their own battles, but those closest to the bars are usually too hungry, tired or disenfranchised to stand up for themselves.

And although I usually stay comfortably out of politics, it's hard to ignore the warning voices that span decades.

Generations ago, Harriet Tubman said she would have freed more slaves if she had been able to convince them they were slaves.

Much more recently, I saw a novelty item for sale. It's a cup with the words "civil liberties" written on it. When liquid is poured in, the words disappear.

Prognosticators tell us that in just a few years, human beings will have microchips with medical information implanted in their bodies. Should we really be concerned that "they" might also plant global positioning devices to keep track of our whereabouts? They're already available for dogs and science fiction plots.

We've been told that if we put a frog in a pan of cold water and gradually turn the heat up, he will sit there until he is boiled. If we see bubbles forming, should we not jump? No one likes to be considered a Chicken Little, but nonetheless, shouldn't we holler "ouch" when we're hit with an unmistakable piece of sky?

If indeed we are all being held captive, who are the jailers? Is it the government or is it our own indifference, ignorance and inertia? Whatever the questions, whatever the answers, there's no get out of jail free card.

The Fourth of July season is a perfect time to reflect on the status of our freedoms. Right or left, apathetic or vigilant, prisoners or not, we're being called to the tower window to look.

* * * * *

[121]

A plethora of plurals
July 22, 2007

After motor-tripping across Kansas, lifelong city slickers might tell friends they had seen a bunch of cows. We Kansans would snicker, knowing that although bananas come in bunches, cows congregate in herds.

Who got to name the animals anyway? Considering monikers like orangutan and platypus, one might think names were thought up by a government subcommittee.

But however it happened, all God's creatures have names by now and the committee disbanded.

Recently, thanks to a San Diego Zoo website, I've become entranced not with animal names but with their creative plurals. What are critters called when, like bananas, they show up in bunches?

We're all familiar with designations for some of those groups such as army of ants, swarm of bees, flock of sheep, school of fish and pack of dogs. But how about these actual names? A congregation of alligators, an obstinacy of buffalo, an intrusion of cockroaches, a mob of emus, a bloat of hippos and cackle of hyenas.

Birds often congregate with lovely names: a parliament of owls, a murmuration of starlings, a charm of finches, and best of all, an exultation of larks. On the other hand, some committee with a grudge must have decided on a murder of crows.

Happily, the zoo list reminded me there's still room for us to participate in expanding the Queen's English. So I'm taking over the determination of plurals for inanimate objects and abstract ideas. Feel free to join in.

When the custodian lumbers down the hall, his bunch of keys is referred to as a jangle. On a particularly bad day we commit a bungle of errors. And on an especially affectionate evening we might exchange a whole pucker of kisses.

Get it? If you do, and if you care, sign up for my committee. With a little creativity and campaigning, our phrases might become common usage and end up in the dictionary. New words and phrases sprout from grass roots, you know. If "blog" can make it, anything can.

Besides the distinction of having our names attached to new plurals, we might assist with political campaigns. Imagine the subliminal implications if we referred to gatherings of politicians as dens of Democrats or slithers of Republicans. And when they gather for weekly meetings, dare we refer to city fathers as a ruckus of councilmen?

Obviously, this business of creating plural forms isn't child's play. It demonstrates even to the usually unimpressed just how powerful words can be and, not incidentally, how much care we must exercise in choosing them. A group of emus probably doesn't object to being called a mob, but a group of peaceful protesters might not be so forgiving.

I no longer regret not being around to name the animals or even groups of them. There's still much work to be done. Create your own plethora of plurals while enjoying a blessing of breezes during the sizzle of summer days.

* * * * *

[122]

Too much of a good thing
August 26, 2007

Well, it's just as I predicted. The inevitable finally happened.

Unfortunately, I didn't get around to warning everyone, but fortunately am way too mature to say I told you so. The wisdom of my prognostications was confirmed by a recent story on public radio. It seems that large companies are having trouble with their workforce of employees between the ages of eighteen and twenty-five. Even though well educated and competent in their chosen fields, they require so many positive strokes from supervisors that it's become a burden.

Designating an Employee of the Month will no longer suffice. There has to be an honored Employee of the Day. At least one company has champagne breakfasts for employees and, of course, had to hire someone to oversee the ever-expanding rewards program. I presume this was someone over twenty-five.

I'm the first to acknowledge that many young workers don't fall into this category and can perform excellently without getting gold stars regularly stuck on their foreheads. I also know the importance of employees receiving deserved recognition from superiors rather than being sought out only when they've done something wrong.

So what was my warning?

With all good intentions, loving, conscientious parents had bought into the fashionable emphasis on self-esteem and went overboard. Toddlers were rescued from falling on their bottoms, never allowed to hit the floor. They were applauded each time they piled two building blocks on top of each other and were called great artists with every scribble.

Of course I believe in fostering a child's self-esteem! I even got paid for spreading the word. But the best way to do that isn't simply by showering them with praise or micro-managing their every move. And that was my concern.

We mature into productive and confident adults as we develop and embrace internal self-evaluation rather than relying on external validation of our behavior.

Ideal employees of any age are those who can initiate projects on their own, see the project through to completion and then, without rewards of M&M's or pats on the back, be able to feel pride in the accomplishment. They are self-initiators, self-perpetuators, self-evaluators. That process starts early in life and helps build a strong foundation for positive self-esteem. Just as we're cautious in our use of criticism, we need to use praise wisely, too.

The moral of my story is that somewhere between all the cozy hugs and warm fuzzies, children need time to invent their own fun, to be given time and space to explore without instruction or interruption, and finally to say to themselves, "Well done."

I guess there's no reason to stop telling a child his every move is brilliant – as long as we can guarantee to be there to do that the rest of his life. Otherwise, his boss will have to crown him permanent Employee of the Day.

Sorry. I just can't help it. I told them so.

* * * * *

[123]

In the swim of things
September 23, 2007

One imaginary afternoon, I rested on the edge of a grassy river-bank miles above the earth.

Looking down from that vantage point I saw that Life is not walls and clocks and calendars, but is a winding, majestic, endlessly flowing River. So immense is the River that neither end was visible, even though I strained to see its beginning and end. There were stretches of peaceful flow, areas of challenging whitewater, occasional falls and whirlpools; the colors ranging from a sparkling blue to muddy brown. But most amazing of all were the people – the Swimmers.

It seemed at first that one Swimmer was indistinguishable from the other; but even though all were making the same journey, they traveled in decidedly different fashions.

In the center of the River, Swimmers progressed rapidly with strong, measured strokes, permitting no deviation from their path. As though in a race, they were single-minded about their goal – splashing others or elbowing them aside in their own desperation. In contrast, a few casual Swimmers floated downstream on their backs – whistling and oblivious to life around them. Others bobbed up and down at the whim of the River, forever in a dead man's float.

Conspicuous were those who struggled to swim upstream against all odds, ignoring the hoots and warnings of those who noticed. Many formed groups and maintained a synchronized routine as they traveled mechanically downstream. A large contingent swam as though they were being judged – checking the fit of their bathing suits and frequently glancing up as if to see the scores they were being given for style. But, clearly, there were no judges; only other Swimmers engaged in their own struggles to stay afloat.

Some of the scenes brought tears to my eyes. Weary Swimmers treaded water until they floundered and then sank beneath the surface. Heroic Swimmers made their way while pulling a weaker companion along, slowing their own journeys by accepting others' burdens. Along each bank, there were timid, frightened non-Swimmers clinging to the rocky edge, too fearful to leave the shore or enter the mainstream.

I had questions.

Where does the River begin and where does it end? Does it empty into some vast warm reservoir? Is there a final gigantic falls over which Swimmers tumble like lemmings into oblivion? Or is it possible the River is a circle so that Swimmers resurface for another trip after they have once been pulled under? Is there a Navigator who determines when each of us enters the River and signals when it's time to leave?

Swimmers preceded us. Swimmers will follow. And since we're all sharing the same River, I'd like to think we'll stop to help each other on the journey. Perhaps we can dive deeper, swim more confidently, and show greater compassion for fellow Swimmers – remembering that when things get tough, we can rest a while on that grassy riverbank.

* * * * *

[124]

It's so hard to forget
October 28, 2007

It's been pretty well established that as we age, we retain old memories while our short-term memory starts slipping. Quick now – what did you have for breakfast?

Well, I've been downsizing again. Having rid myself of non-essentials from the attic and basement, I'm trying to clear out my brain to make room for short-term information. The process is rather like defragging the computer or permanently deleting useless data.

There's already been some progress. I can remember only two of the counties in Ohio although the seventh-grade geography teacher made us learn names of all of them. I have also forgotten details (everything) about the square of the hypotenuse and why I should care. The same goes for theorems of all varieties and any numbers with x's and y's attached.

Sizeable remnants of some ancient memories remain. I can still recite names of the U.S. presidents in order from Washington through Truman – which is where my mnemonic trick runs out. And if the audience isn't too compulsive about detail, I can recite the books of the Bible in order, too. We had to learn them because, back in the day, no one coddled us by printing page numbers for the scripture readings in Sunday's order of worship.

In spite of these breakthroughs, however, there is still much to be forgotten. And apparently some things are harder to delete than others. For instance:

Would you like to hear me sing "There is a Tavern in the Town" (in its entirety) – in Latin? Or how about requesting two or three verses of dozens of hymns? There's simply not much call for either. My aging brain still retains the rules for Pig Latin, which I have spoken fluently since junior high. Even pigs don't speak it any more.

Since coaching my son for his participation in spelling bees, strange words are stuck in crevices of my brain and are hard to remove. Perhaps I'll be on a quiz show some day and win prizes for spelling syzygy.

Or maybe you would like to know my 1950s phone number. It had only four digits but won't surrender and erase itself.

I would have claimed I didn't listen to popular music in the '40s and '50s, but when golden oldies play on the radio now I can sing every word. Those might well qualify for eradication.

So why do I need the brain space? To remember my current phone number. To remember all three items when I go to the grocery store. To remember where I'm going when I drive off in the car. To remember the name of the person I met just ten minutes ago. And of course to recall what I had for breakfast this morning.

It occurs to me that I could clear even more memory space if I were to forget old hurts, disappointments and seeming slights. But I digress. That's probably for another project.

Now let's see. Where was I?

* * * * *

[125]

Thanksgiving flip side
November 25, 2007

It was a tough day in first grade. Deviating from my usually excellent work, I answered every single question on a reading workbook page incorrectly. I was in shock. Nonetheless I had the foresight to shove the paper into the very back of my desk and, literally, forgot all about it until we cleaned out desks at the end of the semester.

Years later I learned how forgetting often protects us against painful memories and helps us cope with trauma or embarrassment.

Still later, I became aware that entire nations sometimes deliberately bury the past in order to save face or escape blame. But it's equally clear that amnesia doesn't necessarily begin with intentional deception. Often, parts of the truth simply drop out of consciousness to help us bear what would otherwise be an unbearable reality.

Otherwise how does one account for efforts to deny the Holocaust? How many details of slavery have we been sheltered from hearing? And how long before mention of Japanese-American internment during WWII drops out of history texts? I shudder to think which present-day events will fall victim to national amnesia. There are so many to choose from.

All this thinking got stirred up when, somewhere between the turkey and the pumpkin pie, someone told me about a neglected chapter in the first thanksgiving story.

Now, I'm no historian and am usually slow to believe the worst. Just recently I conceded that Nixon maybe was a crook after all. So don't take my word for this addendum to the usual story. There's plenty of information available for those who care to do the research themselves.

History books tell us the Pilgrims landed on Plymouth Rock in 1620 and that there was indeed a feast shared by the Pilgrims and natives. It is probably this feast we recollect as we refer to the first thanksgiving. But this feast was not repeated annually until 1637.

Why those seventeen years later?

Well, in1637 the Pequot Indian tribe of Connecticut had gathered for their annual Green Corn Dance ceremony. English and Dutch mercenaries attacked and surrounded their village, burning it to the ground and killing those who tried to escape. The next day, the Governor of the Massachusetts Bay Colony declared a day of thanksgiving, thanking God they had eliminated some seven hundred Native American men, women and children. "This day forth shall be a day of celebration and thanksgiving for subduing the Pequot."

Some call it the first Thanksgiving. Some call it the Pequot massacre.

We desperately need to treasure and retain our national day of gratitude as proclaimed later by President Washington but also need to reflect on the injustices that accompanied the origins of our country… lest they be repeated.

I can't vouch for the details of the 1637 massacre since I wasn't there. But it's much too important to shove into the back of my desk.

* * * * *

[126/166]

Adding a pinch of salt
December 23, 2007
December 5, 2011

Even though I'd heard that old age ain't for sissies, I had always looked forward to senior citizenship. I planned at that juncture to forget convention and become a full-fledged salty old woman. Since there was no clear criterion for earning the designation, I practiced in small ways through the years, making it up as I went. The motto on my refrigerator read, "Calculated mischief is invigorating."

Unfortunately, when I finally reached those golden years the Universe intervened and made it physically difficult to kick up my heels or hoot and scoot as my plan required. That slide from salty toward bland drastically reduced mischief potential. To compensate, I've devised a list of fantasy plans for the New Year. And who knows? Stranger things have happened.

* First of all, I want to fall in love. Not that sit-on-the-porch-swing-and-hold-hands sort of love, but the passionate-take-my-breath-away sort. Torrid comes to mind – at least torrid enough to embarrass my children.

* I want to visit my ocean again, either riding the waves or floating peacefully at low tide with guardian seagulls hovering nearby.

* And how can someone get this old without ever having skinny-dipped? I plan to remedy that in some body of water bigger than my bathtub.

* I've seen an amusement park ride on television that shows riders strapped in harnesses being flung in great circles in the air, while lying on their bellies like Superman. There's no cage surrounding them – they're just flying through the air. I want to buy a string of tickets for that ride.

* I'm also going to buy a lottery ticket and win the big one. After paying for my trip to the ocean, the amusement park tickets and a fresh pair of sneakers, I'll distribute the money to unsuspecting people simply for the selfish joy of giving it away. Maybe I'll strew it randomly and anonymously on street corners.

*I might start my own church. Details are sketchy but someone suggested I call it The Church of the Cheerful Sinner. The name itself inspires ideas for zany ritual and liturgy. Finally! Milk and cookies for communion!

*They say that everyone who enters our life has done so because they have a lesson to teach us. This year I'm going to ask everyone outright what their mission is so that I can quit worrying about it.

* I'm going to dance – in ballrooms, on street corners and table-tops. Watch for me in a restaurant near you.

There's lots more. And once again, I'll be making it up as I go, so stay tuned.

For now, I have to work on my costume for the New Year's Eve party. I promised my skydiving class I'd come dressed as Baby New Year.

* * * * *

[127]

Good for what ails you
January 13, 2008

The Universe handed me an unexpected assignment last month. I was sent undercover to investigate two area hospitals – literally undercover. Details aren't important since many of us have done such investigations with minor variations. We can compare surgical scars some other time – or perhaps not.

It had been my intention to evaluate medical staff and define characteristics essential to optimal care. It was ordinarily difficult to corral physicians for more than a few seconds, so I had to eliminate them from the pool of subjects. Or is their elusiveness an evaluation in itself?

At any rate, I observed the habits and dispositions of those on the front lines of care – those who wiped bottoms, pushed wheelchairs and took vital signs until I feared having none left. From this motley crew I isolated three characteristics of those I want around me when I am out of commission.

The first two are Competence and Compassion. The former can be taught, but I suspect Compassion springs from somewhere deep with no clear origin. Each caretaker acknowledged and prescribed to the philosophy of patience, but sometimes a tone of voice or rapid movement of the hand suggested otherwise.

In getting to know those folk attached to the end of my call button, I became acutely aware of their lives and interests beyond vital signs. During my undercover stay, December storms hit Kansas. Many employees were without electricity at home for several days. Some stayed overnight at the hospital, unable to travel safely because of icy conditions. As they worked, they were concerned about Christmas shopping, childcare, dysfunctional sump pumps and final exams. They must have had aches and pains themselves, but I heard few of them.

Sometimes several patients at once pushed call buttons – a festive event I compare to a noisy neighborhood where one dog's barking sets off a string of others. Yet help showed up.

Compassion is difficult to quantify, but I will always remember one nurse at each hospital who sang to me. There are conventional medicines and then there are gestures that surpass definition. I received hundreds of smiles and healing acts of kindness that outweighed any negatives.

Besides those two big C's, I add the necessity for a Sense of Humor. Even during difficult or tedious times there was laughter, and I found myself seeking out those who could see the lighter side of life. I think they sought the same from me.

So what lesson are we to gain from all of this? I wrote a limerick to summarize the results of my investigation.

> A patient's condition will worsen,
> requiring tonics and nursin'
> if his medics don't know
> what the x-rays can't show –
> that under the skin there's a person.

* * * * *

[128]

Those voices in my head
January 27, 2008

Two conversations, decades apart, replay in my brain.

The first took place one long-ago February as my daughter and I prepared Valentines for her kindergarten class party.

I picked up one particular card, read it to her and explained, "This one says 'to my teacher' so you'll want to give it to Mrs. Nelson."

She asked politely, "But since they're my valentines I can give them to whoever I want. Right?"

Following my quick affirmation, she said, "I think I'll give it to Mrs. Nelson."

She wasn't arguing or being disrespectful. She was reconfirming her selfhood and freedom to make decisions. It was my job to determine which decisions were age-appropriate and this was certainly one of them. I silently applauded her growing strength and immodestly took some credit for it.

The other conversation took place decades later when my mother was ninety. During that exchange she warned me, "When you get as old as I am, you just do what people tell you." She had previously fought the good fight and just recently reprimanded a wedding photographer who insisted upon calling her "Grandma" and periodically suggested she rest.

Officially a senior citizen now, I find myself lodged between those two conversations, struggling to keep a strong sense of self, yet having to decide which issues are still worth the energy to pursue. Do I care anymore whether someone pronounces my name correctly? Do I accept a wrong order at the restaurant rather than speaking up? Do I nap when someone tells me I'm tired? How much life does each pursuit cost when the currency is self-respect?

Mother was right in one regard. In spite of our wide personality differences acknowledged during middle age, something happens when hair turns grey, steps become unsteady and voices weak. Old folks are often automatically referred to as "honey" or "sweetheart" and are sometimes helped across the street even when they don't want to go. From now on if someone calls me honey or sweetheart they had best be prepared to kiss me full on the lips. Terms of genuine endearment are one thing – a word used generically in place of my name is another. It would be easy to succumb and give up bits of me. Perhaps when others begin making the larger decisions for our lives, we cling more tenaciously to the smaller ones.

A third voice also resonates loudly in my head. My earliest literary hero was Ralph Waldo Emerson, and I recently discovered one of my adolescent underlinings in his essay on "Self Reliance":

"Let a man then know his worth," he said, "and keep things under his feet."

His voice remains a strong influence in my life and supports my efforts to retain self-hood when fatigue or circumstance might allow me to get lazy.

I want always to remember that I can send those valentines to whomever I choose and decide for myself when to nap.

* * * * *

[129]

A matter of purpose
February 24, 2008

Even Tuesdays have a purpose. We don't hear cries of, "Thank God it's Tuesday," and there's not much said about Tuesday night football. Nevertheless, Tuesdays quietly and reliably serve their purpose by keeping Mondays from crashing into Wednesdays.

It's all about purpose. Still reeling from that weighty epiphany, I've been considering how our own purposes change over a lifetime. And I'm wondering now if it all, like Tuesdays, has something to do with keeping things from crashing into one another.

As children with poorly defined purpose, we run about crashing into Wednesdays and grownups and furniture without much thought. Then, all too soon, we are routinely asked what we want to do when we grow up – asked to declare our purpose. At least by young adulthood we are expected to consider the venue in which we want to serve and then spend the next decades fulfilling that purpose to one extent or another.

In pursuing our careers, we challenge ourselves to keep the wolf from crashing through our door. In caring for our families, we strive to keep boogey men from escaping through closet doors into our children's bedrooms. High purpose indeed!

During my own middle-aged prime I had some retired older, empty-nested friends who sometimes expressed their newly felt lack of purpose and asked me, in my infinite wisdom, what they were useful for anymore. I recall telling them, "You don't have to do anything at all. You just have to be." In retrospect, I'm surprised at how well they took this from a young whippersnapper since I don't think that answer would satisfy me now.

But happily I have a young mentor-friend who offers a more helpful answer as I myself approach the customary criterion of uselessness.

She speaks of those times throughout life when it isn't necessary to be the speed bump or buffer for the problems of the world—that sometimes for an hour, day, week, year, or for the rest of our lives our role is to "rest and receive." That maybe it's all right to take our finger from the hole in the dike and, at least temporarily, let others hold back the flood.

God bless and keep those elderly folks who, by choice, continue to fight battles for the rest of us. On our behalf they keep crooked politicians from crashing into democracy, greedy moguls from breaking into our bank accounts and unethical persuasions from seeping into our code of morality.

But God bless and keep the rest of us, too – those who by choice or circumstance have redefined our purpose and lead less dramatic, quieter lives. We still listen, laugh, care and regularly spout both wisdom and nonsense. But at the same time we are practicing the fine, difficult art of resting and receiving with grace and gratitude.

Like Tuesdays, we remain quietly, unobtrusively useful even if for the moment our loftiest purpose is to keep lunch time from colliding with our nap.

* * * * *

[130]

It's all in your head
March 23, 2008

Among the mysterious medical diagnoses recorded, my all time favorite is the pre-Freudian explanation of hysteria among women. Female patients were thought to be overly emotional because they had a floating uterus. Doctors often prescribed pregnancy as the cure, hoping this condition would anchor the uterus and reduce the intensity of emotions.

But, as wrong as they were, at least the prognosticators didn't resort in their ignorance to saying the problems were all in the patient's head. Now that the uterus theory has been abandoned, one of the most frustrating diagnoses given by physicians is that our symptom is all in our head or is caused by some psychological fluke or ill-advised parenting method. We leave his office discouraged and unsure of ourselves. Is he saying we're crazy? Could it please be the uterus after all?

When I worked with children and participated in the evaluation of Attention Deficit Hyperactivity Disorder, I was struck by how many physicians didn't believe the condition was real. They said under their breath (or louder) that, "All this kid needs is a good spanking."

Parenting patterns were also believed at one time to be responsible for schizophrenia, homosexuality and autism. Although research has made progress toward correcting these false notions, a new set of health conditions moves in to be doubted and scrutinized and blamed on the head.

Fibromyalgia patients, for example, describe widespread pain in their muscles, ligaments and tendons. They experience constant fatigue often to the point of exhaustion. Yet they appear to others to be perfectly normal. Laymen and medical professionals alike are prone to call the patient lazy or malingering. Chronic Fatigue patients face the same chorus of doubting Thomases.

Another mysterious malady, Morgellons Disease, was first described in 1600 but just recently took the spotlight. Symptoms include painful sores that erupt all over the body. Furthermore, the sores ooze blue fibers, white threads and black specks of sand-like material. As horrific as that is, patients say the worst symptoms are the chronic fatigue and creepy sensation of bugs crawling under their skin. Since no one knows whether the disease is contagious, many sufferers isolate themselves socially.

Having little information about this condition, physicians often lack compassion and frequently diagnose the patient as delusional.

Small research studies have been carried out and have identified at least one very real microscopic critter in the majority of patients studied. Analysis of the emerging fibers has also begun but the CDC reportedly has undertaken no large-scale explorations.

It's been said that if an etymologist finds a bug he can't classify, he steps on it.

I'm thinking we can do better than that. Perhaps both the medical community and laymen can be more open to what we don't yet understand and more empathetic with those who struggle with strange maladies.

And who knows? We might even learn something.

* * * * *

[131]

Venturing outside of the box
April 27, 2008

Among my favorite zanies is the warm-hearted fellow who stands on a busy street corner in New York City while wearing a sign that says "Free Hugs." Dangerous, you ask? Yes it is. He apparently has to protect himself from bodily harm by those who come rushing at him to collect their free hugs.

Similarly, another enlightened soul sits on a park bench in a well-traveled area. The sign beside him reads, "Stop and talk to me." Imagine the variety of contacts. And who knows what needs it may fulfill for those who pause to chat… or what beautiful lies they might tell each other.

Given the variety of human beings surrounding us, I cheer for the zany ones. These inventive folks with exposed funny bones manage to break out of the box of convention. Some balance full time on the silly edge while others make just periodic forays into silly territory. Either way, their harmless escapades invite others to make human contact and participate outside their own usual boundaries.

On the grandest scale, organized groups of people perform what I'd call street performances – novel ways of pulling folks out of their box to see the world from a different angle.

In one such instance, about a hundred people, calling themselves "Improv Everywhere," dressed in the colors of Best Buy employee uniforms, filtered into a Best Buy store and simply loitered or walked the aisles. "Clerks" seemed to outnumber customers for those bizarre minutes before the caution police arrived.

The same zany group, two hundred strong this time, scattered themselves at random in Grand Central Station. At an agreed upon time, they froze in position for five minutes – then came to life again. The surreal scene elicited confused, amused, stunned reactions from passers by. I hope some of them joined the exercise.

But, happily, we can all enjoy zaniness intervals on a smaller scale.

Amateurs can begin by reaching out to touch someone (figurative-ly) in public elevators. For this venture we need only make eye contact with a stranger and ask, for instance, "Would you like to smell something gross?" Can they – will they – accept the invitation to play along?

Have I personally ever experimented? Well, of course. Sometimes when my mind tilts on its axis, I enjoy approaching information booth clerks to ask for information. Like "What's the capitol of Ecuador?" or "How can I get chewing gum out of my hair?" I've also tried to charge elevator passengers for their ride, but that's a hard sell. We both win when they drop the day's tensions and play along.

What all of these ventures, large or small, have in common is that human beings step out of the box and invite others to join them – if only for a zany instant.

When we're lucky enough to get a playful invitation, it's important to crawl out of the box and RSVP "yes." Reality will close the lid again all too soon.

* * * * *

[132]

Guess who's coming to dinner
May 25, 2008

If there's one thing that helps when I get impatient for the summer season, it's remembering the uninvited guests who showed up last year.

Unfortunately, for an especially lengthy week, I played reluctant host to Drosophila Melanogaster. No, that's not an Italian tenor or Russian ballerina. It's the species name for the common fruit fly.

Immaculately birthed by a ripening banana, one single fly (or maybe two) begat and beget a swarming colony overnight. So tiny they were just short of invisible, they flew in close formation in what seemed to be a random pattern. They didn't buzz or bite but made me itch all over just to watch them.

They obviously were looking for food and were bold and creative. As I ate dinner, one audacious soul rode up and down on my fork handle. Another flew behind my glasses, probably hoping for a better view through the bifocals. Several lined up on the sink faucet waiting for dinner and one found something interesting on my chin. Essentially, they drove me crazy and I called them a name I'd never before called a living creature.

Since the enemy didn't respond to my polite but desperate plea of "Shoo fly," I checked the internet to see if anyone else cared. Two fruit flies followed me to the computer where a visit to Google netted over two million references. I no longer felt alone.

Being primarily interested in how to get rid of them and reclaim my kitchen, I had already sprayed the intruders with flying bug killer on four different occasions, probably doing myself more harm than I did them. I had begun putting all trash into plastic bags but they soon learned to unwind twist ties.

The experts recommended that housekeeping be crumb-free, but my fondness for snickerdoodles clearly eliminated that possibility. Those experts soon became more desperate and creative, suggesting remedies using vacuum hoses or ovens. Trapping the flies in a glass jar using banana bait was the most humane suggestion. But then what does one do with a jar full of fruit flies? I finally decided to let geriatrics take care of the problem, and the Melanogasters soon died off or left for sweeter fields.

I had been right about their speedy multiplication. A single pair can produce hundreds of offspring in a couple weeks, and those offspring become sexually mature in just seven days, ready to start their own families. The eggs, laid on fruit, hatch into maggots, some of whom consumed my bananas. All of this is more than I wanted to know, let alone experience.

As warmer weather approaches, I'm trying to stay optimistic and would like to keep bananas in my diet without fear of another ambush. But I already hear snickering in the kitchen, and that's definitely a bad omen.

* * * * *

[133]

Taking another look
June 22, 2008

Is it too late for a Mother's Day tribute?

Apparently, our family was quite poor, and I give my parents all sorts of credit for essentially keeping that a secret from me. I never went hungry and didn't know I wasn't wearing the right clothes or living in the right neighborhood.

Through grade seven, I lived "in town" in a spacious enough house with my own bedroom. "Town" was an Ohio village of 3,500 people, the county seat with a bandstand at its hub. I walked the relatively long trek to school, but since there were no options, I didn't know it was long.

Apparently, money grew even tighter than usual and, on our downwardly mobile slide, we moved to a tiny village eleven miles away; a community with only fifty residents. Here we paid minimal rent, and my older brother and I rode with my father the eleven miles to school every day and stayed with Grandma and Grandpa until we were picked up at five o'clock when Dad finished work.

I don't recall being unhappy about our new house, and at the time couldn't understand my mother's quiet dissatisfaction. But now I know. Our new home had just four miniature rooms for the six of us. There was no heat except for a wood-burning stove in the living room; no running water; of course no indoor toilet; one tiny bedroom that barely held single beds for my two oldest brothers; a larger bedroom with a double bed for my mother, father, and youngest brother to share, and a bed all for me in that same room.

We brought water in from the outside pump, and in the winter it often froze in the pans in the kitchen sink. How my mother washed clothes and how we ever took baths remains a mystery. We're talking Little House on the Prairie here. Maybe we took baths at our grandparents' home. Let's pretend we did.

We had no telephone, and technology hadn't quite kept up in that rural area. But if we had a call to make, we used the crank phone at the neighbor's and our call was put through by the operator at the general store.

I loved the two years we spent there. The residents quickly became my extended family and the little country church was a second home. When my parents made trips to town to look for another house, I sat in the outhouse and prayed they wouldn't find one.

Now from a distance I can understand why my mother didn't enjoy those lean years as much as I did. If she grumbled, it was quietly – or perhaps she sometimes said desperate prayers of her own in the outhouse. It's easy, as an adult, to imagine her relief when we finally moved back to relative civilization.

I used to call her a martyr and didn't consider the label a compliment. Now I call her amazing and am grateful.

* * * * *

[134]

Heart full of memories
July 27, 2008

As if to confirm the illusion that time flies, I recently realized it's been a dozen years since retiring from my thirty-year stint as a child psychologist. To commemorate the occasion, random vignettes have been parading across my memory. Though each child was memorable in his/her own way, they variously left me with memories that still make me smile… or cry… or wonder. In their honor, I share a few indelible moments.

*In the little tyke category, a five-year-old bopped from chair to chair, finally landed in front of me and challenged," My neighbor has a cow that's bigger than you are."

*Another little boy, now a successful professional, had some trouble with toilet training. Occasionally, when I answered my phone, I heard him say in his tiny voice and without identifying himself, "Dr. Patterson, I pooped in the potty."

*A totally beautiful four-year-old girl came into my office doused in toxic perfume, reeking of cigarette smoke, compliments of her mother and grandmother.

*When I pulled out a stopwatch to time his performance on an IQ test, one little boy asked, "Are you going to make me run?"

*Another worried about the infestation at his house by critters whose name began with the letter K. Turns out it was the dreaded kockroach.

*Teenaged boys had perhaps the most unique ventures. One of them, in a creative moment, spray-painted his pet chicken – blue.

*Another, in an effort to mimic spiked hairdos and lacking money to pay for the customary goop, used wood glue. His spikes lasted… a really long time.

*An adolescent who was afraid in the dark said he appreciated the flashlight I gave him because he could use it to look for lice in his body hair.

*Before much formal attention was paid to bullying, one gentle patient was forced to lick the bottom of his tormentor's shoe. How long does it take to get over that?

*One little girl's family opened Christmas gifts without her, not noticing she wasn't there.

*A special confrontation involved a preadolescent girl who didn't want to be seeing me. At that time I had a huge table-tray holding cleaned wheat. The children used this like a sand box and it was easier to clean up after the session than sand would be. To express her dissatisfaction, she scooped up a pail of wheat and dumped it over my head. I hope she remembers this. I rained wheat all day long.

*After a session with another dissatisfied customer, I went into the waiting room to find he had carved "I hate Dr. Patterson" into the arm of his chair.

All in all, I apparently got mixed reviews, but terminating with patients was not always easy and never taken lightly. An articulate eleven-year-old lamented at her final session, "You're leaving and walking away with all my stories in your head."

She was almost right. But it's heart, not head.

＊ ＊ ＊ ＊ ＊

[135]

Thanks, but no thanks
August 24, 2008

One of my favorite cartoons shows a husband and wife standing on their front porch. He's holding a basket full of kittens. A smug looking woman is hurrying down their sidewalk toward her car. The husband says to his wife, "I don't really believe that was the welcome wagon."

Sometimes it's clearly better to give than to receive. But how do we get rid of gifts we don't want to keep? How do we refuse gifts we don't want to accept in the first place?

Friends recently spoke of receiving starters for "friendship bread" – from friends, of course. Having been given the starter package of dough, they were to add multiple prescribed ingredients, knead the bag at specified intervals throughout the week, and on the 10th day use the dough for baking. But they also were instructed to reserve enough dough to take starters to three other friends who'd perpetuate the cycle. Someone called this a pyramid scheme. I call it an edible chain letter. Either way, if everyone cooperated, every household would eventually have starter in their refrigerator.

Poet Marge Piercy explores a similar problem in her poem, "The attack of the squash people." How do gardeners rid themselves of their prolific harvest? She claims that among other trickery, these desperados drop their excess zucchini into other people's gardens, into baby buggies parked at church and in mailboxes. They approach strangers and plead, "Please take my zucchini, I Have a crippled mother at home with heartburn."

And what does one do with the fabled much maligned gifted fruitcake? One family, sharing the burden, passes the same cake from member to member year after year.

A socially acceptable way to get rid of unwanted gifts is to offer them at a white elephant exchange. Legend tells us that a king of Siam owned sacred white elephants whose upkeep was expensive. To exact punishment on his enemies, he gave them an elephant. Because elephants were considered sacred, the new owner couldn't get rid of the creature and went bankrupt in the process of providing for it.

If we give in to a peddler's pleading looks and accept his zucchini in the first place, what are our options? Is it all right to give away a gift someone has given to you? I vote yes. A distant relative used to send me a poinsettia every Christmas. Although I always appreciated the thought, I've never appreciated poinsettias, so I'd routinely swoop it up and take it to the hostess of the next holiday party.

Similarly, when I've given something to another person, it's theirs to do with as they choose – to keep, give away or put in a garage sale with their other treasures.

But if we ultimately discover we're too softhearted or weak-kneed to reject or dispose of unwanted gifts, there's still hope. We can always feed the zucchini and friendship bread to our elephants.

* * * * *

[136]

Mail from guess who
September 28, 2008

My friend is hurting – and it's your fault. Oh, she'll soon be over it and is already working to get her head screwed on straight again. But you started it when whoever you are sent her that uncomplimentary anonymous letter. Always caring and careful with relationships, she spent valuable time guessing who the sender might be. There was lots of soul-searching about whom she may have offended.

Of course no one can bring us low without our participation, but it's a long hard lesson. In my friend's case, the accusation was totally unfounded and she would have liked to explain or, if appropriate, apologize for the misunderstanding. You left no opportunity for that. You simply took a shot and ran.

Having had two such experiences myself, it's easy to empathize with her struggle.

My first experience with the phenomenon occurred when I was teaching seminars for educators and mental health workers. As is customary, at the end of the session, participants were asked to fill out evaluation forms – anonymously if they chose.

Well, among 150 ratings of excellence with songs of praise penned in the margins, there would occasionally be one evaluation score low enough to crash off the chart. Who, I would wonder, wrote this? Everyone was suspect since no one seemed to have fallen asleep and, until I regained perspective, I suffered a bit of paranoia and bruised confidence.

Later, in a response to one of my columns someone sent a lengthy anonymous letter outlining some of my inadequacies and making recommendations for my betterment. He went to great trouble to disguise his identity, using green ink for the letter and disguising the handwriting on the envelope. I was reminded of an eleven-year-old playing with a spy kit and this made me smile.

At first, I suspected everyone and that's an uncomfortable way to live. But as a student of words, I re-read the letter out loud. Miraculously, by context, grammar, vocabulary and tone, this person spoke aloud to me from the greenish page, and I knew immediately and surely who it was. Even his thinly veiled arrogance seeped through.

I'm puzzled by the mean-spirited cowardice of those otherwise good people who send anonymous letters. Mature people take responsibility for their behavior and this includes responsibility for their words. The only time we don't have to sign our messages is when we're composing ransom notes. Maybe we should require of everyone, as we do for politicians in pre-election commercials, that they acknowledge personal responsibility for opinions their ad expressed.

In the meantime, my friend is doing fine, thanks. It's a painful lesson but she's learning slowly like the rest of us that criticism, like flattery, can hurt us only if we inhale and that whatever the content of an anonymous letter, it says far more about the sender than the recipient.

If this column hits home and makes you squirm, let me add, "I'm Naomi Patterson and I approve of this message."

* * * * *

[137]

Forget about it
October 26, 2008

Author Robert Fulgham suggests that all we ever really needed to know, we learned in kindergarten. These lessons teach us, for example, to share everything, play fair, don't hit people, put things back where we find them, clean up our own mess, don't take things that aren't ours, and say we're sorry when we hurt somebody.

If we've followed his advice, we probably stayed out of jail and made some good friends. But except for his suggestion that we take naps and eat milk and cookies, they mostly relate to our interactions with other people. In my work over the years, however, I discovered that some of the greatest difficulties arise in learning to deal with ourselves. We don't learn how to handle these issues in kindergarten and often spend a lifetime practicing.

For one thing, we worry too much in spite of the fact that, clearly, there are two things it doesn't pay to worry about: those things we can do nothing about and those things we can do something about.

Most of all, we worry about what other people think and try too hard to please them. We are wise enough to know that in the long run it doesn't matter much unless we're running for public office and, even then, people soon forget. We sometimes have an exaggerated sense of how important we are and how much we are on other people's minds. One columnist recently advised teenagers, "Don't worry about what others think of you because they aren't thinking about you." There ought to be some relief in that realization. I like considering the idea that what other people think about me is none of my business.

We also tend to paint the worst possible scenario in our heads when looking for something to fret about. But since many/most of the things we worry about don't ever happen, we need a way to decide which concerns deserve our tizzy. It helps to make the distinction between which outcomes are simply possible and which are probable. If we choose to worry about everything that's possible, we'll worry full time. When I read that a frozen side of beef fell from a truck on an overpass, went through the roof of a car below and killed the driver, I realize absolutely anything is possible.

When an actual problem arises, we can err in perceiving the problem as larger then it really is. Even children grasp this concept when we demonstrate with a dime. Close one eye and hold the coin directly in front of the open eye and it's the only thing we can see. It visually fills our world. But if we hold the dime at arm's length, we see the dime in relation to the larger world. It's a simplistic exercise but has restored perspective more than once.

So, what if we try all the tricks but are so human that we find ourselves fretting anyway? Don't worry about it.

* * * * *

[138]

A song for the unsung
Nov. 23, 2008
(Reprint of #83, May 23, 2004)

* * * * *

[139]

It's time for a time out
Dec. 28, 2008

Is it safe? Is it over? Can I come out of hiding yet?

Oh, I'm not talking about the lengthy election brouhaha or recent holiday frenzy. I managed to muddle through those stressful weeks like everyone else. No, I'm talking about the everlasting football season.

Although I enjoy most individual sports, team sports and their fanatic disciples are omnipresent, noisy and annoying. Football tops my black list. I swear a sportscaster once announced there were forty-one games to select from during that one weekend. Not yet brain dead, I still enjoy keeping an eye on tight ends, regardless of which position they play. But that's small consolation.

I don't remember going to high school games, but since I know some cheers for the Blue Devils, I might have attended a couple times. Or maybe I learned team cheers at the obligatory pre-game rallies. I mostly remember feeling sorry for whichever team lost, so I wasn't an enthusiastic cheerleader. I attended just one college game, remembering only that I wore a new fuzzy blue sweater for the occasion.

As a graduate student at Ohio State University, I was offered a discounted season football ticket for twelve dollars. I turned it down, but since realized I could have scalped those tickets for enough money to pay my tuition.

One late afternoon I had at least a close encounter with football. I left home to go to dinner and headed toward campus. Shortly I was confronted with a wall of several thousand sports fans just leaving the stadium. I recall turning around toward home.

Why my fanatical aversion to the game? First of all, players get hurt – sometimes badly. (I know. Someone could get hurt playing dominoes, too, but we're talking odds here.) Secondly, the game's too complicated. Even when I'm paying attention I can't find the ball until I see the pile of people. And I still haven't figured out how many touchdowns make an inning.

Thirdly, even though these teams provide entertainment for millions of fans, I can't help but remember that these are grown men and should be over it by now... they should be playing nice and keeping their clothes clean. Have they ever noticed that as they are carried out on stretchers, fans are acting as though they themselves had won the game and are the heroes?

I'm sure these comments won't make me popular in certain circles. But others who escape to malls and city parks during game time will understand. And we are legion. It's my contention that fully half those filling the bleachers are there primarily to ingest the atmosphere and hot dogs. That motivation is as sound as any – and judging from televised scanning of the crowd it looks like they're having fun.

I actually have a solution to the whole football problem but so far no one has listened. Ever the peacemaker, I say give each team their own ball and they won't have to fight over it.

* * * * *

[140]

She's no party animal
December 28, 2008

If I were going to get any New Year's Eve party invitations, you'd think they would have arrived by now. But no.

And that's okay because I've never considered myself to be a party animal. Unless it's an evening with good friends, I studiously avoid social situations that require holding a cocktail while wearing shoes and making idle conversation. That's just excessive multi-tasking. If I feel obligated to make an appearance, I spend some pre-event time planning an exit strategy. The routine includes being first to leave, offering polite thanks and regrets to the host. And although my exit is always unobtrusive, a minor exodus often follows as though other reluctant guests have awaited my cue.

One notable New Year's Eve I arrived at a party at eight p.m., drank one cup of hot buttered rum, went immediately home to bed and slept ten hours... the life of the party for sure.

I've certainly attended my share of comfortable, celebratory evenings hosted by generous friends but otherwise am left to figure out the origins of my seeming asocial stance.

As a child, my friends and I once performed a synchronized vomiting routine at a Halloween party, spewing remnants of doughnuts and pre-digested cider in every direction. Might that have made a lasting impact?

Interestingly, however, that trauma left me with a strong interest in children's parties – perhaps in an unconscious effort to get it right this time. I enjoyed devising parties for my children so much that I once thought of starting a small side business as party planner for parents who didn't relish the task.

We made the rounds of skating, swimming and bowling venues, but the best parties were at home.

One favorite was a backward party. We designed the invitations in mirror writing, and guests entered by the back door wearing their clothes on backwards. Creative mothers had wrapped gifts with the ribbon inside the box instead of on the boring outside. Guests gathered for the obligatory photo, backs to the camera of course.

Two party dreams went unfulfilled. I thought often of what fun it would be to have a mud-day gala with all the activities that idea inspired. But we had no place to make enough mud, and maybe I didn't have enough courage. The idea for a themed costume party didn't come to fruition either.

I'm thinking maybe it isn't too late. I know I have some zany adult friends who would appease me by attending the mud session. What a great way to start a new year.

And I've already chosen the theme for my costume party. I'll ask that guests dress as their favorite prepositional phrase. Admittedly, attendance might be low, but I could count on a couple retired English teachers to participate.

For now, I'll check the mailbox for invitations a couple more times and, with any luck, can schedule an early bedtime on New Year's Eve.

* * * * *

[141]

Whine and cheese party
February 1, 2009

As you read this column, I will be puffing my cheeks, preparing to extinguish yet another birthday cake conflagration. It's a three-alarm fire this time, with seventy-five candles, and I can't say I'm totally thrilled with how everything is going.

You see, I had plans.

This is the decade I was to be crowned "Feisty Old Woman." I'd hustle between skydiving lessons and yoga classes, never running out of breath, but perhaps allowing short Sunday naps. I'd "oooh and ahhh" at my vitality and, frankly, would encourage others to do the same.

Though never a health fanatic, I had routinely taken good care of myself and avoided some common pitfalls. I didn't like alcohol and in my lifetime smoked just part of three cigarettes and ten minutes' worth of cigar. I didn't have to keep my doctor's phone number on speed dial and regularly left annual check-ups with a clean bill of health. My ancestors didn't even leave me much medical history to worry about.

Then a surprise diagnosis with symptoms that grounded me in spite of all my expectations. And I hate it... hate the limitations, the helplessness and the blow to my confidence.

In considering the "why," all sorts of answers beyond the medical are offered without my twisting anyone's arm. Very few folks suggest I'm being punished by an angry deity, but someone told me, "We make plans and God laughs." It doesn't really help to picture Her in stitches at my plight.

I'm intrigued by a friend's idea that maladies fall randomly on the population like confetti on our parade. And someone else shared the mysterious theory that somehow we actually chose our present illness in a previous life. A word of advice: If you're ever aware of having a choice, choose dandruff.

I certainly am not alone in this leaky boat and, yes, things could be worse – but tell me that only at your own risk. I can't think of a single instance in which that comment would be helpful.

Those of us who traveled in the fast lane only to become speed bumps don't spend much time complaining because nothing drives friends away faster than an organ recital. And we don't dwell on details with each other. But don't mistake this silence for stoicism or dub us all role models. We have enough to do without having to serve as good examples.

I always told myself I wouldn't use my column to complain about my health. But, as the old song says, "It's my party and I'll cry if I want to." It feels good to get it out of my system and maybe it helped flush out other people's systems as well. I'm apparently out of whine for now, so pull up a chair, have a chunk of cheese and slice of cake, and tell me what's happening in the real world.

As for me, "Doing fine, thanks. And how are you?"

See? I'm already smiling again.

* * * * *

[142]

Giving them the shirt on your back
February 22, 2009

So, how do you feel about advertising? Do you replay commercials for the sheer pleasure of it? Do you read every flyer ad and enjoy pop-up offerings on your computer? Probably not.

There may be nothing new to say about the deluge of advertising thrown our way via every medium available. And it's undeniably a big business. Super Bowl advertisers paid the networks two million dollars for just thirty seconds of airtime. Geesh! Sometimes I don't make that much all year.

My question is why do we consumers so willingly become a part of this nonsense? We probably would not agree to a job that paid zero but required us to wear a sandwich board day after day in public advertising someone's product. Yet we pay to wear sweatshirts emblazoned with the name of clothing companies and breweries, thereby offering them free advertisements. I understand that these companies not only get the profits from the sweatshirts but are able to claim tax deductions for shirt production as an advertising expense.

Mine isn't by any means a new campaign. When my children were young I didn't permit them to wear designer clothes with expensive logos on the pockets. I tried to teach them that if their self-esteem was based on the picture on their pocket or the brand name embroidered on the rear end of their jeans, there was a problem. Besides, I objected to subsidizing the advertising companies without compensation. In fact, we have to pay for the privilege, since designer labels cost more. I had the added advantage of having witnessed how children used labels as a means of cruel discrimination in school settings, and I didn't want to be part of that.

Colleges, rock groups and sports teams toss their hats and sweatshirts into the advertising ring as well. And consumers don't have to prove their affiliation in order to sport the logos. I've been surprised to see Jesus advertised on shirts and jackets. Who gets the tax break for that venture?

Recently I read of a company soliciting bald men who would be willing to have an advertisement emblazoned on the top of their heads. I don't know how many bought into this scheme, but my immediate thought was that this would provide a logical supplemental income for obstetricians or shoe salesmen. And it stirred my imagination.

Little had I realized how much I might personally be missing by not entering the advertising field. Through all my thoughtful years, I had never thought of a message I'd agree to spread via my sweatshirt. But in view of the lucrative possibilities and the world's seeming eagerness to wear those virtual sandwich boards on their backs, I'm considering a message I might accept for my own shirts; something like, "This space for rent."

More thought on that later. For now I'm just pleased to have gotten though the column without giving free advertising mention to Nike, Old Navy or Budweiser.

Oops!

* * * * *

[143]

American Idol wannabe
March 22, 2009

Perhaps I was born too early or perhaps I lack talent. Or probably I just need a better agent. At any rate, I failed to make it through tryouts for the American Idol talent show again this season, and have been relegated once more to the sidelines to cry with the winners and cry with the losers.

My mother, accused of being tone deaf, taught me all the nursery songs, and I seemed to get them right in spite of her alleged disability. I also learned some unorthodox tunes at her knee. Scheduled to sing a solo in the second grade, I found myself standing out in the hall where the teacher had mercifully let me go to recall the tuneless melody for my scheduled piece. It was a tearjerker about a little boy looking for his mother who had run away from home. "Poor song choice," today's judges would say. I obviously needed a new agent.

In fourth grade, asked to sing at a women's church function, my father convinced me to sing, "Coming in on a Wing and a Prayer" and "Moonlight Becomes You." He dubbed this combination a medley and I sang without accompaniment. New agent comes to mind again.

In junior high I free-lanced. As the only child my age in the small town where we lived, I routinely gathered the gaggle of neighborhood children and taught them songs. At one count, 115 oldies but goodies. I hope those grown children sometimes wonder where they learned "K-k-k Katy" and other hits – and I hope they remember me.

During middle school, a choir director heard me vocalize and advised, "You have a lovely voice. Wouldn't you like to learn to sing?" Never quite able to hear this as a compliment, I didn't pursue the options.

My big breaks came in high school. A good friend and I regularly sang in the church choir. We sometimes handled duets, but complained about the minor role of our vocal part in "Ode to Joy." That didn't get us expelled, but later we were emphatically denied our request to sing "Ten Cents a Dance." This rebuff could have meant the end of my singing career.

But wait! There's more!

The premier young male vocalist in town was a preacher's kid two years my senior. I stood anonymously in line with all the girls who had crushes on him, but by some fluke was asked to sing an Easter service duet with him at his father's church. I'm certain we practiced, but when our turn to perform arrived, something went so badly wrong that, no kidding, the organist realized she was only adding to the confusion and stopped playing. Though no accusations were made aloud, everyone assumed they knew who was responsible for the fiasco, and I haven't been bothered by invitations since.

Position now open for enthusiastic agent with fresh outlook and rose-colored glasses.

* * * * *

[144]

Still the best medicine
April 26, 2009

Let's call her Ellie. Though not her real name, it suits her. Round, brown, and thirty-eight, she's taken precious time to curl her hair and knows she's looking especially fine today.

She announces herself with "Good morning" – her prelude to opening my drapes and my day. Her mission is to help with chores that challenge my own energy and capabilities, and she executes them all with ease. As an added bonus, she sees what needs done without being told (a rare gift, indeed) and tackles unpleasant jobs with the same acceptance as more neutral ones.

Anyway, without prompting she hurries across the room and shuts off the radio with its dreary morning news. When later I ask, "What's going on in the world?" I am treated to a visit to Ellie's own universe. No international incidents, governmental crisis, or global warming – but a glimpse into the real world of a decidedly real person with tangible struggles and triumphs.

A single parent, Ellie lives with her teenage daughter and a herd of dogs, both of which demand attention to their own set of problems and needs. She fights off creditors and wrangles with school personnel, works two jobs and frequently allows others to take advantage of her. She enjoys having silly, spontaneous fun, but if there's ever an outright war, I'd like to be on her side.

Interestingly, when Ellie tells her crisis stories, she laughs. Not a laugh of desperation but the laugh, perhaps, of someone watching a funny cartoon, knowing things will eventually turn out all right. Think of Gilligan. Remember him? Shipwrecked on the island, he repeatedly encounters some crisis he personally created but eventually solves the problem and emerges as hero in his own drama.

Ellie is a bright woman, brighter than she probably suspects. Under better circumstances she'd like to be an architect or artist. She paints and watches foreign films. But she is sometimes prone to Gilligan antics like the rest of us. The difference is that she apparently sees through the plot, assumes it will turn out all right in the end – and she laughs. I can almost hear her telling herself, "A fine kettle of fish you've gotten us into now."

So while the dogs tear up her house and creditors park on her doorstep, Ellie laughs. Oh, and sometimes sings. As she works, I often hear her humming a tune. Regardless of the season, it's Jingle Bells.

[148]

Huh? What did you say?
August 23, 2009

I hurried down the crowded corridor, leaning a bit to the left from the weight of a carry-on bag. Eager for exercise, toddlers darted in and out among scurrying passengers while less enthusiastic parents struggled to keep up. A tearful "goodbye" on the left and a line at the yogurt stand on the right. As I whisked by the reunions and passed others en route in the opposite direction, snatches of conversation surfaced for brief moments as though someone were flipping a radio dial from station to station:

"... if that's all you can expect from your credit card company... "

"... but I haven't heard from him since."

"... it's just a matter of principle."

"... some french fries and a hamburger maybe."

"... and did you see the look on her face?"

"... well, before you decide to sleep with somebody... "

Hustle, hustle, hurry.

What? What did she say? "Before you decide to sleep with somebody?" How was she going to finish that sentence? The side of me with the heavy baggage slowed a bit and considered turning to pursue the conversation, but the side with the purse and ticket propelled me down the hallway to make the 2:11 flight.

Soon, safely settled on flight 225, nine hundred miles from Anywhere and six miles above Everything, I was left to fill in the blanks.

"Before you decide to sleep with somebody"... make sure that he's only going to sleep.

"Before you decide to sleep with somebody"... call your parents to see if it's all right.

"Before you decide to sleep with somebody"... check for an untanned mark on his ring finger.

"Before you decide to sleep with somebody"... ask to see his recent medical report and physician's release.

"Before you decide to sleep with somebody"... get married, for God's sake.

"Before you decide to sleep with somebody"... find out where he'll be sleeping tomorrow night.

"Before you decide to sleep with somebody"... make sure he's no crazier than you

"Before you decide to sleep with somebody"...

The musings got me nowhere. Who was giving the advice and who was her companion? Was a mother offering farewell wisdom to her college-bound daughter? Was a single woman talking with another single friend? Was a much-maligned wife scolding her unfaithful husband?

Sad to say, I may never know. On the other hand, I like to imagine that whoever made that comment is sitting now on another flight, miles from Anywhere and miles above Everything, holding the rest of her sentence in a state of suspended animation.

Next Wednesday, rushing to board our return flights, we'll pass again near gate A-4. And with any luck at all, she'll finish the sentence for me when she hurries by.

* * * * *

[149]

The trouble with silence
September 27, 2009

In spite of being repetitive, loud and annoying, television commercials are sometimes instructive. A recent advertisement series featured cell phone users, suddenly disconnected when their calls are inadvertently dropped. The caller is left wondering at the reaction of the person with whom she/he had been talking because their response goes unheard.

In one instance, a young woman on the phone told her husband she was pregnant. We television viewers witnessed his excitement as he danced and babbled happily at the announcement. The dropped call, however, left his clueless wife to guess at his reaction.

Did he not hear her? Was he too upset to respond? Did he pass out? Was he so thrilled he was rendered speechless? She couldn't tell.

And that's the problem with silence. It's open to a multitude of interpretations.

I have two male friends who frequently don't respond to comments others make during conversations. This is frustrating and can be intimidating. Their silence forces others to play detective. Are they stunned by our eloquence? Is there nothing we said worth responding to? Are they deaf? Preoccupied? Asleep?

All of us learn as children what silence means. If our parents used the silent treatment as punishment, we tend to interpret silence in a negative way. If silence in our family of origin meant everyone was content, we are more at ease with non-responders. Those television phone commercials document the frustration that often ensues when messages are met with no outward response.

Certainly, pauses are important in good conversation and best friends can safely leave much unspoken. Silence, in those cases, is an intimate, almost sacred gift. But ordinarily if there's a supposed conversation and only one person speaks, it's either a monologue or psychotherapy.

I've heard husbands boast that they don't ever argue with their wives – that when she's angry, they just keep quiet. Perhaps they euphemistically categorize themselves as the strong silent type. Silence, however, can be one of the cruelest and deadliest weapons – louder than any shout.

Communicating is difficult enough without resorting to guessing games. Maybe we need to tell our non-verbal friends the same thing we'd tell a frustrated whining toddler who points wildly at the cookie jar: "Use your words."

In a recent public radio show, Garrison Keillor suggested a solution to communication problems by way of an invention. He touted a device similar to a set of jumper cables. The terminals are attached to the brains of each person in the conversation and, without spoken words, they communicate directly by reading minds. He called it the jumper synapse.

I'd like to have a set of those cables for my non-responsive friends. But I'm guessing they won't be available to the public until approved by the FDA and pigs fly. So, please, until then, just grunt or something. Speak to me.

* * * * *

[150]

Those terrible twos – the sequel
October 25, 2009

Remember? They want what they want when they want it. They demand their own way and in the choir of toddler voices sing their anthem, "Do it myself." They grab the steering wheel of the car because they are unstoppable and assert their independence and competence long before we old folks consider them capable. Terrible. Just terrible. The terrible twos rear their ugly heads – just like the book predicted.

Just about the time we're getting back to normal, the toddler has become a teenager, and it's déjà vu. He wants to drive the car, date some scary people, and in general feels himself capable of more than we give him credit for. If we're smart enough we finally realize we're dealing with the same terrible twos struggle – a demand for independence. In this second edition of the game, he fears being held captive, never to be free. He wants independence and wants it now.

I should confess that I never had much interest in geriatrics until it recently imposed itself without warning. Life has been pretty kind, but no one warned me that I would have to deal with yet another stage of those terrible twos. This time in my role of old person, I followed the usual formula to carry out the same mission —working for continued independence. Without even being told and without any police involvement, I easily had given up driving and moved from my home to a retirement community. These transitions went smoothly, but then I discovered a third terrible twos. I don't have to have to fight like an adolescent and don't have regular tantrums to flaunt my independence. But the underlying dynamics of all three periods are similar.

My feisty mother summed it up when at ninety years she complained, "When you get old, you just do what they tell you to do." She didn't and I don't want to either.

What I find is that most people are kind and thoughtful – their only motive being to help. And they do. I get an abundance of assistance from others and wouldn't want to be without them. Getting to know one another is crucial, and it's my job to help them learn what things are helpful and which are not. Out of their caring there can be a tendency to do too much. And, honestly, I sometimes welcome the indulgence. But like the toddlers and teenagers before me, the grownups-in-charge don't necessarily rate my competence as high as I do.

Mostly, I want to stay involved in all my affairs as much as possible – everything from bathing to banking. Those who cross the line might hear the mantra I've borrowed from toddlers and teenagers.

"Me do it."

* * * * *

[151]

Role model resigns
November 22, 2009

Some years ago, while losing her battle with cancer, my friend won rave reviews as Role Model. Acquaintances marveled at her emotional strength, her valiant fight, and above all, perhaps her continuing good nature and quiet acceptance. She had many regular visitors who unanimously agreed that they felt better after talking with her. The adulation continued. At her memorial service, speakers related how she taught them not only how to live but how to die.

During my own final visits with her we usually obeyed the neutral chitchat rule, but twice, in brief exchanges, she shared some of the grief and frustration at her helplessness. Once she allowed herself to exclaim, "Phooey on this cancer." I offered to lend her stronger expletives, but she politely declined.

I told her she made it easier on everyone else by being so seemingly valiant, but that I wasn't sure it was fair or particularly helpful to her. Certainly no one likes being around a chronic complainer and it isn't always healthy to answer every "How are you?" with a full organ recital. But there seems to come a time when we have to loosen our Wonder Woman tights and allow ourselves some vulnerability. I hope this friend gave herself those opportunities with other friends even if not with me.

So I've thought a lot about Role Models and am trying to clarify the definition. Thus far in my thinking, I've decided I don't want to be one. Folks sometimes toss us the laurel whether we want the responsibility or not. I guess if I'm being honored, I'd prefer having my face put on money.

When one gets as old as I am, we tend to mingle with others whose cake candles burn as hot or even hotter than our own. And it's becoming increasingly clear that each one of us carries some burden, physical or otherwise, that renders us less than the powerhouses we were in our prime. In our day we bustled about doing our thing as Role Models whether we posed as parents, teachers, politicians or pole dancers. We seldom defined what we would be modeling when the great fatigue eventually sets in.

Frankly, I have observed that people in general don't want to hear details of our coming common demise. It's been around so long that death shouldn't surprise them. (But some of these folks are surprised by Christmas every year, too.)

Among my treasures are friends and family who allow me to remain honest about death and help undo the embroidered Wonder Woman crest on my pajamas. I'll be filling out the forms to resign as incumbent Role Model. I am not qualified to teach other people how to die and will be content to continue the quest for how to live.

This resignation leaves a vacant position, but as a final bit of advice from the mountaintop – don't apply.

* * * * *

[152]

A vote for the goat
January 24, 2010

On behalf of all those who have already banned "The Little Drummer Boy" from background music and insisted he take that noisy flute with him, thanks. The fat lady has sung, and I am declaring the new post-holiday era.

Newscasters have already announced the obligatory list of last year's "ten most everythings." Barbara Walters shared the names of the ten most fascinating people making news in 2009. Unfortunately I was passed over again. This glaring omission encouraged me to compile a list of my own. I originally offered recognition for three entries but eventually realized there was only one story that deserved my attention, and I hope to provide its fifteen minutes of fame.

The subject is goats. Yep, you heard me right. Goats.

I hadn't even thought of goats since reading the tale of the Billy Goats Gruff – and that was some time ago. But recently frolicking through cyberspace, I was introduced to Fainting Goats. Wikipedia, an internet encyclopedia, made the initial introduction. Looking basically like the goats we all know and love, this variety has a peculiar, you might say "fascinating," characteristic.

"A fainting goat is a breed of domestic goat whose muscles freeze for roughly ten seconds when the goat is startled. Though painless, this generally results in the animal collapsing on its side without losing consciousness. The characteristic is caused by a hereditary genetic disorder called *myotonia congenital*. When startled, younger goats will stiffen and fall over. Older goats learn to spread their legs or lean against something when startled, and often they continue to run about in an awkward, stiff-legged shuffle."

Excuse the giggling when the video camera catches these critters in action. The little goats frolic as little goats should. Then, startled by something as routine as being fed, several of them abruptly fall over on to their side, all four legs sticking rigidly out ahead of them. It's probably not politically correct or even nice to laugh at this behavior, but it would take a more mature person than I not to giggle. The lucky ones often become family pets, and the rest are invited to dinner – so to speak.

Some might argue that goats don't belong in the fascination category. But there's something to be learned here, and I'm determined to learn it.

After I was gifted with a surprise diagnosis, those in the know asked, "Have you fallen yet?" I asked "Is it obligatory?" Having since lost a

239

few battles with gravity, I've decided that it is. I'm comforted to know that the older fainting goats learn to spread their legs or lean against something when startled, and often they can continue running about in an awkward stiff-legged shuffle. It sounds like a reasonable alternative if staying vertical isn't an option.

I just might attend Tennessee's annual Fainting Goat Festival in October. I'd like to learn more about those older goats who ward off falling and continue to run with back legs locked together rigidly in place. Fascinating.

* * * * *

[153]

Lazy and loving it
February 28, 2010

"… Don't give up your dream," they say, "Anything is possible. If at first you don't succeed, try, try again."

You'll just have to forgive me – or not, but while the world is busy swaddling me in support and encouragement, I'm gearing up to tell some of them to leave me alone. Of course every cheer is cheered with good intent, but how does one retire from this regiment? Aren't seventy-five duty years (okay, it's seventy-six) enough?

Each time I'm about ready to shift gears from driven to cruise to stop, someone tells me some heartwarming story meant to propel me into action. As I recall it, the last inspiring example was a blind woman, age 127, who had sky-dived while reading the Bible and knitting socks for the homeless. What an example for us old folks. I hate her.

Contrary to conventional wisdom, the central tenet of my philosophy has always been, "If at first you don't succeed, give up." It's touching to learn how many failures Edison suffered on the way to a light bulb. Writers spend retirement days submitting their work for publication and keeping a tally of rejection letters. I applaud their contribution and perseverance.

But what about the rest of the would-be inventors and other dream chasers? I think first of the man who sunk the family into bankruptcy, designing a suit that would withstand a bear attack – if indeed he ever encountered one.

And don't forget the farmer whose corn crop had been superior for many years. But one shiny day, he looked to the sky and saw that white clouds had formed two letters: P C. He dropped to his knees as he interpreted God's message to "preach Christ." Well, he tried, but he was no

Billy Graham. Back home he realized the PC might have meant Pick Corn after all.

As a graduate student I was paid to be companion to a wealthy widow who had taken up knitting. It was her only therapeutic activity and she hated it. Each time she stood up, the ball of yarn fell to the floor. She shuffled across the room dragging the yarn, cussing out loud as she went. Maybe it was time to give it up. Or as Dr. Phil would ask: "How's that working for you?"

Maybe we take ourselves too seriously. The work ethic and demand for perfection often make us inflexible. Do we really have to spend our days trying to improve ourselves? How about a rest? I'm still smarting from the promise that some mail order potion would make a man of me in thirty days.

Maybe Kenny Rogers warns the over-focused and driven among us to "know when to hold 'em, know when to fold 'em, know when to walk away – and know when to run." For now I'll pass up scuba diving lessons and take a nap.

* * * * *

[154]

Beyond Georgie Porgie
April 25, 2010

There was one in every school. We all knew his name and cowered if he headed in our direction. He was the official Bully and held the position without many challenges; the first bully mentioned in nursery rhymes was perhaps Georgie Porgie who kissed the girls and made them cry.

Lately, television news segments reveal the extent of the problem, and girls sometimes earn the bully title in their own right. Just look at how far we've come!

We were deceived. Names do hurt... just as bad as the sticks and stones. Did grownups not know the truth?

A light is currently being shined on the problem of bullying, and it's been recognized as leading to suicide among some of the victims. The numbers are sobering. Since the bullying epidemic has been acknowledged, the world scrambles to understand the source and solution.

I don't know the answer and apparently closed my eyes to all that has taken place under wraps of silence. But having just spent dozens of hours staring at television fare, I am sadly up to date on the immensity of the problem and maybe have an insight or two.

For light fare, I have always enjoyed seeing programs that feature family videos. Much of the videos feature accidents when people take stupid risks and (if their entry is the stupidest) they get prizes – like ten thousand dollars. I don't know what makes these videos qualify as funny, but we all laugh together.

Well, I've quit laughing at many of the videos of children sent in by their parents. Two examples haunt me.

Picture this. A baby not ready to walk but was a gifted crawler was making his run on a treadmill. At the end, the video revealed that a pacifier was left dangling in front of him on a string.

Another prizewinner showed two preteen boys asleep in bed. Their parents had allowed them to watch the movie, "The Texas Chainsaw Massacre." In the morning when the father woke them, he was wearing the mask of one of the movie monsters, turned a real chainsaw toward the bed, and let it roar. The boys awakened screaming and even ran into the wall trying to escape.

In other story lines, the father went outside the house to frighten his young children by showing up at the window near their play area.

No, I haven't lost my sense of humor, and no, I'm not out to badmouth parents or other adults. I am positive that the majority of the perpetrators loved and sheltered their children.

But as I reviewed these stories, I found myself saying, "That's mean." It seemed that occasionally parents took a little longer than necessary to rescue the child when he was being filmed for the judging.

Bottom line? What if we examined our interaction with others? How kind are we?

And what if it all has something to do with teasing and tormenting and had something to do with creating bullies? Interesting idea.

* * * * *

[155]

Have some more s'mores
May 23, 2010

If the phone rings, don't answer! Not usually an alarmist, I am reminded this time of year that just because you aren't paranoid doesn't mean they aren't after you. My experience with "them" transpired nearly forty years ago, but springtime phone calls still make me tremble. I fear I may be too late with my warning because their campaign starts early.

First the caller spouted innocent pleasantries. Then the wind up (I see your daughter will be attending our day camp this summer). And then the pitch (We'd like to give you the opportunity to be a leader for your daughter and her friends that week).

It happened quickly and I didn't have time to dig my heels in. She was good!

My protests didn't appear to concern her even though I had no experience with camping. She wore me down with promises that there would be two other mothers helping with the session.

Being a neophyte, I pictured these "other mothers" as hardy daughters of the earth – women who cook over a backyard campfire, women who know the identity of every tree and plant in this hemisphere. Somewhat later I learned that they, too, sought the outdoors only when their kitchen was on fire.

In view of our inexperience, we attended training sessions. The camp's Indian name reportedly meant "A good place to scratch chiggers."

Having been promised a basket of supplies, we found only an empty Clorox bottle, a sucker stick and two dead beetles. Upon entering the campsite, five girls immediately asked to go to the latrine – a complicated request since five didn't come out even under the buddy system. It soon began to rain, but we had planned an activity for those rainy hours. We discovered, however, that most of the girls didn't enjoy drinking coffee and playing bridge. Our efforts at hiking tied in nicely with the day's first craft, which consisted of making designs on one another's legs with bug spray.

Preparing dinner took most of the day. There were twigs in the tatters, spaghetti on the benches and an oil slick on the Kool-Aid. We found that dessert like applesauce was easier to divvy up than cookies. Math failed a harried counselor when she had to divide nineteen cookies among eighteen hungry girls. If you think we could have just eaten the extra cookie ourselves, you still haven't got the picture of day camp.

It happened here. It could happen to you. But if you get the call, don't turn it down. It's worth every chigger bite when at the end of each day, you gather for closing ceremonies. About a hundred girls singing inspirational songs like "Fried Ham, Cheese and Baloney." You will never forget the touching moment when the dirty-faced color guard retires the flag. Hardly anyone noticed it had been hanging upside down all day long – the international sign of distress.

* * * * *

[156]

Not just a senior moment
June 27, 2010

Years ago I was lucky enough to inherit a wise older woman living next door. Since computers had not yet reared their arrogant heads, she was Information Central for our family. Not content with her eighty years of learning, she was up for new experiences as they presented themselves. We kept in touch when she moved out of state.

One letter held the usual family news, then an unusual tale. In her unflappable calm mode she wrote, "I've had a new adventure."

In words worth a thousand pictures, she explained that she had been spending some time in the unfamiliar realm of hallucinations. She attributed these side trips to a new medication and was relieved to be back to her usual rational self.

These years later, I am glad to remember her story because I recently visited that uncomfortable place myself. I took some comfort in finding that all my symptoms were listed on the label of my new medication as possible side effects.

I had promised myself not to focus columns on my own problems, but found the experience of my Big Adventure eager to be shared. You will have to forgive any self indulgence for now.

The two main villains in my cast were co-conspirators, Time and Memory. Previously functioning normally, they now joined forces to deceive me. When Mornings disguised themselves as Evenings and Saturdays morphed into Tuesdays, I found myself arguing with someone over the details of the day – and lost. I feared losing all credibility and feared my struggles would translate my brilliant attempts at humor as fraudulent.

Having always considered words a playground, I was surprised and frustrated to learn that I had no words to explain what was happening. I had learned long ago that some people aren't reliable and that the best advice was from Shakespeare, who advised, "To thine own self be true." I had lost my closest confidant and literally didn't know the time of day.

My daughter gave me an atomic clock. It automatically sets itself for the correct time, and when I push a silver button the tiny man inside tells me the date and time of day. I've come to rely on him. We sometimes play detective, gathering evidence of the world's reality. He's my new best friend.

Looking at the world in a different light probably has a funny side. But you'll just have to be patient. I did indeed get to look for my own

Easter eggs this spring. I'll share that magic when this interesting journey takes a rational turn some Saturday or Monday morning or night. Whenever.

Believe me. Of all the things I've ever lost, I miss my mind the most.

* * * * *

[157]

Amazing grace, how sweet...
August 2, 2010

It isn't my fault my neighbor's living room couch faded from the sun. Barb realized one afternoon years ago she was missing too much excitement at my house and declared, "I don't care if my couch does fade. I'm not closing the drapes anymore." She had missed plenty, but the lawn mower incident precipitated her resolution.

I was simply mowing the lawn. Guiding the power mower around the corner to the side of the house, I noticed the back yard gate was closed. So I parked the mower in neutral and headed toward the gate. The gear immediately slipped back into drive, and the mower chased me several yards down the side of the house until I gained sufficient sense to dodge right, letting the mower crash into the fence.

I was glad to be alive to tell Barb another episode. I had backed my van into the carport, the trunk lid facing the closed garage door. Needing something from the van, I stood with my back to the garage door and began raising the trunk lid. That feat required a little more space than I calculated, and the rising trunk lid lodged under my chin, pinning me to the garage door. From that position, it was difficult to get sufficient leverage either to breathe or to shut the lid again, but I escaped to tell the story.

It must be a thing about garages. In closing the garage door one other afternoon, rather than properly using the handles, I chose to hurry things along and grasped hold of the door by sticking all eight fingers into one of the hinged cracks and pulling downward. Yes, it hurried the process, and yes, all eight fingers were crushed as the door closed.

Another rushed day, I hurried out the back door into the driveway, jumped into my car and put it in reverse. I had gone no more than three feet when I heard a crash and felt a jolt. I had backed my car into our second car that was parked behind it in the drive.

Or is it a thing about fingers? Our bathroom had a window several feet above the tub – a little high for purposes of short people. Standing in the empty tub, (why for heavens sake?) I reached to lower the open window and it fell shut on those same eight fingers, holding me prisoner. Luckily I was fully dressed and my preschool son was there to run for a neighbor's help. The fingers must have hurt a little because I left shoe prints on the wall above the bathtub.

Am I more prone to such mishaps or just more likely to tell on myself?

At any rate, Barb didn't even bat an eye when I caught my hair in the car door or let the mailbox lid fall shut on my nose.

I soon noticed it wasn't just Barb anymore. Thereafter none of my neighbors pulled the drapes, and I had the only unfaded couch on the block.

* * * * *

[158]

Chicken Little was right
September 22, 2010

It was a dirty job, but we all know someone has to do it; so I volunteered. It was hot out there, or so they tell me. Most of the population dragged themselves inside for relief and then outside in the heat again. Complaining seemed to lower the heat index, if only briefly.

Luckily, I was left out of the fray. Being long since retired, I had few entries in my appointment book. I planned to hibernate until November hunkered down in air-conditioned splendor. I tried not to mention this perk to the suffering masses, but they saw my sweat-free brow as a sign of laziness and were not amused.

To soothe their overheated selves and not incidentally to get back in their good graces, I told them I hibernated through summer for their benefit. Mostly I kept a straight face, but it was hard to maintain a solemn attitude when I mentioned the big recliner that saw me through my ordeal.

My assignment was to monitor television at least eight hours a day and pass on news to the overheated masses. I hoped that news reports from the real world would take their minds off the heat. And the news wasn't good. One crisis piled on another – a collage of floods, a sagging economy, scary product recalls, earthquakes, murders, avalanches, crimes, oh, and a couple wars in between commercials.

Sports took up entirely too many research hours. I recommend that each team be given their own ball and thus eliminate competition and heat stroke in one fell swoop. That move could free up time for soap operas. Devotees were told to take heart, since every actor and plot will be right where they were left six months ago.

Ben Casey, MD is alive and well, channeled through contemporary physicians. Having watched a multitude of birthing stories, I think I am qualified to perform C-sections. Quiz shows offer prizes in millions of dollars – up considerably from the loot on Queen For A Day. Reality shows of all sorts make most viewers appreciate their own reality. Granted, I was addicted to helping a hapless group of adventurers who were struggling to survive on an island without cell phones or water bottles.

My greatest fear was for the children both as actors and observers, but this fear deserves its own space and sadly appears not to go away.

I'm not one to send out alarms or warn periodically that the sky is falling. But recent news has me scared with the rest of mankind and incidentally taking a break from TV viewing. There is apparently an epidemic of bedbugs coming to a bed near you – or even worse, to me. All I can suggest at this point is that you stay vigilant and if a black dust bunny blows across your path, step on it.

* * * * *

[159]

Who's in charge here?
November 9, 2010

Our son was about a year old when we moved into an upstairs apartment in an old frame house. To reach our rooms we had to climb an exceptionally steep and narrow staircase. For safety's sake we installed a baby gate at the landing and "always kept it locked." One morning I heard the baby crying frantically from the hall. I found him sitting at the top of the steps apparently worried about our negligence in not locking the gate. That was my best first example of an appreciation of controls from outside ourselves.

Later I met many children who on the night their grounding was over, deliberately broke a rule to be back again in the structure of the consequence. And if there needed to be more evidence, when my daughter was a teenager, she was angry because I had permitted her to go to a party even against my own good judgment.

Volumes have been written about control. Do we have full control over our lives or maybe none at all? Recently, I have been working on an answer to that larger problem, but for now everyone will just have to wait.

When we were toddlers ourselves, we gradually learned about controls and gradually assessed how much independence we really have. We start as toddlers testing the gates and soon adopt the battle cry of independence.

In my dotage I have reluctantly agreed to give up Diva status but still insist upon playing a major role in my own life's drama. Relatives, friends and strangers come to my rescue if they see me struggling. Because their motives are pure, sometimes they feel unappreciated if I ask to do it myself. The request may seem like bossiness, or an attempt to control them.

At other times I need their help. Then I want to convey the swimmer's call from the ocean. "I'm not waving, I'm drowning." It probably isn't easy trying to read my mind.

Everyone wants to be taken seriously. In my case this means to be able to touch my money as it flies by, to rip up my own junk mail, to speak for myself (as well as I can), and stay involved in decisions that impact my life. Let me be absurdly silly without adding some even sillier diagnosis. Let me cry at the smallest touching moment – including commercials.

I welcome the gates someone hangs to insure my safety and am grateful for those who double-check the locks when my wellbeing is at stake.

You may notice that dates on my calendar sometimes shuffle themselves, refusing to follow conventional rules. I promise to try keeping them in line.

But please, sometimes, let me have three Wednesdays in a week if I choose.

* * * * *

[160]

A basket full of love
December 27, 2010

If there were chestnuts roasting on an open fire and spicy smells of basted turkey filling the air, I missed them. I know there wasn't mistletoe hanging in the doorway, nor poinsettias woven through pine branches on the staircase banister. There was an upright piano gathering dust, but I don't recall its gathering carolers around to sing holiday songs. In one corner of the living room, a Christmas tree, about three feet tall, stood atop an old library table. The decorations could have been homemade or purchased at the five-and-ten-cent store. I simply don't remember. There were gifts beneath the table for my three brothers and me, and no doubt the ones wrapped for me pleased my eight-year-old taste, but I can't recall the contents of one single box.

Yet that holiday was a special one, with an unexpected event that imprinted itself on my mind forever and spoke volumes about love, family, and the Christmas spirit itself.

After the gifts had been opened and we were left to decide what to do with the rest of the day, there was a knock at the front door. I ran to open it and was surprised to see that no one was standing there – nor anywhere on the porch or on the sidewalk. But at my feet was a wicker basket. Inside there lay a baby doll, surely the most beautiful one ever born, dressed in a lacy blue dress and partially covered by a soft, flannel blanket. Attached to the basket was a note, with my name on it, saying, "Please take care of me." I took care of her. The only surviving photograph of that Christmas shows a solemn eight-year-old mother, cradling her new charge.

But the Christmas mystery didn't end there. It wasn't until I was an adult that I learned where the special gift came from – rendering the adopted doll even more precious.

In our large family, cousins were everywhere and family reunions resembled an elementary school playground. None of us was rich. Some of us were poor. I had the distinction of being the only girl for several years and enjoyed a special relationship with my warm, funny, nurturing, beloved grandmother.

On that Christmas day, not being able to afford gifts for all the grandchildren, she somehow had the doll anonymously left on my doorstep, satisfied with seeing my pleasure and needing no recognition beyond that. She would have been pleased to know I took care of my adopted charge well into adulthood and that her special gift elevated that eighth Christmas above all the rest.

* * * * *

[161]

When no news is good news
February 14, 2011

It's February – usually time for valentines. But not this year. My heart is just too tired.

Ordinarily, I've handled crises one at a time as they appeared, counting on them to resolve themselves as I waited and regained perspective. This time optimism is slow to return. As a fellow poet observed, "how much the heart can bear and yet not break." Mother Nature flexed her muscles to get our attention and with all due respect, I think she overdid it. Fires, floods, earthquakes, freezing rain and snow have plagued us, and the year has just begun.

Hunger, disease and homelessness followed each tragedy as our hearts stretched to include the new arrivals.

Lest we forget, newscasters reminded us there was still war in Afghanistan. Did the world forget that conflicts are supposed to be over in Korea? Now Mexico and Egypt vie for heart space.

The ocean turned black, and miners were trapped underground here and abroad. Old familiar crimes (murder, theft, rapes) played on as incidental music.

But wait! There's more!

A new story broke through the clutter without much fanfare, but it both fascinated and horrified me. Birds – hundreds, maybe thousands of birds lying dead in the streets of an Arkansas community and in four other counties. Mostly black, flashes of red feathers added drama. The sight was compelling – the accompanying story eerie.

The flock of birds had fallen from the sky – their deaths not a result of falling, but falling because they were dead. Experts hadn't figured out the cause of the deaths and were making educated guesses at the time of the report.

Frankly, I haven't been comfortable with more than one bird at a time since seeing Hitchcock's scary movie. But dead bird in the singular elicits my sympathy. It's hard to paint a word picture of hundreds of dead birds lying close, neatly in tidy formation down the road. Could it be the equivalent of a Jonestown mass suicide? Am I losing the last sliver of my mind? Probably not, because a follow-up news program reported a similar, simultaneous happening somewhere in Europe.

On my list of selfish wishes, I have always fantasized about driving down the highway in a downpour of rain and then crossing an invisible magical line where the rain stopped abruptly. It hasn't happened yet or I'd still be talking about it.

So I figure, someone surely drove down that highway when he or she was suddenly bombarded by dead birds falling from the sky. Did someone call 911 – or their mother? Was there a camera within reach? Were they frightened? Just seeing the photograph made me wonder if someone's eye was still on the sparrow.

To my knowledge, scientists haven't released any more informa-tion. Maybe they just don't know. Or maybe it's just easier to deal with our accustomed evils. Maybe I'll send valentines after all.

* * * * *

[162]

I'm doing just fine, thanks – how about you?
April 4, 2011
(Reprint; see #88, October 24, 2004)

* * * * *

[163]

Beauty found in quietness
May 23, 2011

May has a reputation as a quiet month. It usually marks the end of those well-advertised April showers. This year, April turned on all her faucets at once. Could this be the flood that will drown out all our muskrats?

Browsers and buyers passed through the narrow aisles of the craft show. The huge gymnasium was hot and, since there was no relief from the tiny fans high in the vaulted ceiling, most shoppers hurried about their business, eager to get outside where they could hope for an occasional breeze. One person began blending into the next and there was little sense of joy.

The sterile mood was broken by the gentle voice of a child saying, "Look, mama, look!" I turned to see a slender, blond boy about four years old. He had paused in the aisle and, with wonder in his eyes, pointed to the ceiling. Those around him stopped to see what he had discovered.

High in the rafters, at the opposite end of the gymnasium, was a green balloon that had apparently escaped someone's grasp earlier in the day. It, too, was hot – and seemed to have lost some of its life-giving helium. As we focused on the balloon and shared for a moment in the boy's pleasure, the balloon mysteriously started travelling slowly across the giant room. It stayed at ceiling height until it reached our end of the gymnasium, then drifted downward across the bleacher section, then across three rows of craft booths, and floated directly to the little boy.

It hung in front of him, its string dangling below, while bystanders looked on in amazement and became believers. Too stunned and shy to respond, the child neither spoke nor moved. Someone shouted, "Grab it!" And I heard myself urging more quietly, "You can have it. It's yours."

Even though May has a reputation as a quiet month, it sometimes flows over its banks with beauty. Could this really be the flood that will drown out all our muskrats? Perhaps not, but we keep searching for peaceful moments that give our lives meaning. As for the little boy, he reached out to claim his prize, grasped the string, and resumed his walk down the aisle with the magic balloon. Boy and balloon were rescued from the heat and tedium of the day.

And for a moment, so were we all.

＊＊＊＊＊

[164]

It only hurts when we laugh
Date: July 11, 2011

She just couldn't help it, Ordinarily sympathetic and kind, my mother broke out laughing when she saw someone fall down.

I recall having once known a couple theories explaining why this happens, theories long ago moved on, but I've found the mother lode of falls during my recent television research – plenty to make someone die laughing.

The show is based on home videos that the viewing audience sends to them. Why participate, you may ask. Could it be to win prizes of up to $100,000? The stars in the family videos are mostly caught doing something stupid, embarrassing or downright dangerous. I think they used to advertise that no one featured got hurt. But I haven't heard that claim lately. Scenes of piñatas, bicycle crashes, and falls of every genre seem to prevail, then the laughter of the studio audience.

Why do I watch? Because among the videos there are some genuinely funny, tender sequences of children learning about life sometimes the hard way. One little girl cried because she was afraid of her shadow that pursued her as she ran down the driveway. Another child cried when a magician announced he was going to turn her into a butterfly. And – ouch! – a couple of two-year-olds crashed repeatedly into the wall with buckets on their heads. Several others collided out of control with fences or mailboxes, not yet competent to operate their miniature motorized vehicles.

Taking time to reflect on the videos, the sadness rolled in. Four examples stood out for me:

1. Those wielding the camera don't react as quickly to rescue the child in distress as they might without the prize. Do those people carry their cameras at all times?
2. At least one mother deliberately broke a promise to her son by insisting he do an embarrassing dance for the camera.

3. Fear tactics are plentiful. One father dressed in costume and woke his two young teenage sons by running a chainsaw beside their bed. Less dramatic but equally persuasive are fathers who go outside at night and peer in the windows to frighten the children. How much prize money would this fear be worth?

4. Saddest of all in my estimation is the three- or four-year-old boy brought to tears trying to convince his father to return his nose. Father was a hard sell but eventually reunited boy with nose.

No, I haven't lost my sense of humor, and yes, I'm aware that most of the antics taped are just teasing and won't send parents with cameras to some video hell. I like to believe that what counts in parenting isn't the occasional goof up. It's the thread of things running through our relationships that's critical. Kindness will be the answer when we get life figured out. And in this regard, home schooling beginning at birth is recommended.

* * * * *

[165]

Keeping up with karma
August 29, 2011

I've been advised by friends not to write this column lest indignant readers abandon me. So perhaps I should at least acknowledge past transgressions in hopes of appeasing Karma before it's too late.

My warning came years ago from a serious dog lover who put her affection where her money was. She took it upon herself to make regular rounds with food for animals she thought to be neglected. As far as I know, there was no award or human recognition for her devotion and care.

She was not entirely excited when she learned that I wasn't an Animal Person, but was kind enough to offer a warning. At Heaven's entrance, she said, we'll find that the gates are operated by two large Saint Bernards. Animal Lovers (especially dog lovers) will enter, and the rest of us will be assigned warmer quarters.

I can take a hint and am old enough to be planning for that ultimate trip. My defense is ignorance. As a child I had no real association with critters except for lightning bugs sacrificed as bling for my jewelry. I thought gerbils were fish – but they weren't.

I later learned that children are animal magnets, and some creature or other is always following them home. The animal parade at our house began with Frederick, a horned toad from Oklahoma. God rest his soul.

Two turtles were sacrificed in the incinerator before I learned about hibernation, and I was present during the final days of numerous pet death scenes.

The accidents included a lethal mix of parakeet, gerbil, canary, gold fish, flea spray, boiling water and ignorance. But no malice or premeditation.

We eventually promoted ourselves to ordinary pets, having learned at least something basic like keeping them alive. Cato, a canine named after the Green Hornet's assistant, arrived as a pup and was with us for thirteen years. He had full house privileges until he grew into his huge paws. We found him a rental home in our backyard in a warm shed and saw to it that he was well fed. Big mistake – and here comes the guilt enough to attract the Saint Bernard's attention and maybe lose points with those Animal People.

Cato spent his days alone – essentially abandoned by his humans. He chased squirrels and (I'm guessing here) spent time looking in the window trying to get the cat's attention. He died one winter leaving behind his identification tags, a lesson, and, I hope, forgiveness.

The cat, however, quickly elevated herself to the status of Queen and dropped her given name, Puff. She thrived on our attention and, according to the children, developed talents uncommon to her breed. Her status only swelled with her marriage to the Invisible King of the Universe, the ceremony attended by all available humans. She was fluent in several languages, excelled in ballet and went on vacations with us. She died in my lap while I thanked her for the years she took care of our human family, and I think I got it right this time. She left samples of fur on the furniture she denied climbing on… perhaps enough to knit another cat.

When Karma reviews my life, I hope I'm given the benefit of the doubt. And please – if you know any Saint Bernards, put in a good word for me.

* * * * *

[166]

Adding a pinch of salt
December 5, 2011
(Reprint, see #126, Dec. 23, 2007)

* * * * *

[167]

It's been a year of small potatoes
January 23, 2012
(Reprint; see #78, Dec. 28, 2003)

* * * * *

[168]

Things are looking up
March 12, 2012

I've always been short and have never complained because my legs always reached the ground. But my world is even shorter now, since I've essentially been relegated to a wheelchair. From this perspective, the world is different, both for me and my pusher. Since the wheelchair is a companion variety, I don't go anywhere alone. Not only are there changes in me, but others' reactions to me change significantly also. A wheelchair seems to make people say, "You're looking good," and one person was even reduced to telling me I had pretty eyelashes. If my speech is garbled in any way, a universal look of desperation toward my caretaker asks silently for help in understanding.

The pushers are assigned the task of avoiding crashes, and often I find their head on my shoulder, straining to hear. I'm not used to being pushed around; one might think I would be a reluctant traveler. Sometimes indeed I may get a little testy, but depending upon the pusher and whom we run into or the fantasies we create, the mood of the ride can be amusing. We've made plans for a bank robbery and shenanigans after hours. We've considered regularly scheduled food fights in the dining room and ring-the-bell-and-run games at the doors of other residents at the facility where I live.

Shopping is an adventure and a challenge for both my companion and me because of the distance between us. When I signal to stop or look at merchandise, we're often far past it already. Point of view is everything, and the shopping experience makes me wonder how much it guides our lives even when we are upright. I'm reminded of those old 3D puzzles; looking at them one way, we see nothing but dots, but if we focus just right, intricate pictures appear. It's rather spooky but certainly illustrates the role of perspective in judging our universe.

Often I tire of hearing people tell me that it's all about attitude, even if they are correct. I still make efforts to keep a good perspective. A sense of humor helps, as does a tiny streak of orneriness. If my companion is brave enough, I often suggest an activity not advised or probably even consistent with the rules. But I can sit in the wheelchair at the end of a long hall and break every rule in the book by holding both arms out wide and ordering my companion to fly like the wind. When they oblige, I genuinely fear for my life. One wobbly wheel on the chair is the only damage so far. With this confession, I probably risk reprisal, but perhaps not as severe as the bank robber's would be. While I would never dare try this in crowded spaces, it does make me wonder if I've missed opportunities by sticking to too many rules. I find myself enlisting others to join the band of would-be miscreants, and in safe places, I tell them, "Run! Run! Fly like the wind!"

* * * * *

[169]

Taking it with me
April 30, 2012
(Reprint: see #103, Jan. 24, 2006)

* * * * *

[170]

Wagons ho!
June 14, 2012

Our family's welcome to Kansas was obviously not orchestrated by the state Tourism Bureau.

That August day in 1971, we pioneers made the long, melancholy trek from Colorado to homestead in this unfamiliar land. Most of the stories we'd heard so far featured flatlands, tornadoes, cattle, red shoes and wizards. I'd flown to Topeka earlier to scout the city and purchase a home but knew nothing of territories west of Topeka city limits.

Our immigrant wagon train consisted of two automobiles to be followed later that day by a moving van packed with our worldly goods. My husband drove the lead car, with our nine-year-old son David, and dog, riding shotgun. I drove the second car with my six-year-old daughter, Carol, keeping me company and, just to be on the safe side, looking out for wild animals.

After ten hours on the trail, relieved, tired, and eager to reach our new home, we finally pulled into the driveway, one car behind the other.

Naturally, everyone was excited upon arrival, but apparently no one was as excited as the dog. As soon as the car door opened, he jumped out, ran back to the second car, and promptly bit our daughter in the leg.

Where in the world are welcome wagons when you need one?

The four of us stood in the driveway pondering our emergency but without a single resource to our name. Carol cried and bled while Cato reveled in the excitement. After all, it was his very first bite.

Perhaps etiquette prescribes that established settlers make the first approach to newcomers. But, breaking all the rules, we quickly introduced ourselves to a neighbor and explained the move and the dog and the daughter and the bite… probably in random order.

Fortunately, the natives were friendly. The neighbor immediately called her children's pediatrician and he agreed to see us right away. In the meantime, the moving van, surely ambushed by highwaymen somewhere on Interstate 70, didn't arrive for three days. Without beds, we spent our nights camping out on the hardwood floor and spent our day without a pot to cook in. Eager to get the new settlers oriented, another neighbor showed up while we were roughing it and offered to lend us mowers and edgers to get our raggedy lawn in shape. It was difficult to reject his untimely offer with the politeness it deserved, but we smiled and requested a rain check.

We posted the events of that day in our diaries more than forty years ago. The dog and daughter both survived, the moving van finally arrived, and we eventually relieved the lawn of its ragged edges.

We stayed in Kansas.

Through ensuing years, those helpful neighbors became and remained friends, and the pediatrician continued to care for the medical needs of our children.

Although we didn't exactly make a graceful entrance into the state, I've always been thankful that when we stumbled into Kansas, we ran into genuine Kansans.

* * * * *

[171]

What's wrong with these people?
August 6, 2012

One mid-afternoon as usual I had sarcastically announced that I was going to see how my war was going. Then my remote flicked to CNN and my companion and I prepared to review the war, politicians, murderers and assorted violence. In the midst of these all too familiar scenarios, my companion asked me, "What is the matter with these people?" She had seen it all before but suddenly was fed up and wanted an answer. I was nearly out of solutions, but I recalled a previous time when another friend asked me to explain what evil was, and that time I wrote him a short verse with my idea of an answer. It said, in defining evil:

> evil is
> an absence
> an emptiness
> a void
> a barren core
> where empathy belongs
> where fear
> patrols perimeters
> and stomps its
> toxic footprints
> on our lives

It still expressed my feeling that evil is not something piled on, but something that is missing. If this is true, we only have to look to identify what is missing and especially how we get it. Is there some way to change large groups of people? Probably so. Before my time there was a program to stop people from spitting on the sidewalk. The message was inscribed on bricks. More recently a campaign against littering was seemingly successful, and now there are programs against bullying. "Just Say No" didn't really help, and "no-smoking" hasn't taken hold. Is it possible to redirect the world with prohibitions?

I'm not the first to attempt an answer to the question of what's wrong with these people. Many years ago the subject was tackled by Pogo of comic strip fame. His conclusion was, "We have met the enemy and he is us."

The problem is where to start, and things seem to be getting worse. One problem is that this venture is like trying to change the engine of a plane in mid-air. Among the recent remedies is one program where young children are introduced to infants. The theory is that this is how children will learn gentleness and caring for others. Perhaps this would be a good starting place, but a seemingly endless task.

A new television show of the candid-camera sort features rigged situations that pose problems for unsuspecting participants. Contestants are forced to handle different moral situations with the results taped for every-one to see. If nothing else, these programs show how far we have to go toward peace both privately and globally.

The task is to remember how much each moment means even on an individual basis and how it impacts the whole world in ways we'll never know. A good starting point may be to recognize that Pogo was right. We have met the enemy and he is us. Or as writer/artist Brian Andreas more eloquently says, "He said who invented evil? & I said I wasn't sure anybody invented it, it just happened when somebody got tired of all the effort it took to live right." Amen.

* * * * *

[172]

Dying to know the answers
September 24, 2012

"Do you ever think when a hearse goes by that sooner or later you're going to die?" Those irreverent lines are the first of two lines we sang as children… probably to upset the adults. I think of that sometimes recently because it's been interesting to contemplate my own nonexistence.

My thinking falls into two categories. First of all, what's going to happen to cause my demise? I used to think it would be interesting and appropriately climactic to be shot by a jealous wife. I abandoned that idea. Others seem to think they prefer to die quietly in their sleep. Dylan Thomas advises, however, to "rage, rage against the dying of the light."

The timing of all of this is difficult. As one tombstone epitaph explains, "I expected this, but not just yet."

The second part of my thinking is, what's next? I have carefully considered some alternatives without reaching a decision. In addition to more prominent belief systems, there is the creative belief of the Frisbee-tarians, who believe that when we die our souls go up on a roof and we can't get them down. Regardless of when and how, "death has so many doors to let out life." Death is always inconvenient. For a while I wondered if I would know how to die, much like the time long ago when I wondered if I would know how to give birth, but that seemed to take care of itself without my micromanagement.

Since I spend a lot of time with old people, I'm surprised that no one mentions having similar thoughts. It's not for lack of intellect or energy, but the tendency toward aversions of the subject.

And it's not because they lack adventure. Seniors sometimes take "mystery tours" for recreation. They aren't told the destination, but anticipate the excitement and discuss it amongst themselves. It seems to me that dying will be the most exciting trip of all. Maybe this gets discussed when people are at their house of worship. Are they afraid of upsetting others? I personally have spent some interesting minutes considering everything from meeting people on the other shore to spending eternity as a sparkling electron.

Besides the question of our destination, the process of dying itself leaves a lot of room for imagination, too. We children also had a line for that, but I'll spare you. Obviously I've not completed my inquiry but will consider all suggestions at this point. My conclusion is, like Woody Allen said, "I don't mind dying, I just don't want to be there when it happens."

I'm always considering that death is the central fact of my life. The only sure thing is that (except for taxes) that's all we are certain of. But sometimes folks seem startled to realize that. I'm thinking that's the same people who are surprised every year when Christmas comes.

So I'm dying to know the answers. Surely I can't be the only person wondering about this adventure. Stay tuned; I may be in touch.

* * * * *

Obituary
(largely self-written)
October 19, 2012

Naomi Bruey Patterson

Naomi Patterson passed away on October 17, 2012 in Topeka, Kansas at the age of 78. She was born in Lisbon, Ohio, to Ralph and Helen Shive Bruey, both deceased.

She married Tom W. Patterson in 1961; they divorced in 1999. Naomi is survived by her children, David Patterson of Oak Park, Illinois and Carol Baldwin of Tecumseh, KS, as well as by her brothers, Fred Bruey of Jackson, MI, Ron Bruey of Cornelius, NC and David Bruey of East Troy, WI.

She earned her bachelor's and master's degrees in clinical psychology in Ohio and her Ph.D. from the University of Nebraska. She worked primarily with children, at first in Fort Collins, CO and in Topeka beginning in 1971, where she was employed by the Shawnee County Health Center, The Topeka Psychiatric Center, and Pediatrics P.A. She also offered parent training workshops for thirty years in addition to child-parent counseling.

Naomi was an accomplished writer and poet. She began writing columns for The Topeka Capital Journal in 1997; her last column on the topic of death appeared only a few weeks ago. She published three books of poetry and won numerous prizes for prose and poetry in both state and national competitions. In 2005 she was awarded a fellowship by the Kansas Arts Commission. She was also a volunteer writing teacher at the Topeka Lutheran School. Always artistic and creative, Naomi was known as well for her work in stained glass and her appearances as an amateur magician.

Naomi was a member of the First Congregational Church, the Kansas Authors Club, American Pen Women and the Minerva Club. She was also a former member of Sam's Club.

Naomi will be cremated by Penwell-Gabel. The date and time of her memorial service will be announced in the near future.

In lieu of memorial contributions, Naomi asked that friends surprise someone with a bouquet or single flower in her memory.

* * * * *